CW00926272

NAPOLEONIC ARMY HANDBOOK

The French Army and Her Allies

Also by Michael Oliver and Richard Partridge

Battle Studies in the Peninsula

Napoleonic Army Handbook: The British Army and Her Allies

NAPOLEONIC ARMY HANDBOOK

The French Army and Her Allies

Michael Oliver and Richard Partridge

CONSTABLE • LONDON

Constable & Robinson Ltd
3 The Lanchesters
162 Fulham Palace Road
London W6 9ER
www.constablerobinson.com

First published in the UK by Constable,
an imprint of Constable & Robinson Ltd 2002

A copy of the British Library Cataloguing in Publication data is available from the British Library

ISBN 1-84119-223-6

Printed and bound in the EU

This book is dedicated to all the soldiers of Imperial France and her allies, who lost their lives in the pursuit of their nations' ambitions, protection and necessity.

Contents

Acknowledgements

Our thanks are extended to the following people for their patience and forbearance:

Our wives who saw too little of us in the last stages of writing and soon will see too much; Carole O'Brien of Constable & Co. who has waited and waited; our colleagues at Southend Wargames Club who looked to heaven as yet another reference book was brought out in the middle of a wargame and pored over; and virtually everyone else who knows us!

In addition, we would like to express our immense gratitude to J.P. Perconte, who has one of the most informative websites on Italian (Napoleonic) Army matters anyone could imagine. When our sources revealed highly conflicting data and we desperately needed some prime source information, he dropped everything and consulted the National Archives in Paris on our behalf. The result was that the clouds parted and we were able to eliminate the confusion to determine what was right and what was wrong. For those wishing to discover more on this subject, we strongly recommend that you visit *www.histunif.com* and spend a little time browsing. There were many others, too numerous to list, who gave of their time and advice, to whom we should give thanks and this we do unreservedly.

Preface

When we set out to write these two volumes, little did we realize what we had taken on. Our objective was to correlate as much as possible of the enormous volume of work that, over the years, has been published on the various armies that took part in the Napoleonic Wars. We wished to provide, in two moderately sized books, a list of every regiment that fought and a little of the background to their involvement – their nations' military organization and recent history and something of their methods of fighting and where they fought.

We anticipated that the literature available would largely agree, subject to a few minor discrepancies, and that these could be resolved by a little logic and further research among other contemporary references where necessary. How wrong we were! The discrepancies and differences were legion, almost every reference had something different to say and there was seldom a full coverage of a regiment's history in any one place. As a result, this second volume took almost twice as long to write as we anticipated.

Much discussion has taken place among historians as to the dubious value of tertiary and even secondary level sources as opposed to primary ones. It is generally accepted that primary sources are best. This can be understood, in that those writing are closer in time to the events described and sometimes had personal involvement. However, often these writers have reason to slant their writings in one or more directions to give the desired impression of events, to answer criticism or to embellish or mitigate their own part. If written at a time much advanced from the events, memories are apt to be affected by age or infirmity. Those writing at the secondary level, on the other hand, can compare the writings of various primary authors and, hopefully, point out, and suggest resolutions for, serious discrepancies. Professor Oman's History of the Peninsular War is one such secondary source (of which we made considerable use). Yet even he was prone to error or misunderstanding and, sometimes, was the victim of undiscovered typographical mistakes.

This is one of the main reasons for the delay between volumes one and two of the *Napoleonic Army Handbook*. We do not claim that they are without error. What we do claim is that, where we have found inconsistencies and obvious mistakes, we have tried to resolve them by going deeper into them – either through searching other people's work until a picture emerges or by consulting experts in other countries who have access to sources in their own language. We are not linguists, although between us we speak one or two European languages, and to have done our research with solely primary sources would have taken two lifetimes and the learning of several more languages. However, we accept that, should there be mistakes in our work, they are of our making and not the ultimate responsibility of the authors whose work we have consulted. Where we were still in doubt at the end of our efforts, we have either indicated an arbitrary selection or have left interpretation open for the reader.

We took as a slightly off-key compliment, one of the (thankfully few) criticisms we received on Volume I, which we approached in the same way. The criticism took us to task over the fact that we had given the facing colour of one Russian infantry regiment as 'orange'. With some heat, the critic informed us that the correct translation from the Russian was 'flame'. We were relieved that he could find little else to mention specifically and take comfort that, if a figure painter went to ask his supplier for the colour 'flame', he would probably receive something that was some shade of orange. Nevertheless, we have learned something from the criticism (although we have not yet checked the critic's accuracy) and are grateful.

Many readers have told us that they found Volume I a useful reference and we hope Volume II will prove to be equally valuable.

CHAPTER 1

The French Army, 1803–15

1. BACKGROUND

THE YEAR 1802 has been chosen as the starting point for the French Army because this was the year when, following Napoleon's *coup d' état* of 1800, which made him head of the French state, the multitude of changes which affected the army finally settled down. Consequently it seems an appropriate point in time to begin an examination of the French Napoleonic Army. None the less, it is worthwhile to spend a little space in examining what had gone before; the better to understand what took place subsequently.

The revolutionary armies used a divisional structure which embodied the concept, adopted later (1800) in Napoleon's Corps d'Armée, of combined arms within the single organizational entity. However, largely because of ignorance on the part of the average general on how to handle the various arms, towards the end of the revolutionary period, a division was rapidly becoming a formation made up either entirely of infantry or of cavalry plus its own artillery, thus losing the full benefits of combined arms.

Revolutionary armies, formed from the *levée en masse* (conscription), adopted the concept of 'clouds of skirmishers' – persistent and effective niggling harassment by swarms of light infantry, using cover and dispersed formations, of their enemy's rigid linear formations – a legacy of Frederick the Great's successes earlier in the century. To such an 'unfair' tactic, the enemy was unable to reply without 'wasting' ammunition and breaking its own ranks, thereby forfeiting its ordered deployment. The hard-pressed close-order enemy – by now in a state of some disorder – would suddenly be confronted by advancing columns of men screaming revolutionary slogans and with bayonets fixed on their muskets. Morale simply collapsed. The training of French infantry in close-order drill was not seen by the new state as a priority responsibility and so substantial numbers of recruits were used in a skirmishing role where training for formal manoeuvre was less critical. The need to provide some training for the bolder men who formed the light troops was met by divisional commanders' arranging for training on campaign and then sending the troops on outpost raids to gain experience and confidence (or die). Gradually, however, French tactics were developed and refined by experience and necessity and a use of the skirmish screen supported by formed columns together with lines, where appropriate, became the norm in an army superior in its morale and mobility to any in mainland Europe.

Organizationally, the infantry was composed of demi-brigades (the rough equivalent of a regiment), two of which would form a brigade. Two brigades made up the infantry complement of the division. Since the members of a division tended to be fixed, its strength could vary depending on its involvement in fighting and what recruits its constituent units could amass. Artillery was attached to the lower formations as support. Cavalry were organized in regiments and squadrons, much as later.

As a result of the varying competence of their commanders, the divisions, although frequently successful in battle, always suffered from a lack of supply and, as time went on, this proved to be their undoing. Consequently, the soldiers who mutinied in 1799 were a hardened, professional and veteran army of disenchanted men.

2. ORGANIZATION

i) The Guard

THE CONSULAR GUARD 1800–03

As well as the infantry and cavalry detailed below, the Guard contained a company of light artillery and a detachment of horse artillery. Additionally, the Mamelukes were incorporated, following the campaign in Egypt, with three companies each of 100 horsemen.

UNIT	STRENGTH	UNIT	STRENGTH
Grenadiers à Pied	2 battalions	Grenadiers à Cheval	2 squadrons
Chasseurs à Pied	1 company	Chasseurs à Cheval	1 company

In addition, there was a company of about 100 veterans and a company of light artillery (4 pdrs). The year 1804 saw another milestone in the history of the French Army with the formation of the Garde Imperiale from the old Consular Guard. It must be said that Napoleon enjoyed 'tinkering' with the Guard. Its structure was constantly changed and nomenclature adjusted. Consequently, when one consults various sources, each appears to have differences of detail. These almost certainly derive from the numerous Imperial decrees and orders issued in rapid succession – not all of them being adopted by the formations – and so, one receives a series of 'snapshots' often at variance with one another. We have tried to rationalise all of this by giving annual summaries at the end of various years. If, as a result, we are judged guilty of adding to the confusion we can only say this was not our intention.

THE IMPERIAL GUARD MAY 1804 TO APRIL 1806

The company of Veterans now numbered 166. Towards the end of the above period, the Guard Dragoons were raised with three squadrons (expanded to five in July 1807) plus a squadron of *vélites*.

A number of additions and changes occurred over a period of about eight months culminating in the organization shown in the table on p. 4. The Guard Fusiliers were first raised in April and expanded to two regiments in December of 1806 by re-naming the *vélites*. In the early part of this period, the term 'Old Guard' was first introduced as a term for the Grenadiers and Chasseurs.

THE IMPERIAL GUARD MAY 1804 TO APRIL 1806

INF. TYPE	BNS	CO./BN	MEN/CO.	CAVALRY	SQNS	MEN/SQN
Grenadiers	2 + 2 Vélites	4 (Vél = 5)	200 (Vél = 172)	Chasseurs	4 + 2 Vélites	240
Chasseurs	2 + 2 Vélites	4 (Vél = 5)	200 (Vél = 172)	Grenadiers	4 + 2 Vélites	240
Marins	1	5 + depot	120	Mamelukes	1	123
Gendarmes à Pied	1/2 (accounted with Cav.)	2	121	Gendarmes à Cheval	2	177
ARTILLERY	**SQNS**	**COS**	**GUNS PER CO.**			
HORSE	3	2 per sqn	4 x 4 pdr, 8 pdr or 12 pdr + 2 x 6" howitzers			
FOOT	Not created until 1808					

THE IMPERIAL GUARD AT END 1806

INF. REGT	BNS	CO./BN	MEN/CO.	CAVALRY	SQNS	MEN/SQN
1er Grenadiers	2	4	140	Chasseurs	4 + 2 sqns Vélites	240
2e Grenadiers	2	4	140	Grenadiers	4 + 1 sqn Vélites	240
2e Fusiliers	2	4	140	Mamelukes	1	124
1er Chasseurs	2	4	140	Gendarmes d'Elite à Cheval	2	177
2e Chasseurs	2	4	140	Dragons de l'Impératrice	2[1] + 1 sqn Vélites	
1er Fusiliers	2	4	140	**ARTILLERY**	**FOOT**	**HORSE**
Marins	1	5 + depot	140		No changes	
Gendarmes à Pied (to mid 1806)	$^1/_2$ (accounted with Cav.)	2	140			

[1] Grehan, J. and Gaffney, L., ('France – The Imperial Guard', p. 10 [*Age of Napoleon* article]). Nafziger, G. F., (*The French Army – Royal, Republican, Imperial,* Vol. IV, p. 85) gives the number as three, with two more squadrons raised in July 1807 but, on page 86, he gives the same organization as Grehan and Gaffney.

THE IMPERIAL GUARD AT END 1806

In 1807, the Régiment de Chevau-légers Polonais (Polish Light-Horse) was raised with four squadrons each comprising two companies of 120 men and five commissioned officers. (See table on p. 5.)

The year 1808 was relatively quiet as preparations were made for the venture into the Iberian Peninsula. The 1st Sqn Chevau-légers de Berg joined but only lasted until disbandment in January 1809. They joined the Grand Duke of Berg's Chasseur regiment which, itself, became, in December 1809, a 'new' Chevau-légers de Berg, in the Guard, armed with the lance. There was a re-organization of the Grenadier and Chasseur regiments, the 2nd of each being amalgamated with the 1st. The Artillerie à Cheval was reduced to two squadrons and the Artillerie à Pied was created (see 1809 organization).

The advent of 1809 saw some additions and changes to the organization. The Polish light cavalry were armed with lances and the *Tirailleurs* and *Conscrits* were raised, both conscripted troops with the former being given the name '*Tirailleurs*' as a result of concern over the effect of the word 'conscript' (this concern seems to have been allayed in a matter of weeks with the introduction of the latter regiments). Two further units, contingents supplied by the regents of Turin and Florence were raised and admitted to the Young Guard. The artillery was increased by the addition to the Young Guard of three companies of Conscrit Artillerie.[2]

THE IMPERIAL GUARD AT END 1809

The Gardes National de la Garde was created on 1 January 1810 and comprised four battalions each of four companies but recruiting difficulties forced a reduction to two battalions of six companies each at the end of May the same year. Each company contained 140 men.

When Holland became a metropolitan district of the Empire, the Dutch guard infantry, in September 1810, became 2e Grenadiers à Pied in the French Imperial Guard. It comprised two battalions each with four companies of 200 men. The Guard cavalry was augmented

[2] Nafziger, G. F. op. cit., p. 33 gives an order of battle for Wagram which shows the artillery equipment we use later (see footnote 4). Grehan, J. and Gaffney, L. op. cit., p. 16 say they were '. . .frequently armed with 8 x 4 pdrs'; their source is not given and they do not conform with Nafziger, whom we prefer.

THE IMPERIAL GUARD AT END 1809

INF. REGT	BNS	CO./BN	MEN/CO.
Grenadiers	2	4 + depot	200
Fusiliers-Grenadiers	2	4	200
1er Tirailleurs-Grenadiers	2	4	200
2e Tirailleurs-Grenadiers	2	4	200
1er Conscrits-Grenadiers	2	4	200
2e Conscrits-Grenadiers	2	4	200
Chasseurs	2	4 + depot	200
Fusiliers-Chasseurs	2	4	200
1er Tirailleurs-Chasseurs	2	4	200
2e Tirailleurs-Chasseurs	2	4	200
1er Conscrits-Chasseurs	2	4	200
2e Conscrits-Chasseurs	2	4	200
Vélites de Turin	1	6	120
Vélites de Florence	1	6	120
Marins	1	5 + depot	200

CAVALRY	SQNS	MEN/SQN
Chasseurs	4 + 2 sqns Vélites	240
Grenadiers	4 + 1 sqn Vélites	240
Mamelukes	1	124
Gendarmes d'Elite à Cheval	2	177
Dragons de l'Impératrice	2 + 1 sqn Vélites	250
Chevau-légers Lanciers (Pol.)	4	240
Chevau-légers de Berg[3]	4	240

ARTILLERY

FOOT

UNIT	COS	GUNS/CO.
Art. à Pied	6	1er, 2e, 5e & 6e Cos: 4 x 6pdr + 2 how. 3e & 4e: 6 x 12pdr[4]
Conscrit Art.	3	8 x 4 pdrs

HORSE

SQNS	COS	GUNS/CO.
2	2/sqn	4 x 6pdr + 2 how.[4]

[3] Von Pivka, O., (Armies of the Napoleonic Era [Taplinger]) says (p. 164) these troops were 'attached to the Imperial Guard'. Grehan, J. and Gaffney, L. op. cit., p. 11 say that 'on 17th December 1809 they were admitted to the Guard'. Nafziger does not show their formal inclusion until August 1813, whilst Johnston, R., (*Napoleonic Armies, a Wargamer's Campaign Directory*, Arms & Armour Press, 1978) says they were admitted to the Guard in 1809 (1 sqn., 'quickly raised to 4').

[4] This is the equipment shown as at Wagram in July 1809.

by the erstwhile Dutch Guard Hussars, who became the 2e Chevau-légers Lanciers with the Poles being designated as the 1er Regiment. Dutch artillery was also incorporated into the Guard.[5]

A third, French-manned, Grenadier regiment was raised in May 1810 which eventually became 2e Grenadiers, whilst the Dutch became 3e Grenadiers.

Although no changes in structures or strengths were instituted, at the end of 1810 some re-naming of units occurred: the Tirailleur-Grenadier regiments dropped the 'Grenadier' designation and the '*Conscrit*' equivalents did likewise, becoming the 3e and 4e *Tirailleurs* in February 1811. There was an exactly similar re-naming in the Chasseur regiments which adopted the titles 1er to 4e *Voltigeurs* between December 1810 and February 1811. The *Vieille* (Old), *Moyen* (Middle) and *Jeune* (Young) distinctions were formalized at this time. There were a multitude of organizational changes and changes of nomenclature during the year.

THE OLD GUARD AT END 1811

In addition, the Compagnie d'ouvriers pontonniers and Compagnie de sapeurs were classified 'Old Guard'. (See table on p. 9.)

THE MIDDLE GUARD AT END 1811

(See table on p. 10.)

THE YOUNG GUARD AT END 1811

The '*conscrits-canonniers*' were the corporals and gunners from the batteries attached to the Young Guard. (See table on p. 11.)

In 1812, there were some additions to the Guard cavalry in the form of a fifth squadron for each of the lancer regiments and the raising of a third regiment – itself with five squadrons – from Lithuania, to which was attached a squadron of Tartars. The *vélites* were disbanded and their men used to bring the Grenadiers, Dragoons and Chasseurs up to five squadrons – each, now, of 250 men. At the end of 1812, the Guard had a paper strength of just over 56,000. By the end of the disastrous invasion of Russia, this magnificent corps was down to just a few thousand exhausted, frost-bitten men.

[5] Although this event is recorded by all the sources we consulted, none gives details.

THE OLD GUARD AT END 1811

INF. REGT	BNS	CO./BN	MEN/CO.
1er Grenadiers à Pied	2	4 + depot	200
1er Chasseurs à Pied	2	4 + depot	200
Co. of Veterans	–	–	200[6]

ARTILLERY

UNIT	COS	GUNS/CO.
1er Art. à Pied	6	(2 Cos) 6 x 12 pdr 2 x Howitzers (4 Cos) 6 x 6 pdr 2 x Howitzers
1er Art. à Cheval	4	4 x 6 pdr 2 x Howitzers

CAVALRY	SQNS	MEN/SQN
Chasseurs	4 + 2 sqns Vélites	240
Grenadiers	4 + 1 sqn. Vélites	240
Mamelukes	1	124
1er Chevau-légers Lanciers (Polish)	4	240
Dragons de l'Impératrice	2 + 1 sqn Vélites	250
Gendarmes d'Elite à Cheval	2	177
Marins[7] 1 Bn	6 Cos + depot	200/Co.

[6] The actual strength of the company was 62, according to Johnston, R. op. cit., p. 23.

[7] Nafziger, G.F. op. cit., p. 43 does not list the Marins as part of the guard organization but, on the following page, lists them as on the guard strength. We suspect a typographical error.

THE MIDDLE GUARD AT END 1811

INF. REGT	BNS	CO./BN	MEN/CO.	CAVALRY	SQNS	MEN/SQN
2e Grenadiers à Pied	2	4 + depot	200	2e Chevau-légers Lanciers (Dutch)	4	240
3e Grenadiers à Pied	2	4 + depot	200			
2e Chasseurs à Pied	2	4	200			
Fusiliers-Grenadiers	2	4	200			
Fusiliers-Chasseurs	2	4	200			
Vélites de Turin	1	6	120			
Vélites de Florence	1	6	120			
Train d'artillerie (2 Bns)						

THE YOUNG GUARD AT END 1811

INF. REGT	BNS	CO./BN	MEN/CO.	INF. REGT	BNS	CO./BN	MEN/CO.
1er Tirailleurs	2	4	200	1er Voltigeurs	2	4	200
2e Tirailleurs	2	4	200	2e Voltigeurs	2	4	200
3e Tirailleurs	2	4	200	3e Voltigeurs	2	4	200
4e Tirailleurs	2	4	200	4e Voltigeurs	2	4	200
5e Tirailleurs	2	4	200	5e Voltigeurs	2	4	200
6e Tirailleurs	2	4	200	6e Voltigeurs	2	4	200
Flanquers	2[8]	4	200	Pupilles	8 + Depot	4	200 (Depot 400)
Conscrits-canonniers		3 Cos	?	Gardes Nat.	2	4	200

[8] One bn was the Flanquers-Grenadiers, the other the Flanquers-Chasseurs.

Napoleon addressed the necessity for reorganizing the Guard in 1813 by the issuing of a number of Imperial Decrees. These not only restored the previous year's numbers but increased the theoretical total, by the end of the year, to almost 92,500. Much of this was achieved by recruiting from the regiments in Spain, which at least provided experienced troops, although substantial quantities were new conscripts. The Guard had risen, like the phoenix, from the ashes but its stout old heart lay cold and still in the snows of Russia. Nevertheless, in the campaigns to come, these new soldiers were to give good account of themselves and rekindle the reputation and *esprit* of their predecessors.

The following tables give the Imperial Guard order of battle for the invasion of Russia in the summer of 1812 (it includes attached line units).

INFANTRY

1ère (YOUNG GUARD) DIVISION	OFFICERS	MEN
1ère & 2e Bataillons 5e Voltigeurs	28	917
1ère & 2e Bataillons 6e Voltigeurs	25	621
1ère & 2e Bataillons 5e Tirailleurs	28	1,011
1ère & 2e Bataillons 6e Tirailleurs	22	548
4e Compagnie Cannoniers conscrits	3	81
5e Compagnie Train d'Artillerie	1	143
2e Compagnie 5e (Ligne) Sapeur Bataillon	2	90
Divisional Total	109	3,411

2e DIVISION	OFFICERS	MEN
1ère & 2e Bataillons Régiment de Flanquers	25	1,134
1ère & 2e Bataillons 1ère Voltigeurs	25	788
1ère & 2e Bataillons 1ère Tirailleurs	22	928
1ère & 2e Bataillons Fusiliers-Chasseurs	33	1,322
1ère & 2e Bataillons Fusiliers-Grenadiers	30	1,391
13e & 14e Compagnies 8e Artillerie de la Ligne	8	178
6e Compagnie 4e (Ligne) Train Bataillon	1	97
2e Compagnie 7e (Ligne) Train Bataillon		41
Sapeurs	5	104
Train d'Équipages		44
Administration	2	44
Divisional Total	151	6,071
3e (OLD GUARD) DIVISION	**OFFICERS**	**MEN**
1ère & 2e Bataillons 1ère Chasseurs à pied	34	1,452
1ère & 2e Bataillons 2e Chasseurs à pied	41	1,245
1ère & 2e Bataillons 1ère Grenadiers à pied	31	1,294
1ère & 2e Bataillons 2e Grenadiers à pied	33	1,079
1ère & 2e Bataillons 3e Grenadiers à pied	41	1,165
3e Compagnie (Young Guard) Artillerie à pied	4	77
1ère & 2e Compagnies (Old Guard) Artillerie à pied	8	182
3e & 4e Compagnies (Old Guard) Artillerie à pied	9	199
3e Compagnie 2e Train Bataillon	1	108
1ère Compagnie 1ère Train Bataillon	2	125
4e Compagnie 1ère Train Bataillon	1	152
Train d'Équipages		23
Ambulances	11	39
Divisional Total	216	7,140

CAVALRY

UNIT	OFFICERS	MEN
1ère - 5e Sqns Chasseurs à Cheval	70	1,107
1ère Compagnie des Mamelukes	8	67
1ère - 5e Sqns Dragons de l'Impératrice	64	1,015
1ère - 5e Sqns Grenadiers à Cheval	70	1,096
1ère - 4e Sqns 1ère Chevau-léger Lanciers	69	887
1ère - 4e Sqns 2e Chevau-léger Lanciers	57	1,095
1ère & 2e Sqns Gendarmes d'Elite	28	363
1ère & 2e Cies 1ère (Ligne) Artillerie à Cheval de la Ligne	5	124
2e & 3e Cies 7e (Ligne) Train Bataillon	2	146
Cavalry Total	373	5,900

RESERVE ARTILLERY

ARTILLERIE À CHEVAL (YOUNG GUARD)	OFFICERS	MEN
2e, 3e & 4e Cies à Cheval	7	173
1ère Cie 1ère Train Bataillon	1	125
1ère & 5e Cies à Cheval	6	157
5e & 6e Cies 1er Artillerie à Cheval de la Ligne	5	134
4e Detachment 7e (Line) Train Bataillon	1	110
ARTILLERIE À PIED (YOUNG GUARD)	**OFFICERS**	**MEN**
3e & 4e Cies à Pied	6	195
3e & 4e Cies 2e Train Bataillon	2	267
5e & 6e Cies à Pied	7	214
1ère & 5e Cies 2e Train Bataillon	2	226
15e & 16e Cies 8e Artillerie à Pied de la Ligne	5	174
5e Cie 7e (Line) Train Bataillon	1	150
Artillery Total	43	1,925

ENGINEERS

UNIT	OFFICERS	MEN
6e Cie 5e (Ligne) Sapeur Bataillon	3	117
1ère Cie Sapeurs de Berg	3	118
1ère Bataillon (Naval) Ouvriers	16	824
1ère & 7e Cies Marins de la Garde	8	211
3e Cie Equipages de la Garde	8	516
1ère - 6e Cies 7e (Ligne) Equipage	15	705
Engineers Total	53	2,491

Later, the 4e Voltigeurs and 4e Tirailleurs joined the 1ère Division.

At the start of 1813, prodigious efforts were made to heal the wounds of 1812. Heavy recruitment and reorganization were undertaken. The Grenadiers now comprised 1er and 2e Grenadiers, the Veteran Co., the Fusilier-Grenadiers, 1er to 7e Tirailleur Grenadiers and four companies of the Fontainebleau Bataillon d'Instruction. The Chasseurs were made up of 1er and 2e Chasseurs, Fusilier-Grenadiers, 1er to 7e Voltigeur Grenadiers and four battalions of Pupilles. The 1st regiments of Grenadiers and Chasseurs were old guard, whilst the 2nd regiments were regarded as middle guard (the 3rd Regiments were disbanded and used to bolster the strengths of the other two). A single depot company was established for the Grenadiers whilst the Fusilier-Grenadiers had one and the Tirailleurs two depot companies. Each of these companies was 300 men strong. Similar arrangements were made for the Chasseurs. Flanqueur and Fusilier regiments were reorganized into six 120-man companies.

The campaigns of 1813 took their toll on the restructured Garde which resulted from Napoleon's strenuous efforts after the retreat from Moscow and, during the ensuing armistice, more recruiting and reorganization was required. This resulted in the following order of battle by 1 August:

CIC: Marshal Mortier

Old Guard Division: Général de division Friant:

1ère BRIGADE: Général de division Curial	OFFICERS	MEN
1/1ère Chasseurs à Pied	23	648
2/1ère Chasseurs à Pied	14	599
1/2e Chasseurs à Pied	26	414
2/2e Chasseurs à Pied	14	195
2e BRIGADE: Général de brigade Michel		
1/1ère Grenadiers à Pied	25	625
2/1ère Grenadiers à Pied	17	587
1/2e Grenadiers à Pied	25	461
2/2e Grenadiers à Pied	8	333
Vélites de Turin	15	438
Vélites de Florence	25	403
ARTILLERIE: Chef de bataillon Courin		
1ère Cie Artillerie à Pied de la Vielle Garde	3	112
6/1ère Train Bataillon	1	100
Division Total	196	4,915

1ère Division:[9] Général de division Dumoustier:

1ère BRIGADE: Général de brigade Mouton-Duvernet	OFFICERS	MEN
1ère Fusiliers-Chasseurs	21	697
2e Fusiliers-Chasseurs	16	722
1ère Fusiliers-Grenadiers	23	586
2e Fusiliers-Grenadiers	18	604
2e BRIGADE: Général de brigade Tindal		
1/1ère Voltigeurs	19	527
2/1ère Voltigeurs	11	498
1/2e Voltigeurs	21	444
2/2e Voltigeurs	12	458
3e BRIGADE: Général de brigade Lanusse		
1/3e Voltigeurs	19	704
2/3e Voltigeurs	13	672
1/6e Voltigeurs	20	665
2/6e Voltigeurs	17	655
1/7e Voltigeurs	19	620
2/7e Voltigeurs	12	577
ARTILLERIE: Chef de bataillon Levic		
1ère Cie Artillerie à Pied de la Jeune Garde	3	116
2e Cie Artillerie à Pied de la Jeune Garde	3	120
8e Cie Artillerie à Pied de la Jeune Garde	2	111
4/1ère Train Bataillon & 3/2e Train Bataillon	3	283
2/5e Bataillon des Sapeurs (Ligne)	3	127
Train d'Équipages	2	124
Division Total	257	9,310

[9] Johnston, R. op. cit., p. 35 refers to this as a Young Guard division but Nafziger op. cit., p. 52 does not classify it in the same way.

2e (Jeune Garde) Division: Général de division Barrois:

1ère BRIGADE: Général de brigade Rothemberg	OFFICERS	MEN
1/1ère Tirailleurs	24	523
2/1ère Tirailleurs	12	489
1/2e Tirailleurs	18	459
2/2e Tirailleurs	11	445
2e BRIGADE:		
1/3e Tirailleurs	18	512
2/3e Tirailleurs	13	551
1/6e Tirailleurs	19	483
2/6e Tirailleurs	12	471
1/7e Tirailleurs	19	658
2/7e Tirailleurs	11	517
3e BRIGADE: Général de brigade Boyeldieu		
1ère Flanquers-Chasseurs	18	601
2e Flanquers-Chasseurs	12	578
1ère Flanquers-Grenadiers	23	681
2e Flanquers-Grenadiers	12	661
ARTILLERY: Chef de bataillon Lefrançois		
3e Cie Artillerie à Pied de la Jeune Garde	3	89
4e Cie Artillerie à Pied de la Jeune Garde	2	100
12e Cie Artillerie à Pied de la Jeune Garde	1	108
9/1ère Train Bataillon & 9/2e Train Bataillon	2	288
3/7e Bataillon des Sapeurs (Ligne)	3	237
Train d'Équipages	1	115
Division Total	234	8,566

3e (Jeune Garde) Division: Général de division Roguet:

1ère BRIGADE: Général de brigade Gros	**OFFICERS**	**MEN**
1/4e Voltigeurs	19	649
2/4e Voltigeurs	13	594
1/5e Voltigeurs	23	696
2/5e Voltigeurs	12	694
2e BRIGADE: Général de brigade Combelle		
1/8e Voltigeurs	19	703
2/8e Voltigeurs	11	667
1/9e Voltigeurs	21	717
2/9e Voltigeurs	11	685
1/10e Voltigeurs	18	725
2/10e Voltigeurs	12	711
3e BRIGADE: Général de brigade Dulong		
1/11e Voitigeurs	19	556
2/11e Voltigeurs	9	550
1 & 2/12e Voltigeurs	–	–[10]
ARTILLERIE: Chef de bataillon Faivre		
5e Cie Artillerie à Pied de la Jeune Garde	3	96
6e Cie Artillerie à Pied de la Jeune Garde	2	92
7e Cie Artillerie à Pied de la Jeune Garde	3	90
1 & 2/2e Train Bataillon	2	257
Division Total	197	8,482

[10] This unit was assembling in Mainz.

4e (Jeune Garde) Division: Général de division Friant:

1ère BRIGADE: Général de brigade Boyer de Rebeval	**OFFICERS**	**MEN**
1/4e Tirailleurs	21	610
2/4e Tirailleurs	10	599
1/5e Tirailleurs	17	653
2/5e Tirailleurs	12	593
2e BRIGADE: Général de brigade Combelle		
1/8e Tirailleurs	19	652
2/8e Tirailleurs	13	624
1/9e Tirailleurs	16	650
2/9e Tirailleurs	12	566
1 & 2/10e Tirailleurs	29	1,545
3e BRIGADE: Général de brigade Pelet		
1 & 2/11e Tirailleurs	28	1,277[11]
1 & 2/12e Tirailleurs	–	–[12]
ARTILLERIE: Chef de bataillon Oudin		
9e Cie Artillerie à Pied de la Jeune Garde	2	102
10e Cie Artillerie à Pied de la Jeune Garde	1	104
11e Cie Artillerie à Pied de la Jeune Garde	1	103
4e & 5e Train Bataillon	2	325
Division Total	183	8,403

During the year, a Polish battalion was organized with 200 men per company but it was never recruited up to strength and was disbanded early in 1814.

11 Marching to join Brigade.
12 This unit was assembling in Paris.

The Cavalry are noticeable by their comparative absence. The old regiments still existed on paper but there was a dearth of mounts and recruiting could not bolster the strengths of the old regiments nor provide full complements for several new units decreed by the Emperor. The old regiments comprised, in April 1813, 1ères (530 men) & 2e (700 men) Lanciers, Grenadiers à Cheval (550 men), Chasseurs à Cheval (750 men), Dragons de l'Impératrice (550 men) and Gendarmes d'Elite (50 men). The Mamelukes were reorganized as a single squadron of 250 men and took on the Empress Dragoons' organization and the Chevau-léger de Berg were incorporated. With much recruiting and reorganization, including the substantial increase in the number of lancer squadrons, the following organization was achieved by 1 August:

REGIMENT	NO. OF SQUADRONS	NO. OF MEN
1ères Chevau-léger Lanciers Polonaises	7[13]	1,383
2e Chevau-léger Lanciers Hollandaises	10	1,576
Chevau-léger de Berg	1ères, 3e[14] & 4e	599
Chevau-léger de Berg	5e	235
Chevau-léger de Berg	6e	235
Chasseurs à Cheval	9 + Mamelukes	1,837
Dragons de l'Impératrice	6	1,365
Grenadiers à Cheval	6	1,272
Gendarmerie d'Élite	2	510
1ères Gardes d'Honneur	5	1,245
2e Gardes d'Honneur	5	1,257
3e Gardes d'Honneur	5	1,218
4e Gardes d'Honneur	5	1,149

[13] Johnston, R. op. cit., p. 35 says there were only five squadrons but we have followed Nafziger op. cit., p. 95 who gives more precise references.

[14] Nafziger op. cit., p. 96 indicates the absence of 2nd Squadron, whilst Johnston, R. op. cit., p. 35 suggests the 3rd, which he says had been absorbed into the 2e Chevau-léger Lanciers Hollandaise.

The Gardes d'Honneur were the new units referred to above and were forming in Mainz and Gotha. They joined the army after Dresden. Also attached to the cavalry were four horse batteries (Old Guard) each comprising 4 x 6pdr cannon and 2 x 5.7" howitzers, plus the 1st & 7th Train Battalions. At the end of the year, three regiments of *Éclaireurs à Cheval* were raised, each with four squadrons of two companies apiece, each of 130 men.

By the end of 1813, with a substantial increase in the number of Tirailleur and Voltigeur regiments, and an adjustment to the six-company (200 men each) battalion organization with an additional, third battalion for almost all regiments, the Guard comprised:

MEN	UNITS
3,200	2 Régiments: Grenadiers à Pied
200	Cie des Veterans
1,600	Régiment de Fusiliers-Grenadiers
20,800	13 Régiments: Tirailleurs
1,800	Flanqueur-Grenadier Régiment
3,200	2 Régiments: Chasseurs à Pied*
1,600	Régiment de Fusiliers-Chasseurs
20,800	13 Régiments: Voltigeurs
1,800	Flanqueur-Chasseur Régiment
1,136	Bataillon de la Marine
1,600	Pupilles
2,000	Bataillon d'Instruction de Fontainebleau
1,250	Régiment de Grenadiers à Cheval
2,500	Régiment de Chasseurs à Cheval
250	Mamelukes
632	Gendarmes d'Élite (2 squadrons)

MEN	UNITS
1,250	Dragons de l'Impératrice
6,500	2 Régiments: Chevau-léger Lanciers
10,020	4 Régiments: Gardes d'Honneur
6,000	3 Régiments: Éclaireurs à Cheval

*Old Guard regiments

In addition, were the six foot and six horse companies of Old Guard artillery plus the fourteen young guard companies, *pontonniers*, train and *enginiers*.

Some more recruiting was ordered for the defensive campaigns of 1814 with increases in the numbers of Tirailleur and Voltigeur regiments. By the time of the abdication, the Guard had a paper strength as follows:

MEN	UNITS
3,200	2 Régiments: Grenadiers à Pied
200	Cie des Veterans
1,600	Régiment de Fusiliers-Grenadiers
30,400	19 Régiments: Tirailleurs
1,850	Flanqueur-Grenadier Régiment
3,200	2 Régiments: Chasseurs à Pied
1,600	Régiment de Fusiliers-Chasseurs
30,400	19 Régiments: Voltigeurs
1,850	Flanqueur-Chasseur Régiment
1,136	Bataillon de la Marine
1,600	Pupilles
2,000	Bataillon d'Instruction de Fontainebleau

MEN	UNITS
1,250	Régiment de Grenadiers à Cheval
2,500	Régiment de Chasseurs à Cheval
250	Mamelukes
632	Gendarmes d'Élite (2 squadrons)
1,250	Dragons de l'Impératrice
6,500	2 Régiments: Chevau-léger Lanciers
10,000	4 Régiments: Gardes d'Honneur
6,000	3 Régiments: Éclaireurs à Cheval

Plus the artillery, train, *pontonniers* and *enginiers*.

Since the short interim reign of Louis XVIII is not, strictly speaking, Napoleonic and did not see the Guard engage in active warfare, we will not go into any detail here. The main activities of the Bourbons as far as the Guard was concerned was to form Royal Corps of Grenadiers de France and Chasseurs de France from the Grenadiers à Pied, Fusiliers-Grenadiers, Chasseurs à Pied and Fusiliers-Chasseurs. Each regiment had four battalions of six companies. The men from Young Guard battalions were incorporated into the line after disbandment. Many veteran companies were organized to cope with the vast numbers of soldiers leaving the ranks as the army was reduced dramatically in numbers. Napoleon took with him, to Elba, a small body[15] of the Guard comprising a battalion of grenadiers, a company of Marins and the lance-armed 'Escadron Napoléon', some 868 men in all.

The Guard fought the 'Hundred Days' Campaign organized as follows (although not all battalions campaigned and actual strengths did not match the theoretical numbers shown below):

[15] Nafziger op. cit., p. 65. Johnston, R. op. cit., p. 36 says he took '. . .six companies of Grenadiers and Chasseurs (607 men of the Old Guard), 1 squadron of Polish Lancers, and 5 squadrons of Chasseurs à Cheval', although he does not make it clear whether the last-mentioned were Guard units.

NAME	NO. OF REGIMENTS	BNS/SQNS PER REGT	COS PER BN/SQN	MEN PER CO./SQN
Grenadiers à Pied	4	2[16]	4	150
Chasseurs à Pied	4	2	2	150
Tirailleurs	8	2	2	150
Voltigeurs	8	2	2	150
Marins	1 company	n/a	n/a	104
Dragons de l'Impératrice	1	7	2	200
Grenadiers à Cheval	1	6	2	200
Chevau-léger Lanciers	1	5	2	200
Chasseurs à Cheval	1	6	2	200
Gendarmes d'Élite	1	1	2	200
Artillerie à Pied	12 batteries	6 x 12 pdr guns each		
Artillerie à Cheval	5 batteries	6 x 6 pdr guns each		
Train	8 companies			

A company of Mamelukes was attached to the *Chasseurs à Cheval.*

The following tables provide a list of the actions in which units of the Guard were involved.

CONSULAR GUARD

UNIT	ENGAGEMENTS	UNIT	ENGAGEMENTS
Grenadiers à Pied	Marengo[17]	Grenadiers à Cheval	Marengo
Chasseurs à Pied	Marengo[17]	Chasseurs à Cheval	Marengo

[16] Of the 4th Regiment, only one battalion was formed.

[17] Lachouque, H. and Brown, A. S. K., (*The Anatomy of Glory* Arms & Armour Press, 1978, p. 15) indicate both units as being present: '. . .here come the grenadiers and chasseurs of the Guard. . .', although Smith, D. (*The Greenhill Napoleonic Wars Data Book* Greenhill Books, 1998, p. 186) suggests only one Consular Guard battalion – he does not state which. The combined strength of the Consular Guard infantry at Marengo seems to have been about 900.

GUARD INFANTRY

UNIT	SOBRIQUET	ENGAGEMENTS[18]
1er Grenadiers à Pied	Les Grognards (The Grumblers) and The Gaiterstraps	Ulm, Austerlitz, Jena, Eylau, Aspern-Essling, Wagram, Krasnoi,[19] Lützen, Dresden, Leipzig, Hanau, Montmirail, Vauchamps, Craonne, Laon, Arcis-sur-Aube, Paris, Ligny, Mont St Jean (Waterloo)
2e Grenadiers à Pied[20]		Jena, Dresden, Krasnoi, Leipzig, Vauchamps, Craonne, Laon, Paris, Ligny, Mont St Jean (Waterloo)
3e Grenadiers à Pied[21]		Krasnoi, Vilna, Ligny, Mont St Jean (Waterloo)
4e Grenadiers à Pied		Ligny, Mont St Jean (Waterloo)
1er Chasseurs à Pied	Les Grognards	Eylau, Aspern-Essling, *Spain*,[22] Krasnoi, Leipzig, Bar-sur-Aube, Montmirail, Château Thierry, Vauchamps, Craonne, Laon, Paris

* Italics indicate a presence in a general locality rather than a specific battle.

[18] By Waterloo, the honours of Marengo, Ulm, Austerlitz, Jena, Eylau, Friedland, Eckmühl, Essling, Wagram, Smolensk, La Moskowa (Borodino), Vienna, Berlin, Madrid and Moscow appeared on all Guard standards, regardless of any particular unit's involvement. We have shown the 1er Grenadiers with their presence at Ulm, Austerlitz & Jena. The honour 'Madrid' refers to the 'dos Mayo' riots in 1808 and is included in these tables under 'Spain', which represents a presence in the Peninsula without direct engagement. Specific engagements in Spain are given separately (e.g. Bailén).

[19] This was a combat fought by French survivors on the retreat from Moscow. There was little unit integrity.

[20] It should be remembered that, between 1808 and 1811, the 1er and 2e regiments were combined, so the engagements listed for that period under either regiment are effectively for both.

[21] We have discovered a small mystery with regard to a relatively minor combat at Mesa de Ibor in Spain (March 1809). Smith, D. (*Napoleon's Regiments*, Greenhill Books, 2000, p. 28) shows 3e Rgt as present (this unit only joined the Guard in 1810 as 2e Rgt, being re-numbered as 3e Rgt in 1811), although his earlier work, *The Greenhill Napoleonic Wars Data Book*, identifies only 'IR Holland'. This unit would appear to be part of Leval's 2nd division of Sebastiani's Corps and was not part of the Guard.

[22] Bessières' Army of the North contained elements of the Garde and was attempting to keep the guerrillas and remnants of the old Asturian Army from taking and holding the ports of the Biscay coast. Numerous small clashes and skirmishes occurred but the Spanish forces, if bettered, simply melted away into the Sierras to return another day. Smith D., (*Napoleon's Regiments*, p. 28) shows 1er Chasseurs in 1811 as involved in 'three skirmishes in Spain'. It is interesting that Oman, Sir C., (*A History of the Peninsular War* Greenhill Books, 1996, Vol. IV, p. 463) refers to 'eleven regiments of *tirailleurs, chasseurs* and *voltigeurs*' as 'all troops of the Young Guard'. In fact, 1er Chasseurs were Old Guard and it is not clear if these are the troops to which Smith was referring. Oman's orbat for the Army of the North op. cit., p. 641 gives '4 regiments of Voltigeurs, 4 of Tirailleurs, 1 of Chasseurs, 1 of Fusiliers-Chasseurs and 1 *bataillon de marche*'.

UNIT	SOBRIQUET	ENGAGEMENTS[18]
2e Chasseurs à Pied	Les Grognards cont.	Eylau, Lützen, Dresden, Hanau, Bar-sur-Aube, Montmirail, Arcis-sur-Aube, Craonne (1 Bn), Laon (1 Bn), Paris, Mont St Jean (Waterloo)
3e Chasseurs à Pied		Mont St Jean (Waterloo)
4e Chasseurs à Pied		Mont St Jean (Waterloo)
Marins	Les Hussards de la Marine	Austerlitz, Bailén, Beresina

GUARD INFANTRY (2)

UNIT	ENGAGEMENTS
Fusiliers-Grenadiers	Heilsberg, Essling, Krasnoi, Beresina, Dresden, Leipzig, Bar-sur-Aube, La Rothière, Montmirail, Meaux, Fère-Champenoise, Paris
Fusiliers-Chasseurs	Heilsberg, Friedland, Medina de Rioseco, Somosierra, Essling, Krasnoi, Beresina, Reichenbach, Dresden, Leipzig, Bar-sur-Aube, Montmirail, Meaux, Craonne, Paris
Vélites de Florence	Lützen, Leipzig, Montmirail, Meaux, Fère-Champenoise, Paris
Vélites de Turin	Lützen, Leipzig, Haynau, Montmirail, Meaux, Laon, Paris
1er Bn Tirailleurs Grenadiers/ 1er Tirailleurs	Essling, Wagram, *Spain*, Borodino, Krasnoi, Beresina, Lützen, Bautzen, Dresden, Leipzig, La Rothière, Craonne, Soissons, Fère-Champenoise, Paris, Mont St Jean
2e Bn Tirailleurs Grenadiers/ 2e Tirailleurs	Essling, Lützen, Bautzen, Dresden, Leipzig, Brienne, Montmirail, Craonne
1er Bn Conscrits Grenadiers[23] / 3e Tirailleurs	*Spain*, Lützen, Dresden, Leipzig, Laon, Paris, Mont St Jean
2e Bn Conscrits Grenadiers[23]/ 4e Tirailleurs	Krasnoi, Vilna, Dresden, Leipzig, La Rothière, Laon, Paris
5e Tirailleurs	Krasnoi, Beresina, Dresden, Leipzig, Brienne, Bar-sur-Aube, La Rothière, Montmirail, Arcis-sur-Aube, Paris
6e Tirailleurs	Lützen, Dresden, Leipzig, , La Rothière, Arcis-sur-Aube
7e Tirailleurs	Lützen, Würschen, Leipzig, Haynau, Brienne, Bar-su-Aube
8e Tirailleurs	Dresden, Leipzig, Brienne, Bar-sur-Aube, Arcis-sur-Aube
9e Tirailleurs	Dresden, Paris
10e Tirailleurs	Dresden, Leipzig, Craonne, Laon

UNIT	ENGAGEMENTS
11e Tirailleurs	Paris
12e Tirailleurs	Paris
13e Tirailleurs	Dresden, Craonne
14e Tirailleurs	Craonne, **Soissons**, Fère-Champenoise, Paris
1er Bn Tirailleurs Chasseurs/ 1er Voltigeurs	Essling, Wagram, Smolensk, Krasnoi, Lützen, Dresden, Leipzig, Brienne, Craonne, Quatre-Bras, Mont St Jean
2e Bn Tirailleurs Chasseurs/ 2e Voltigeurs	Lützen, Dresden, Leipzig, Brienne, Craonne, Laon, Paris
1er Bn Conscrits Chasseurs[23]/ 3e Voltigeurs	Lützen, Würschen, Dresden, Leipzig, La Rothière, Craonne, Laon, Fère-Champenoise, Mont St Jean
2e Bn Conscrits Chasseurs[23]/ 4e Voltigeurs	Krasnoi, Beresina, Lützen, Leipzig, Craonne, Laon, Fère-Champenoise
5e Voltigeurs	La Moskowa, Dresden, Leipzig, Fère-Champenoise, Paris
6e Voltigeurs	Krasnoi, Beresina, Dresden, Leipzig, Brienne, La Rothière, Fère-Champenoise
7e Voltigeurs	*Spain*, Dresden, Leipzig, Brienne, Craonne, Laon, Fère-Champenoise, Paris
8e Voltigeurs	Dresden, Leipzig, La Rothière, Vauchamps, Laon, Arcis-sur-Aube, Paris
9e Voltigeurs	Dresden, Leipzig, Paris
10e Voltigeurs	Dresden, Leipzig, Laon, Paris
11e Voltigeurs	Dresden, Leipzig, Laon, Arcis-sur-Aube, **Soissons**, Paris
12e Voltigeurs	Haynau, **Maubeuge**, Paris
13e Voltigeurs	Paris
14e Voltigeurs	Craonne, Fère-Champenoise
15e Voltigeurs	Bar-sur-Aube, Laon, Paris
16e Voltigeurs	Brienne, Laon, Paris
Flanquers-Chasseurs	Krasnoi, Beresina, Dresden, Leipzig, Brienne, Montmirail, Craonne, Laon, Paris

* Bold typeface indicates a siege, italics a presence in a general locality rather than a specific battle.

[23] The *conscrits* had a sobriquet of 'Les cts' (Pronounced 'say-tay-ess') from a subscript stencilled on their wagons.

GUARD CAVALRY

UNIT	SOBRIQUET	ENGAGEMENTS
Grenadiers à Cheval	Les Grands Eperons (The big heels or spurs) or Les Dieux (The gods)	Austerlitz, Eylau, *Spain*, Beresina, Leipzig, Brienne, Montmirail, Château Thierry, Vauchamps, Craonne, Laon, Ligny, Mont St Jean (Waterloo)
Chasseurs à Cheval	Les Invincibles or Les enfants cheris de L'Empereur (The Emperor's cherished or spoilt children)	Ulm, Austerlitz, Eylau, Heilsburg, Friedland, Benavente, Wagram, *Spain*, Krasnoi, Lützen, Reichenbach (3 sqns), Dresden, Leipzig, Brienne, Montmirail, Château Thierry, Montereau, Craonne, Laon, Paris, Courtrai, Ligny, Mont St Jean (Waterloo)
Mamelukes	–	Austerlitz, Eylau, Benavente, Altenburg, Weimar, Haynau
Gendarmerie d'Élite	Les Immortels (The Immortals)	Jena, Medina de Rioseco,[24] Beresina, Lützen, Leipzig, Quatre Bras, Mont St Jean
Dragons de l'Impératrice	–	Jena, Friedland, Medina de Rioseco,[24] Borodino, Malojaroslavetz, Krasnoi, Beresina, Dresden, Leipzig, Haynau, Bar-sur-Aube, Montmirail, Château Thierry, Craonne, Laon, Arcis-sur-Aube, Quatre Bras, Mont St Jean
1er Chevau-léger Lanciers		Medina de Rioseco,[24] Somosierra, Essling, Wagram, *Spain*, Russia, Dresden, Leipzig, Haynau, Craonne
2e Chevau-léger Lanciers		Borodino, Beresina, Reichenbach, Dresden, Leipzig, **Antwerp**, La Rothière, Montereau, Craonne, Paris, Quatre Bras, Mont St Jean

* Bold typeface indicates a siege, italics a presence in a general locality rather than a specific battle.

[24] Smith D., (*Napoleon's Regiments*, p.32) suggests that the Guard cavalry present at Medina were the Dragons de l'Impératrice and 1er Chevaux Lég. but does not show the former in his orbat for that battle (*Napoleonic Wars Data Book*, p. 262), instead giving 1er Chevaux Léger. Oman, Prof. Sir C. op. cit. Vol. I, p. 167, merely states that there were 3 sqns. of Guard cavalry present, so we suspect all three regiments could have been represented, each by a single squadron.

UNIT	SOBRIQUET	ENGAGEMENTS
1er Gardes d'Honneur	Les Otages	Leipzig, Courtrai
2e Gardes d'Honneur	(The hostages)	Leipzig
3e Gardes d'Honneur		Leipzig, Haynau, Craonne, Paris
4e Gardes d'Honneur		Leipzig, **Strasbourg**
1er Éclaireurs		Brienne, Craonne, Laon, Arcis-sur-Aube, Paris
2e Éclaireurs		Craonne, Laon, Arcis-sur-Aube, Paris
3e Éclaireurs		Arcis-sur-Aube, Paris

ii) The Line & Light Infantry

In 1800, the old revolutionary nomenclature still existed and the demi-brigade was still the basic organization for French infantry. The Treaty of Lunéville, with the Austrian capitulation on 9 February 1801, saw Britain as the only remaining active enemy to France and this situation was ended on 27 March 1802, with the Treaty of Amiens. An uneasy peace and preparations for war and invasion of Britain occupied the months until 16 May 1803. Later in that year (September) the line demi-brigades were renamed regiments, the léger units having been renamed in 1801 with two two-battalion demi-brigades combining to form one regiment. This does not seem to have been universally implemented since, in 1808, the order was reinforced by an Imperial decree.

FRENCH INFANTRY 1800 TO 1803

APPROXIMATE PAPER STRENGTHS	LIGNE	LÉGER
NO. OF D-BRIGS	110	30
BNS/D-BRIG	4 x 4, 103 x 3, 3 x 2	to 1801: 3; after 1801: 2
COS/BN	Fusilier – 8; Grenadier – 1	Chasseur – 8; Carabinier – 1 (see below)
MEN/CO.	Fusilier – 124; Grenadier – 83	Chasseur – 50; Grenadier – 48

In 1801, with the reduction in regimental size, each of the two battalions converted one fusilier company to voltigeurs (light). When the denomination 'regiment' was reinstated (24.9.03), there were eighty-nine line units in total, many (nineteen) had four battalions (presumably the regulations stipulating three had not been acted upon) whilst the rest had the regulation three. Almost exactly one year later, a reorganization took place converting one fusilier company (2nd) in each battalion to voltigeurs in common with the light units. By 1805, there was little difference in organization between line and light regiments.

INFANTRY 1804 TO MID-1807

APPROXIMATE PAPER STRENGTHS	LIGNE	LÉGER	GARDE DE PARIS	ÉTRANGER & ITALIAN	SWISS[25]
NO. OF REGTS	89	26	2	There were several regiments with varying strengths and organizations. They are dealt with in the notes below this table.	4 (inc. 8pdr art. Bty each)
BNS/REGT	3+depot	3+depot	4		4
COS/BN	Fusilier – 7 Voltigeur – 1 Grenadier – 1	Chasseur – 7 Voltigeur – 1 Carabinier – 1	10		Fusilier – 8 Voltigeur – 1 Grenadier – 1
MEN/CO.	Fusilier – 121 Voltigeur – 120 Grenadier – 96	120	123		100

FOREIGN UNITS 1803 TO 1807

1. There were four *Étranger* regiments, all organized on the basic French lines: 1er 'Tour d'Auvergne' (Austrian POWs); two battalions, raised in 1804. 2e 'd'Isembourg' (Prussian POWs); one battalion raised in 1805. 3e 'Légion Irlandais' (Irish rebels); one battalion, raised in 1803. 4e 'Régiment de Prusse' (Prussians); three battalions, raised in 1806.
2. The 'Légion Hanovrienne' initially comprised two battalions each of five companies of 156 men, raised 1804.

[25] Excluding the Neuchâtel and Valaison battalions.

3. The 'Régiment de Westphalie' (troops from various German provinces, including Prussia, Brunswick and Nassau) had four battalions, raised 1807. Each battalion had four companies of 140 men.
4. In addition to the four Swiss 'mercenary' regiments, two units of Swiss troops were formed: in 1805, the 'Bataillon de Valais' (Genoese); five companies, including one grenadier, of 100 men and, in 1806, the 'Bataillon de Neuchâtel' (Light infantry); a carabinier, a voltigeur and four chasseur companies, each of 160 men.
5. The 'Chasseurs d'Orient' were originally Turks, recruited to police Cairo in the Egyptian campaign. The organization and strength of the battalion was, at Marseilles, in 1801, seven companies, each of eighty men. However, it never boasted a total strength of more than 400, falling as low as seventy-seven in 1807 and ninety-six in 1813. Between 1809 and 1814 it was in garrison on Corfu.
6. An Albanian regiment was raised by Berthier from Greek, Albanian, Italian and Dalmatian nationals in the Ionian Islands. Two battalions of eight fusilier (120 men) and one grenadier (seventy men) companies were established, plus the 'Bataillon Septinsulaire' which had six companies, each of 150 men.
7. As well as the troops raised by Italy for its own army, that country provided recruiting facilities for a number of French regiments and some specifically Italian-manned units. These were: 'Légion du Midi' (Piedmontese); two battalions, raised in 1803. Tirailleurs du Po (Light infantry from the River Po region) – two battalions. Tirailleurs Corses (Light infantry from Corsica) – two battalions.
8. Details of the Vistula Legion and the Spanish Army of King Joseph are given in the tables later in the book, (the Portuguese Legion is dealt with separately, later in the book), whilst the troops forming the Spanish division of La Romana in Denmark are dealt with in the first volume of the *Handbook* (pp. 305 and 306).

In mid-1804, the regiments of the line (*Ligne*) were numbered from 1 to 112, although numbers 31, 38, 41, 49, 68, 71, 73, 74, 77, 78, 80, 83, 87, 90, 91, 98, 99, 104, 107, 109, and 110 were not used. The light (*Légère*) regiment numbering ran from 1 to 31 with 19, 20, 29 and 30 being unused. The 86e and 89e Ligne regiments were amalgamated as a new 86e regiment whilst the 5e and 11e Légère combined as a new 5e Légère. In May 1808, the 113e Ligne was formed as was a 32e Légère, both in Tuscany.

It was the practice to 'strip-out' the grenadier, voltigeur and other companies from the line battalions to form 'élite' battalions. These were initially grouped together as the Grenadier Division under Marshal Oudinot. Each regiment had two battalions of six companies.

Additionally, sixteen Regiments Provisoires were raised. They were formed from independent and unattached companies plus any 'odd' battalions not operating at the front. They could exist for anything up to two or three years, although the practice was discontinued after the invasion of the Iberian peninsula (1808) when the provisional regiments were disbanded or incorporated in the line as 114e to 120e Ligne and 33e Légère (1809) regiments. The grenadier division was also largely disbanded and the élite companies returned to their parent regiments, although the practice of creating *grenadiers réunis* units from the élite companies of line regiments for specific battlefield engagements continued (e.g. Albuera – May 1811).

The year 1807 saw the start of a major change for line infantry units which would become the official organization in February 1808. It reduced the seven fusilier companies to four (but retained the grenadier and voltigeur companies) and raised the number of battalions to four per regiment plus one depot battalion of four fusilier companies.

This year also witnessed the formation of five '*Légions de Reserve*' (*Régiments Supplémentaires*), designed to give protection to the coastal and frontier regions during the absence of the *Grande Armée* on its German campaigns. Each comprised five battalions of eight companies (160 men each) plus an artillery company of 6 x 8pdr plus two howitzers. After being sent on the early Peninsular campaigns and being part of Dupont's defeat at Bailén, the legions were amalgamated and became the 121e and 122e line regiments.

FRENCH INFANTRY 1808

APPROXIMATE PAPER STRENGTHS	LIGNE	LÉGER
NO. OF REGTS	69 (exc. Lég. de Res.)	22 + 32e léger
BNS/REGT	4+depot	4+depot (32e had 3)
COS/BN	6 (depot 4)	6 (depot = 4, 32e = 9)

In early 1808, six additional régiments provisoires were organized, as were the aforementioned Tuscan regiments (32e Légère, which had nine companies, and the 113e Ligne with three battalions, each of six companies). Also, three battalions of 'Chasseurs de Montagnes' were formed in this year. Several Colonial regiments, battalions and companies also became part of the army and the contribution by foreign units was increased.

By 1809, the number of line regiments had increased to ninety-six, whilst the 3/37e demi-brigade had still not followed the nomenclature rules and the 2e Légion de Reserve had yet to be amalgamated into the 121er and 122e line regiments. A number of colonial regiments, some of whose battalions had been sent to the West Indies, or who acted as recruiting depots for the colonies, were counted in the army strength. Light Infantry regiments numbered twenty-seven and there were the following foreign or provincial units included on the strength: Tirailleurs de Po, Tirailleurs de Corses, Chasseurs de Montagnes (8 Bns), Corsican battalions (4), Légion du Midi, Bataillon de la Mediterranée (originally a penal battalion), Garde de Paris, Pompiers de Paris (firemen), Chasseurs d'Orients, Albanian (1) & Greek (1) battalions, Bataillon Septinsulaires, Bataillon de L'Ile d'Elbe, Régiment Tour d'Auvergne, Régiment d'Isembourg, Régiment de Prusse, Swiss (four regiments), Bataillon de Valais, Bataillon de Neuchâtel, Légion Irlandais, Légion Hanovrienne, Régiment Joseph Napoléon (Spanish), Bataillon Piombino (Pauline Bonaparte's principality – ten Cos x 100 men + 8pdr battery), Régiment de Westphalie, Légion Portugaise, two Bataillons Étrangers, twenty-seven Veteran battalions, about 125 independent companies.

In 1810, the numbers and organization of the basic line and light regiments remained as before, the six Croatian regiments of the erstwhile Austrian *Grenz* and two Illyrian battalions became part of the army, reorganizing along French lines, and there were a few changes in the foreign, colonial and provincial strengths and organizations. Additionally, seven Bataillons Auxiliaires were formed for service in Spain. Much of this was the result of the leakage of men from the Spanish theatre. The Peninsula was a running sore which drained men from the regiments prosecuting the war. As early as 1809, fresh recruits were being formed into régiments de marches and sent to Spain, they were then broken up to supply replacements for the engaged regiments; supplementary and auxiliary battalions, with little in the way of staff and no real *esprit de corps*, were hastily put together and sent to bolster the army's strength. Much 'tinkering' with organizations was forced on the Emperor because of the necessity for providing a constant flow of new conscripts into the Peninsula without appearing to change materially the army's overall strength. Another move which improved the army's apparent (and actual) strength was the incorporation of the Dutch line infantry as the 123e to 126e Ligne and 33e Léger (whose original establishment had lasted only a short time) regiments. The Texel Regiment (four battalions of six companies each x 140 men) was formed from the old Zeeland Regiment.

By the time 1811 arrived, the situation had become difficult enough that Napoleon announced the filling of the vacant regimental numbers with actual units – even the names of officers were published – but it was all a smoke screen to disguise the size of France's army. However, there was a small increase in the total number of line and light regiments. One hundred-and-four of the former and thirty of the latter existed by the beginning of April that year. There were one or two that did not have the same number of battalions (five) as the rest: 58e Ligne boasted six battalions, whilst 127e, 128e and 129e had only four each and the 32e Léger still had only three battalions. The 11e Léger – combining the Tirailleurs de Po and Corses plus the Légion du Midi – and the 29e Léger were two of the vacant numbers which were filled, whilst the Chasseurs de Montagnes were reduced to three eight-company battalions. An early increase in the line regiments came as a result of the 'absorption' of the Hanseatic League cities into France, which provided the three four-battalion regiments mentioned above. In March, the 34e Léger came into being by the amalgamation of four Bataillons Auxiliaires, whilst three more were used to form the 130e Ligne. The 131er Ligne was formed from the Dutch van Walcheren regiment.[26] One of the major organizational changes which occurred during 1811 was the increasing of the numbers of battalions in some line and light regiments to six[27] (with six fusilier companies in the new sixth battalion). Interestingly, three regiments (14e and 22e Léger and 6e Ligne) were increased to seven battalions.

[26] Smith, D., (*Napoleon's Regiments*, p. 174). Nafziger op. cit., Vol. I, p. 30 says 131er was formed from Regiment van Walcheren in 1812 as part of the reorganization after the Russian campaign.

[27] Nafziger op. cit., Vol. I, p. 28. Johnston, R. op. cit., p. 24 gives each regiment only three battalions and, on p. 26, says, referring to the year 1812, 'The only changes in organization of the infantry was an increase, in some regiments, of the number of component battalions to five' and, later, 'the Russian campaign forestalled the full implementation of this measure.' We suspect the reason for apparent difference of view is that Johnson ignores the depot and includes only field battalions.

Before the invasion of Russia in 1812, two 3pdr cannon were ordered to be issued to each regiment. This was not fully implemented because of the campaign but many regiments did receive the guns (mostly those stationed in France) – we have no certain information as to how many or which regiments benefited, however. The order of battle for the invasion of Russia is presented in many works which are readily available in public libraries, so it is not our intention to take up valuable space in this volume to reproduce it. However, it is key to understanding the subsequent reorganization of the French Army to appreciate how many regiments were either totally destroyed or so badly damaged that they effectively disappeared from the lists. The following table provides this information:

INFANTRY BATTALIONS LOST OR SEVERELY DAMAGED IN THE RUSSIAN CAMPAIGN

REGIMENT	BNS LOST/ DAMAGED	REGIMENT	BNS LOST/ DAMAGED
7e Léger	1er, 2e, 3e, 4e, 6e	85e Ligne	1er, 2e, 3e, 4e, 6e
8e Léger	1er, 2e	92e Ligne	1er, 2e, 3e, 4e
10e Léger	4e	93e Ligne	1er, 2e, 3e, 4e, 6e
11e Léger	1er, 2e, 3e, 4e	106e Ligne	1er, 2e, 3e, 4e
13e Léger	1er, 2e, 3e, 4e, 6e	108e Ligne	1er, 2e, 3e, 4e, 6e
15e Léger	1er, 2e, 3e, 4e, 6e	111er Ligne	1er, 2e, 3e, 4e, 6e
18e Léger	1er, 2e	123e Ligne	1er, 2e, 4e
22e Léger	6e	124e Ligne	1er, 2e, 3e
24e Léger	1er, 2e, 3e, 4e	125e Ligne	1er, 2e, 3e
26e Léger	1er, 2e, 3e, 4e	126e Ligne	1er, 2e, 3e, 4e
29e Léger	1er, 2e, 3e, 4e	127e Ligne	1er, 2e
33e Léger	1er, 2e, 3e	128e Ligne	1er, 2e
2e Ligne	1er, 2e, 3e, 4e, 6e	129e Ligne	1er, 2e
4e Ligne	1er, 2e, 3e, 4e	Neuchâtel	1er
9e Ligne	1er, 2e, 3e, 4e	1er Suisse	1er, 2e, 3e, 4e

REGIMENT	BNS LOST/ DAMAGED	REGIMENT	BNS LOST/ DAMAGED
12e Ligne	1er, 2e, 3e, 4e, 6e	2e Suisse	1er, 2e, 3e, 4e
17e Ligne	1er, 2e, 3e, 4e, 6e	3e Suisse	1er, 2e, 3e, 4e
18e Ligne	1er, 2e, 3e, 4e	4e Suisse	1er, 2e, 3e, 4e
19e Ligne	1er, 2e, 3e, 4e, 6e	Joseph Napoléon	1er, 2e, 3e, 4e
21er Ligne	1er, 2e, 3e, 4e, 6e	1ère Légion Portugaise	1er, 2e
25e Ligne	1er, 2e, 3e, 4e, 6e	2e Légion Portugaise	1er, 2e
30e Ligne	1er, 2e, 3e, 4e, 6e	3e Légion Portugaise	1er, 2e
33e Ligne	1er, 2e, 3e, 4e, 6e	1er Régiment de Croatie	1er
35e Ligne	1er, 2e, 3e, 4e	2e Régiment de Croatie	1er
36e Ligne	4e	3e Régiment de Croatie	1er
37e Ligne	1er, 2e, 3e, 4e, 6e	4e Régiment de Croatie	1er
40e Ligne	1er, 2e, 3e, 4e, 6e	5e Régiment de Croatie	1er
48e Ligne	1er, 2e, 3e, 4e, 6e	6e Régiment de Croatie	1er
51er Ligne	4e	1ère Légion de la Vistule	1er, 2e, 3e
53e Ligne	1er, 2e, 3e, 4e	2e Légion de la Vistule	1er, 2e, 3e
55e Ligne	4e	3e Légion de la Vistule	1er, 2e, 3e
56e Ligne	1er, 2e, 3e, 4e, 6e	4e Légion de la Vistule	1er, 2e, 3e
57e Ligne	1er, 2e, 3e, 4e, 6e	4e Rgt Polonnais	1er, 2e, 3e
61er Ligne	1er, 2e, 3e, 4e, 6e	7e Rgt Polonnais	1er, 2e, 3e
72e Ligne	1er, 2e, 3e, 4e	9e Rgt Polonnais	1er, 2e, 3e
84e Ligne	1er, 2e, 3e, 4e	**Totals:** 40 Léger, 157 Ligne, 53 Étranger	

The reorganization itself started with the formation of twenty-eight provisional regiments from the battalions which had remained in Germany, although these regiments did not remain in being for long.

The 132e and 133e Régiments de Ligne were formed from two penal regiments (2e de la Mediterranée and Ile de Ré) whilst 35e and 36e

Léger regiments were formed from 1ère de la Mediterranée and Belle-Ile, similarly penal units. Three battalions of 134e Ligne came from the Garde Municipale de Paris whilst the fourth was derived from the 4th battalion of the 4/125e (under siege in Stettin); the 5th and 6th battalions came from 4e/ and 5e/126e.

In 1813, the 135e to 156e Ligne regiments were raised from the National Guard, and the Garde Municipale provided the men for 37e Léger, whilst other regiments were given additional battalions partly by bringing forward the Class of 1814 conscription and rigorous recruiting in the various districts of France. Forty-five further provisional regiments were raised from the remains of some of the old regiments and lasted about three months before being reassigned to proper units. It should also be borne in mind that there was a substantial French army still serving in the Iberian Peninsula – which, itself, provided considerable numbers for the new 'Grande Armée'.

As a result of this mammoth undertaking, by mid-1813, the structure of the army was as follows:

Line Regiments (5 battalions)	97	Régiments Polonais (3 battalions)	5e, 10e, 11e
Line Regiments (6 battalions)	26	Bataillons d'Amsterdam	2 (battalions)
Line Regiments (8 battalions)	6e	Rgts. de Pologne et Lithuanie (2 battalions)	4
Line Regiments (4 battalions + depot)	26e, 66e, 82e	Régiment Portugaise (1 battalion)	1
Line Regiments (4 battalions)	127e, 128e, 129e	Albanian Regiment (6 battalions)	1
Light Regiments (5 battalions)	29	Régiment Étrangère (6 battalions)	1
Light Regiments (6 battalions)	4	Régiment Étrangère (5 battalions ea.)	3
Light Regiments (8 battalions)	14e, 35e	Régiment Irlandais (3e Etrang.)	1
Régiment des Marines (10 battalions)	1	Régiment Suisses (1 battalion ea.)	4
Régiment des Marines (8 battalions)	1	Régiment Joseph Napoléon (2 battalions)	1
Régiment des Marines (4 battalions)	2	Illyrian Regiment (2 battalions)	1
Garde Nationale (800+ man battalions)	10	Régiment Croatiennes	6

Garde Nationale (1 Cht x 6 Cos)	12	Bataillon d'Orient	1 (Bn)
Garde Nationale (Urban Cht x 6 Cos)	37	Bataillon Septinsulaire	1 (Bn)
Bataillons des Vétérans	14	Bataillon de l'Ile d'Elbe	1 (Bn)
Bataillons Coloniales	4	Bataillons Étrangères	3 (Bns)
Bataillons Déserters	1	Bataillon de Neuchâtel	1 (Bn)
Régiment de Texel	1	Bataillon de Piombino	1 (Bn)
Chasseurs des Montagnes	3 Battalions	Albanian Battalion	1 (Bn)

Plus 138 independent companies of various type and origin.

Notes on the above table:

1. 'Cht' = Cohorts
2. The total number of men in the infantry was just under three-quarters of a million.

Following the 1813 campaigns, a number of units were disbanded – principally 4th Battalions but, in one case (129e Ligne), an entire regiment. In all, twenty-nine battalions suffered this fate. Much reorganization was necessary and many amalgamations took place. However, where recruitment areas provided enough men, some regiments received additional battalions. These changes did not represent adjustments to the theoretical structures of the infantry but were effectively *ad hoc* arrangements to suit local situations.

The Bourbon reorganization of 1814 (for details, see tables of actions fought) resulted in ninety regiments of the line and fifteen light regiments; four Swiss regiments; three Étranger and one Colonial Étranger regiments; eight Colonial battalions with six companies each and three with five; two Corsican Chasseur battalions and one battalion of Paris Firemen (Pompiers) plus sixty independent companies – in all about 170,000 infantry.

Napoleon's return to the French mainland from Elba for the 'Hundred Days' prompted the Allies to react in an aggressive manner and this, in turn, resulted in the Emperor calling for all the veterans of his old infantry regiments to return to the colours. Details of those regiments participating in the 1815 campaign are in the tables of actions fought. As a result, the line and light regiments were brought up to four battalions each and the Swiss were formed into a single battalion

(2e Étranger [Suisse]). Large numbers National Guard battalions were also planned as an auxiliary force but, by the second abdication, only about 200 had been formed and these were used to provide troops in the French interior. Some other troops were available, being largely from the remnants of some of the pre-1814 abdication units but they amounted to a very small number of men.

iii) The Cavalry

A number of unit types existed within the Cavalry arm and we will deal with these in turn, there being little in the way of regulations which affected the cavalry as a whole after 1800.

CUIRASSIERS

In 1802, the heavy cavalry numbered twenty-seven regiments. That same year, the Emperor ordered the number cut to twenty – eighteen heavy and two carabinier regiments. The remaining units were disbanded and their men distributed among the twenty. The 8e 'Cuirassier' regiment was already armoured and 1er to 5e, inclusive, were supposed to receive cuirasses (with steel breast and back plates) whilst the six remaining heavy cavalry regiments converted to dragoons towards the end of 1803. By the end of 1803, there were six armoured cuirassier regiments but they were 1er, 2e, 3e, 6e, 7e & 8e. In 1804, the 4e heavy cavalry regiment received the cuirass, along with 9e to 12e but 5e did not become armoured until 1805. Cuirassiers were armed with pistols and straight sabre until 1812, with *mousquetons* added thereafter; they were intended for use as battlefield shock troops, charging their enemy in close order. The steel cuirasses were admirable protection against sabre slashes or sword thrusts but could not withstand penetration by a musket ball unless the ball struck the cuirass at a very oblique angle.

In 1809, after the disaster at Bailén, the 1er and the remains of the 2e *Régiments Provisoires* were combined to form 13e Cuirassiers. The two provisional regiments were originally made up of detachments from 1er and 2e Carabiniers, 1er, 2e, 3e, 5e, 9e, 10e, 11e and 12e Cuirassiers. In 1808, a third provisional regiment was formed of detachments from 4e, 6e, 7e and 8e regiments; it lasted until 1811, serving in Spain during most of that period.

CARABINIERS

These two units were formed from the old 1er and 2e heavy cavalry regiments of the Revolutionary army. Initially, they were un-armoured but adopted the cuirass in 1809, at the same time changing their dark blue coats and buff breeches for an all-white uniform. Weaponry comprised a carbine, heavy cavalry straight sabre and a pair of pistols. Essentially, their rôle was similar to that of the cuirassiers but they had the special regard of the Emperor, who considered them '*grenadiers de la cavalerie*'.

DRAGONS À CHEVAL

Non-armoured; originally mounted infantry who were theoretically at home fighting on foot or mounted (usually on strong but slow horses), they were armed with a *mousqueton*, pistols and straight sabre and were considered by Napoleon as 'vital to support the light cavalry in advance guard'. The revolutionary army contained twenty dragoon regiments, a twenty-first being raised in 1801. The change of status of the 13e to 18e heavy cavalry produced the 22e to 27e *Dragons à Cheval* regiments, whilst the conversion of 7e(bis), 11e and 12e *Hussards* created the 28e to 30e regiments. In 1811, the 1er, 3e, 8e, 9e, 10e and 29e regiments were converted to *Chevaux-légers Lanciers*.

DRAGONS À PIED

To a large extent thanks to the shortage of horses, many dragoons were not supplied with mounts. Napoleon, in 1803, decreed that the 1st and 2nd squadrons should give up their mounted status and form foot squadrons; the 3rd and 4th squadrons received their horses. The foot squadrons were combined to form five brigades each with three foot dragoon formations. In 1805, the dismounted companies were reorganized, re-designated and reshuffled until, eventually, they were formed into a division with the following organization, which also included ten artillery pieces:

1er Bataillon, 1er Régiment: dismounted companies of 1er, 2e, & 20e Drag. à Ch.
2e Bataillon, 1er Régiment: dismounted companies of 4e, 14e[28] & 26e Drag. à Ch.
1er Bataillon, 2e Régiment: dismounted companies of 10e, 13e & 22e Drag. à Ch.
2e Bataillon, 2e Régiment: dismounted companies of 3e, 6e[28] & 11e Drag. à Ch.

1er Bataillon, 3e Régiment: dismounted companies of 5e, 8e & 12e Drag. à Ch.
2e Bataillon, 3e Régiment: dismounted companies of 9e, 16e[28] & 21er Drag. à Ch.
1er Bataillon, 4e Régiment: dismounted companies of 15e, 17e & 25e Drag. à Ch.
2e Bataillon, 4e Régiment: dismounted companies of 18e, 19e & 27e Drag. à Ch.

It was not intended that the dismounting of dragoons should be a permanent situation but should only be implemented whilst there were insufficient horses. Eventually the regiments were mounted on horses obtained from the Rhine region.

CHEVAU-LÉGER LANCIERS

As stated above, the first six regiments of this body were converted to dragoons in 1811. In the same year, two additional regiments (7e and 8e) were taken from the Polish Vistula Legion whilst the 9e was formed from 30e Chasseurs à Cheval. The lance was seen by Napoleon as a weapon to be feared after his earlier experiences with Cossacks, although, as well as this weapon, the lancers were issued with *mousquetons* and curved sabres, the latter of which they would have used in close combat where their primary weapon could not be wielded.

CHASSEURS À CHEVAL

Numbering 1 to 25 (with 17 and 18 vacant) during the revolutionary period, the Chasseurs, together with the Hussars, formed the main scouting arm of the French Army. However, they were perfectly capable of spirited action on the field of battle as was proved on numerous occasions. Additional regiments were raised – 26e in 1801 (from the Piedmont Hussars), 27e and 28e in 1808 (from Chevau-légers d'Arenburg and 2nd Tuscan Dragoons respectively), 29e in 1810 from a provisional regiment (3rd), 30e in 1811 from the Maburg Dragoon

[28] Nafziger, G., (*The French Army, Royal Republican, Imperial*, Vol. III, p. 33). Bukhari, E. (*Napoleon's Cavalry* Osprey Publishing Ltd, London, 1979) gives a list 'Amended from a slightly erroneous list of General Baraguey d'Hilliers, dated 9 Fructidor AnXIII', which indicates 2/1er contained 16e instead of 14e and 2/3e contained 6e instead of 16e. We think it unlikely that the 6e would have provided two detachments, so have opted for Nafziger's organization.

Co. (they were shortly after converted to Lancers) and 31er from 1er and 2e Régiments Provisoires again in 1811. Also in that year, the 17e and 18e were raised. Curved sabres, *mousquetons* and, usually only for officers, one or two pistols were the arms issued to chasseurs.

HUSSARS

The fourteen regiments which existed during the Revolution were reduced to eleven with the disbandment of 13e and, in 1802, to ten with the conversion of 7e (bis), 11e and 12e to Dragoons. In 1800, insufficient mounts could be found for all of the regiments plus the large number of semi-independent bodies attached to volunteer units. Consequently, those hussars who could not be supplied with horses were formed into two nine-company foot battalions which were later amalgamated with the 45e Ligne and 14e Léger infantry regiments. By 1803, only ten hussar regiments remained and this was the situation until 1810, when the Dutch Black and Red Hussars combined to form a new 11e Régiment. The 9e (bis) was raised in Spain in 1812 and, the next year, became 12e Régiment whilst, again in 1813 but lasting just under a year, the 13e was reborn from men raised in Tuscany, and later undergoing yet a third life as Jérôme Napoléon's Westphalian Hussars assumed the regimental number for four months. Another regiment which lasted less than a year was 14e which was captured at Dresden but the regiment was raised a second time in Turin early in 1814 – this time lasting only three months!

Hussars were the stuff of legend in the French Army. Not best noted for discipline but more for their bright and variegated uniforms and their undoubted *élan*, they were the dashing *beaux-sabreurs* of story books and exciting tales (many based on fact). Their task was to seek out the enemy advance guards or positions and, by brave skirmishing and the threat of a full-blooded charge, pin them whilst the main body advanced. Alternatively, they could fight dogged and desperate rearguard actions to protect the retirement of their comrades. They were armed with the light cavalry curved sabre, a *mousqueton* (other ranks only) and, if they were fortunate, one or two pistols.

GENERAL ORGANIZATION

The various types of French cavalry were largely organized along the same lines after 1800. Each regiment comprised four squadrons, each of two companies (the first of the first squadron being the so-called '*élite*' company). The main variations seem to have been in the number of men in each company:

FRENCH CAVALRY – NUMBER OF MEN PER COMPANY (PAPER STRENGTHS)

UNIT TYPE	1801	1803	1806	1809	1812	POST 1812[29]
CARABINIERS	86	86	100	120	125	125
CUIRASSIERS	62	86	100	120	125	125
DRAGOONS	88 mounted 52 dismounted	88 mounted 149 dismounted	80[30]	80	109	127
LANCERS	–	–	–	–	128	128
CHASSEURS	116	78	80	80	80	80
HUSSARS	116	78	80	80	80	80

iv) The Artillery

ARTILLERIE À PIED

The French artillery service underwent, shortly before the Revolution, a complete overhaul and reorganization by Gribeauval, who had service both with Prussia and Austria in earlier years. His measures provided for a much lighter, more manoeuvrable gun carriage with standardized (4-pdr, 8-pdr and 12-pdr) projectiles. This gave the French probably the best artillery system in Europe if not the world. At the end of 1801, the French line field (foot) artillery comprised eight regiments of twenty companies each. Each company had six cannon and two 6.4

[29] After the Russian campaign, the 1813/1814 campaigns and the Bourbon reorganization, the old regiments could not be re-established and recruited up to theoretical establishment either in principle or fact. We have been guided by Nafziger's comment that op. cit., p. 41, 'When Napoleon returned to France . . . he confined himself to restoring [cuirassier] regiments to their previous imperial organization and strength.' This must have applied equally to the other cavalry types. Nafziger makes a similar remark regarding Chasseurs and Hussars (p. 30).

[30] Johnston, R. op. cit., p. 12 says, when talking generally of French cavalry in 1805–1807 that, 'Each of the squadrons had a book strength of 160 men.' Nafziger is silent on this aspect of Dragoon strengths for the period.

inch[31] howitzers. The major activity during the ensuing two years was in the colonies and this was addressed by the addition, in 1803, of two companies to each regiment. The sixteen new companies thus formed were sent to the Caribbean and Africa.

The same year saw the Gribeauval system replaced by a new ('Year 11' – 1802/3) one, which replaced the 4- and 8-pdr guns with 6- and 12-pdr versions, although the old weights persisted in various combinations throughout the period.

In 1805, a company of artillery comprised 100 men and each regiment had twenty-two companies plus a staff of thirty and this structure seems to have persisted for the next six years. The most significant event in the intervening period was the addition of the Dutch foot artillery to form the 9e Régiment in 1810. In 1811, the company strength was adjusted, ending the year with 114 men. Four companies were added to each regiment at the beginning of 1813 and, in August of that year, a further two. The year 1814 saw the conversion of some coast-guard companies to provide three more companies for each regiment but by no means all regiments benefited.

ARTILLERIE À CHEVAL

Horse artillery did not form part of French arms prior to 1792, when three companies were raised under two different commanders in separate places but, by 1802, an establishment of six regiments had been decided upon. The 1805 organization provided each regiment except the 6e (which had seven), with six companies of 100 men and a regimental staff of fifteen. In 1808, the other five regiments appear to have adopted the seven-company establishment. In 1810, the Dutch horse artillery formed a seventh regiment which did not last long, its men and equipment being absorbed into other regiments. By 1813, an eighth company had been added to the 4e and 6e regiments with the other regiments taking up this establishment the following year.

The size of the guns served by the horse artillerists seems to be somewhat uncertain. In the early years, mostly 4-pdrs were allocated (six of them, with two howitzers per company). However, when infantry 'battalion guns' were allocated in 1809, these were mostly the 4-pdr variety, with the artillery-proper adopting the Year XI 6-pdrs. However there is evidence that some units used 8-pdrs and even 12-pdrs.

[31] Johnston, R. op. cit., p. 12 erroneously gives these as 5.5" howitzers, which was the calibre used by British batteries.

INFANTRY REGIMENTAL ARTILLERY

As mentioned above, there was a resurrection of the system of allocating guns to infantry regiments. Initially limited to the *Armée d'Allemagne* (six regiments), the decree was not implemented until 1811 by which time, the regiments of the *Corps d'Observation de l'Elbe* was embraced as, gradually, were other regiments. The guns were 4-pdrs and numbered four per regiment. Generally, the foreign regiments did not embrace this system.

TRAIN D'ARTILLERIE

Until 1798, the artillery was transported to and about the battlefield by contractors, who supplied drivers and horses. Thereafter, the facility became militarized, with independent companies being formed that worked directly with the artillery units to which they were attached. In 1800, the train was organized into thirty-eight battalions of five companies each, one of which was designated *élite* and had eighty men and 144 horses whilst the rest comprised sixty men and 106 horses each. The number of men was rationalized to around 100 in 1805, with reduced manning in peacetime.

The organization fluctuated from a war footing to a peacetime one over the years until, in 1811, the establishment of a company was set at 141 men with 272 horses.

3. UNIFORMS

Whilst it is not the main purpose of this book to give full and detailed guides to uniform styles and colours – this information is more than adequately covered in other volumes specifically designed to do that job – we feel that it is important to convey a general picture.

For the line and light infantry, the distinctions from regiment to regiment were not normally made through facing colours. More subtle differences were the order – for example, different shaped cuffs, pockets and flaps or shako plates – and regimental numbers were worn on the shako plates and uniform buttons. The Guard, however, used fairly substantial uniform variations from unit to unit. In general, for all line infantry, where waistcoats were worn, they were white and, for light infantry, blue.

Both line and light infantry battalions had *élite* companies that dressed somewhat differently from the rest of their comrades. Some (but not necessarily all) of these differences are given in the tables on pp. 47 onwards.

GUARD INFANTRY

UNIT	Coats						Trousers		Headgear	
	Main	Collar	Epaul.	Lapels	Turns	Cuffs	Breech.	Gaiters[32]	Cap	Plume
Gren.	Dk Blue	Dk Blue	Red	White	Red[33]	Red	White	White	B/Skin	Red
Chass.	Dk Blue	Dk Blue	Green/Red[34]	White	Red[35]	Red	White	White	B/Skin	Red/Green
Dutch Gren.	White	Red	Red	Red	Red	Red	White	White	B/Skin	Red
Fus-Gren.	Dk Blue	Dk Blue	White	White	Red	Red	White	White	Shako	Red
Fus-Chass.	Dk Blue	Dk Blue	White	White	Red	Red	White	White	Shako	Red/Green
Tir-Gren.	Dk Blue[36]	Dk Blue	Red strap	Dk Blue	Red	Red	White	Black	Shako	Red/White
Tir-Chass.	Dk Blue[36]	Dk Blue	Green strap	Dk Blue	Red	Red	White	Black	Shako	Grn. pom-pon
Volt-Chass.	Dk Blue	Yellow	Green/Yel.	Dk Blue	Red	Red	White	White	Shako	Red/Green
Flanq-Gren.	Green[37]	Green*	Green str.*	Green*	Red*	Red*	White	Black	Shako	Red/Yellow
Flanq-Chass.	Green[37]	Green*	Green str.*	Green*	Red*	Red*	White	Black	Shako	Yellow/Green
Cons-Gren.	Dk Blue[36]	Dk Blue#	Blue strap#	Dk Blue#	White	Red	Dk Blue	–	Shako	Red
Cons-Chass.	Dk Blue[36]	Red§	Green strap#	Dk Blue§	Dk Blue	Red§	Dk Blue	–	Shako	Grn. pom-pon
Garde Nat.	Dk Blue[36]	Red	Blue strap#	White#	White#	Red§	White	–	Shako	Red pom-pon

Footnotes on p. 48.

GUARD INFANTRY (CONTD.)

UNIT	Coats						Trousers		Headgear	
	Main	**Collar**	**Epaul.**	**Lapels**	**Turns**	**Cuffs**	**Breech.**	**Gaiters**[32]	**Cap**	**Plume**
Marins	Dk Blue[38]	Dk Blue	Brass scale	–	–	Red	Dk Blue[38]	–	Shako[a]	Red
Pupilles	Green[37]	Green*	Green str.*	Green*	Green*	Green*	White	Black	Shako	Yell. pom-pon
Veterans	Dk Blue	Dk Blue	Red	Red	Red	Red	White	Black	Bicorne	Red pom-pon

*Piped Yellow #Piped Red $Piped White [a]Orange binding / indicates 'over' in Plume column

32 Occasionally black.
33 Gold grenade symbols on the turnbacks.
34 Green, piped red with red fringes.
35 As Gren. with additional hunting horn symbol for chasseurs.
36 Shorter cut coat.
37 'Spencer' short coat.
38 Hussar-type dolman with orange lace.

DATE	Coats						Trousers		Headgear	
	Main	Collar	Epaul.	Lapels	Turns	Cuffs	Breech.	Gaiters	Cap	Plume
1793–1803	Dk Blue	Red	Blue strap#	White#	White#	Red§	White	Black (short)	Bicorne	Red pom-pon
1804	Dk Blue	Red	Blue strap#	White#	White#	Red§	White	Black (short)	Shako	Red pom-pon
1805	Dk Blue	Red	Fus: Blue strap# Gren: Red strap Volt: Green strap	White#	White#	Red§	White	Black (short)	Shako	Gren: Red Volt: Yell. or Grn. Pom. + Yell/Red or Yell/Green plume Fus: Co. pom.[39]
1806–1807[40]	White	1st,3rd, 4th,5th, 7th,8th	Red	1st,2nd,3rd, 5th,6th,7th	All	1st,2nd, 4th,5th, 6th,8th	White	White or Black	Shako	Gren: Red Volt: Yell. pom Fus: Co. pom.[39]
1807	Dk Blue	Red	Blue strap#	White#	White#	Red§	White	Black (short)	Shako	Gren: Red
1808	Grenadiers replace bearskin by tall shako									

Piped red § Piped white

Musicians wore similar uniforms to fusilier companies until 1812 when a decree was issued for their tunics to be single-breasted dark green 'Spencer' type jackets with red collars and cuffs, decorated with a dark green lace, embellished by yellow discs, and sleeves bearing seven inverted chevrons in the same material.

[39] 1st Co.: Green, 2nd Co.: Sky Blue, 3rd Co.: Orange, 4th Co.: Violet.

[40] Only adopted by a few regiments. The details were what was planned to overcome an indigo dye shortage. The regiments were divided into fourteen groups of 8, each with a distinctive colour worn in various positions by the regiments in the group. The group colours are: Gp 1: Imperial Green, Gp 2: Black, Gp 3: Scarlet, Gp 4: Nasturtium, Gp 5: Violet, Gp 6: Sky Blue, Gp 7: Rose Pink, Gp 8: Gold, Gp 9: Dk Blue, Gp 10: Yellow, Gp 11: Grass Green, Gp 12: Madder Red, Gp 13: Crimson, Gp 14: Iron Grey.

LIGHT INFANTRY

DATE	Coats						Trousers		Headgear	
	Main	**Collar**	**Epaul.**	**Lapels**	**Turns**	**Cuffs**	**Breech.**	**Gait.**	**Cap**	**Plume**
1799–1804	Dk Blue	Red	Green#	Dk Blue$	Dk Blue$	Dk Blue$	Dk Blue	Black	Shako or b/skin (Carab)	Carab: Red Chass: White
1804 (Volt. only)	Dk Blue	Yellow# Yellow$	Green*	Dk Blue$	Dk Blue$	Dk Blue$	Dk Blue	Black	Shako	Yellow/Green
1808	Carabiniers replace bearskin by tall shako									

*Piped Yellow #Piped Red $Piped White [a]Orange binding / indicates 'over' in Plume column

GUARD CAVALRY

UNIT	Coats						Trousers		Headgear	
	Main	**Collar**	**Epaul.**	**Lapels**	**Turns**	**Cuffs**	**Breech.**	**Boots**	**Cap**	**Plume**
Grenadiers	Dk Blue	Dk Blue	Yellow	White	Red	Dk Blue	White	Knee, Black	B/skin	Red
Chasseurs	Green	**Dolman**: Green*		**Pelisse**: Red* Fur Blk		Red*	Buff	Hussar Blk	Colback	Red/Green
1er Lanciers	Slate Blue	Crimson[§]	White	Crimson[§]	Crimson[§]	Crimson[§]	Slate Blue	Black	Czapka	White
2e Lanciers	Red	Dk Blue	Yellow	Dk Blue	Dk Blue	Dk Blue	Red	Black	Czapka	White
Dragoons	Dk Green	Dk Green	Yellow	White	Red	Red	White	Knee, Black	Helmet	Red
Gendarmes	Dk Blue	Dk Blue[#]	White strap	Red	Red	Dk Blue	Buff	Knee, Black	B/skin	White

*Piped Yellow [#]Piped Red [§]Piped White [a]Orange binding / indicates 'over' in Plume column

Musicians usually had different (sometimes 'reversed') colour schemes.

LINE CUIRASSIERS

Until 1804, the cuirassiers wore a bicorne, changing to the steel helmet with black horsehair aigrette and red plume that year. All coats were dark blue with red epaulettes and no lapels.

REGT	Regimental distinctive colours		
	Collar, turnbacks & pocket flap edging	Cuffs & flap trim	Cuff flaps
1er	Red	Red	Red
2e	Red	Red	Blue
3e	Red	Blue	Red
4e	Orange	Orange	Orange
5e	Orange	Orange	Blue
6e	Orange	Blue	Orange
7e	Yellow	Yellow	Yellow
8e	Yellow	Yellow	Blue
9e	Yellow	Blue	Yellow
10e	Pink	Pink	Pink
11e	Pink	Pink	Blue
12e	Pink	Blue	Pink
13e	Lilac	Lilac	Lilac
14e	Lilac	Lilac	Blue

*Piped Blue #Piped Red $Piped White [a]Orange binding / indicates 'over' in Plume column

Musicians had 'reversed' colour schemes (coat in regimental distinctive colour with dark blue facings) until 1812, when the green coat referred to for infantry musicians was introduced.

LINE CARABINIERS

In 1809, the Carabiniers adopted a Roman-style helmet of brass with a red crest and brass cuirass.

LINE CARABINIERS

UNIT	Coats						Trousers		Headgear	
	Main	Collar	Epaul.	Lapels	Turns	Cuffs	Breech.	Boots	Cap	Plume
1804–1809	Dk Blue	Dk Blue#	Red$	Red	Red	Red	Buff	Knee, Black	B/skin	Red
1809 on	White	Sky Blue	Red	None	Sky Blue	1er Rgt Red 2e Rgt Sky Bl.	White	Knee, Black	Helmet	Red

#Piped Red $Piped White

Musicians had 'reversed' colour schemes (coat in regimental distinctive colour with dark blue facings) until 1812, when the green coat referred to for infantry musicians was introduced.

LINE DRAGOONS

All Dragoons wore their regimental distinctives on lapels and turnbacks. The distinctives were allocated in groups of six paired regiments, the first regiment of each pair having lateral pocket flaps and the second vertical. It should be obvious from the table which group of six had which distinctive colour. Coats were dark green, breeches buff and cuirassier-style helmets were worn. The short 'habit-veste' or 'Spencer' coat was introduced in 1812. Elite companies sported a brown fur colback with red plume and red epaulettes.

REGT	Regimental distinctive colours		
	Collar	Cuffs	Cuff flaps
1er & 4e	Red	Red	Red
2e & 5e	Dk Green	Red	Dk Green
3e & 6e	Red	Blue	Red
7e & 10e	Crimson	Crimson	Crimson
8e & 11e	Dk Green	Crimson	Dk Green
9e & 12e	Crimson	Blue	Crimson
13e & 16e	Pink	Pink	Pink
14e & 17e	Dk Green	Pink	Dk Green
15e & 18e	Pink	Blue	Pink
19e & 22e	Yellow	Yellow	Yellow
20e & 23e	Dk Green	Yellow	Dk Green
21er & 24e	Yellow	Blue	Yellow
25e & 28e	Lt Orange	Lt Orange	Lt Orange
26e & 29e	Dk Green	Lt Orange	Dk Green
27e & 30e	Lt Orange	Blue	Lt Orange

Musicians had 'reversed' colour schemes (coat in regimental distinctive colour with dark blue facings) until 1812, when the green coat referred to for infantry musicians was introduced.

LINE CHASSEURS À CHEVAL

Coats were a similar colour to those of the Dragoons. Breeches were in the same shade. Hussar style boots were worn as was a 'mirliton' hussar cap, lined with the regimental distinctive colour. The coats were replaced by hussar dolmans (without pelisses) and, in 1805, mirlitons were replaced by shakos, dolmans by a '*surtout*' jacket which, in 1812, gave way to 'Spencer' jackets. Elite companies had colbacks with red 'bags' and plumes plus red epaulettes. Shoulder straps and lapels were edged in the regimental distinctive. From 1812, the facing distinctives were as shown on p. 56.

Before 1808, there were only twenty-six regiments (although the 17e & 18e were vacant), split into groups of three, and similar distinctives applied prior to 1812 but they were worn only on collars and cuffs in the following sequence: first of group: both locations, second: cuffs only, third: collar only. Musicians had 'reversed' colour schemes (coat in regimental distinctive colour with dark blue facings) until 1812, when the green coat referred to for infantry musicians was introduced.

LINE CHASSEURS À CHEVAL

REGT	Collar	Collar piping	Cuffs	Cuff piping	REGT	Collar	Collar piping	Cuffs	Cuff piping
1er	Scarlet	Green	Scarlet	Green	17e	Green	Sky Blue	Sky Blue	Green
2e	Green	Scarlet	Scarlet	Green	18e	Sky Blue	Green	Green	Sky Blue
3e	Scarlet	Green	Green	Scarlet	19e	Gold	Green	Gold	Green
4e	Yellow	Green	Yellow	Green	20e	Green	Gold	Gold	Green
5e	Green	Yellow	Yellow	Green	21er	Gold	Green	Green	Gold
6e	Yellow	Green	Green	Yellow	22e	Nasturtium	Green	Nasturtium	Green
7e	Pink	Green	Pink	Green	23e	Green	Nasturtium	Nasturtium	Green
8e	Green	Pink	Pink	Green	24e	Nasturtium	Green	Green	Nasturtium
9e	Pink	Green	Green	Pink	25e	Madder Red	Green	Madder Red	Green
10e	Crimson	Green	Crimson	Green	26e	Green	Madder Red	Madder Red	Green
11e	Green	Crimson	Crimson	Green	27e	Madder Red	Green	Green	Madder Red
12e	Crimson	Green	Green	Crimson	28e	Lt Purple	Green	Lt Purple	Green
13e	Orange	Green	Orange	Green	29e	Green	Lt Purple	Lt Purple	Green
14e	Green	Orange	Orange	Green	30e	Lt Purple	Green	Green	Lt Purple
15e	Orange	Green	Green	Orange	31er	Buff	Green	Buff	Green
16e	Sky Blue	Green	Sky Blue	Green		Turnbacks, straps, lapels: Buff, piped Green			

LINE CHEVAU-LÉGERS LANCIERS

Regiments 1 to 6 (inc.) wore dark green 'Spencer' coats and breeches, with a carabinier-style helmet with black crest. The 7e, 8e and 9e regiments, being Polish, wore dark blue coats with white epaulettes and a blue czapka cap. (See table on p. 57.)

Musicians had 'reversed' colour schemes (coat in regimental distinctive colour with dark blue facings) until 1812, when the green coat referred to for infantry musicians was introduced.

REGT	Regimental distinctive colour	Facings on which worn
1er	Scarlet	Collar, cuffs, turnbacks, piping, breeches stripes
2e	Lt Orange	Collar, cuffs, turnbacks, piping, breeches stripes
3e	Pink	Collar, cuffs, turnbacks, piping, breeches stripes
4e	Crimson	Collar, cuffs, turnbacks, piping, breeches stripes
5e	Sky Blue	Collar, cuffs, turnbacks, piping, breeches stripes
6e	Madder Red	Collar, cuffs, turnbacks, piping, breeches stripes
7e	Yellow	Collar, cuffs, turnbacks, piping, breeches stripes
8e	Yellow (Blue Collar)	Collar (blue), cuffs, turnbacks, piping, breeches stripes
9e	Buff	Collar, cuffs, turnbacks, piping, breeches stripes

LINE HUSSARS

Hussar uniforms were much more likely to be treated flexibly by their owners and regimental commanders. Various changes occurred from time to time (for example a regulation, only sketchily obeyed, was issued by the War Ministry – a Col. Bardin was apparently directing matters[41] – that Hussars should adopt bottle green breeches. Also, some regiments (e.g. 1er) adopted red breeches (a colour popular amongst officers from an early period). The following table shows the

[41] Bucquoy, Cdt. E.-L., (*Les Uniformes du Premier Empire*, Ed. Grancher, 1980, p. 88).

uniforms generally thought to be extant from about 1803 to 1812 for the first eleven regiments and from their inception (1813) for the last three. Generally, all élite companies wore colbacks with red 'bag' and plume whilst the rest of the regiment wore mirlitons until 1800 when Shakos were introduced. Hussar boots were worn throughout.

REGT	Dolman			Pelisse	Lace	Breeches
	Main colour	Collar	Cuffs			
1er	Sky Blue	Sky Blue	Red	Sky Blue	White	Sky Blue
2e	Chestnut Brown	Chestnut Brown	Sky Blue	Chestnut Brown	White	Sky Blue
3e	Silver Grey	Silver Grey	Red	Silver Grey	Red	Silver Grey
4e	Royal Blue	Royal Blue	Scarlet	Scarlet	Yellow	Royal Blue
5e	Sky Blue	Sky Blue	White	White	Yellow	Sky Blue
6e	Scarlet	Scarlet	Scarlet	Royal Blue	Yellow	Royal Blue
7e	Dark Green	Scarlet	Scarlet	Dark Green	Yellow	Scarlet
8e	Dark Green	Scarlet	Scarlet	Dark Green	White	Scarlet
9e	Scarlet	Sky Blue	Sky Blue	Sky Blue	Yellow	Sky Blue
10e	Sky Blue	Scarlet	Scarlet	Sky Blue	White	Sky Blue
11e	Royal Blue	Scarlet	Scarlet	Royal Blue	Yellow	Royal Blue
12e	Scarlet	Sky Blue	Sky Blue	Sky Blue	Yellow	Sky Blue
13e	Brown	Sky Blue	Sky Blue	Brown	White	Sky Blue
14e	Dark Green	Scarlet	Scarlet	Dark Green	White	Scarlet

For brief uniform information on the foreign regiments, see the tables dealing with engagements.

GUARD ARTILLERY

The dress uniform of the Horse Artillery was very Hussar-like in style, with dark blue dolman and breeches, the former trimmed with black fur. Frogging on the dolman was scarlet as were the cuff lace and stripes and piping on the breeches. A colpack with a red bag and plume formed the headgear. On campaign, the coat was short in the same colouring but without frogging. Instead, the lapels and collar were piped red. Also on campaign, a dark blue waistcoat was worn. A busby with tricolour side disc made up the headgear.

Foot artillery were similarly attired in terms of the campaign dress except that the coat was somewhat longer and white gaiters to above the knee were worn. Until 1810, the headgear was a shako with red cords, and crown band plus a red plume. After this, the artillery were issued with peaked grenadier-style bearskins again with red cords and plume.

LINE FOOT ARTILLERY

These were attired in the style of the guard foot artillery prior to the issue of bearskins.

LINE HORSE ARTILLERY

Again, the uniform style followed that of the guard with the change from colpack to shako coming for field duty. Small variations in coat style are identifiable from pictures but these are not significant. In general, the shakos were adorned with pom-pons or short tufted tassel-end plumes (in red).

ARTILLERY TRAIN

Dressed in similar fashion to the artillery itself, the drivers wore a paler blue coat with iron grey (almost black) facings on collar, cuffs and turnbacks. Breeches were buff and the shakos bore white eagle plates and blue or red pom-pons.

4. ENGAGEMENTS

Numbers in brackets indicate either the number of battalions involved or, if ordinal (e.g. 1er, 3e), the actual battalions involved.

FRENCH LINE INFANTRY REGIMENTS

Number	Raised	Ancestry & Associations[1]	1814 Bourbon Title	Post '100 days' Formation	Engagements[2] (with at least 1 Bn present) in approx. date order[3]
1er	1569 (Smith D., says 1597)	Rgt de Picardie, Rgt Vivarais (No. 71)	Rgt du Roi	Légion du Rhône	Caldiero, Sacile, Raab, Wagram, Miranda, Arapiles (Salamanca), **St Sebastien**, Lützen, Bautzen, Dresden, Leipzig, Les Echelles, St Julien, Brienne, Sézanne, Montmirail, Vauchamps, Laon, Paris, Quatre-Bras, Mt St Jean (Waterloo)
2e	1776	Rgt de Provence, Gardes Françaises, G. N. de Paris, Rgt Orléans (No. 44), Rgt Lorraine (No. 47)	Rgt de la Reine	Légion de Lot-et-Garonne	Cap Finisterre*, Trafalgar*, Molins de Rey (4e), Aspern, Essling, Wagram, Polotsk, Berezina, Dresden, Leipzig, La Rothière, Fleurus, Mont St Jean
3e	1569	Rgt de Piémont, Rgt Soissonais (No. 40), Rgt Bretagne (No. 46), Rgt Beauce (No. 68)	Rgt du Dauphin	Légion de Puy-de-Dôme	Hollabrünn, Austerlitz, Heilsberg, Friedland, **Thorn**, Schierling, Eckmühl, Essling, Wagram, *Spain*, Vitoria, Bar-sur-Aube, Arcis-sur-Aube, Quatre-Bras, Mont St Jean
4e	1776	Rgt de Colonel-Général, Rgt Flandre (No. 19), Rgt Cambresis (No. 20) Rgt Lyonnais (No. 27), Rgt Maine (No. 28), Rgt Medoc (No. 70), Rgt Boulonnais (No. 79), Rgt Angoumois (No. 80)	Rgt de Monsieur	Légion d'Indre	Ulm, Austerlitz, Jena,[4] Eylau, Heilsberg, Eckmühl, Aspern, Essling, Wagram, Smolensk, Valoutina, Moskowa, Krasnoe, Dresden, Leipzig, Hanau, Brienne, La Rothière, Montereau, Troyes, Ligny

Footnotes on pp. 86–7.

Number	Raised	Ancestry & Associations[1]	1814 Bourbon Title	Post '100 days' Formation	Engagements[2] (with at least 1 Bn present) in approx. date order[3]
5e	1569	Rgt de Navarre, Rgt Boulonnais (No. 79), 109e Inf. de Ligne	Rgt d'Angoulême	Légion de Saône-et-Loire	*Naples*, *Dalmatia*, Mt Kita, Wagram, *Croatia*, *Spain*, Fleurus
6e	1776	Rgt d'Armagnac, Rgt Le Port-au-Prince (2e Bn.)	Rgt de Berry	Légion de l'Ardèche	Calabres, Gayete, Reggio, Mockern, Mesebourg, Würschen, Bautzen, Leipzig, Hanau, R. Mincio, Belfort
7e	1559	Rgt de Champagne, Rgt Picardie (No. 2), Rgt Vintimille (No. 49), Rgt Condé (No. 55), Rgt Beauce (No. 68), Rgt Foix (No. 83)	Rgt d'Orléans	Légion de Puy-de-Dôme	*San Domingo*, **Barcelona**, Cardadeu(2), Valls(2), Molins de Rey(2), **Gerona**, Villafranca, **Tarragona**, **Fort Olivio**, **Montserrat**, **Valencia**, Saguntum, Castalla, Yecla, Bautzen, Jüterbock, Leipzig, Hanau, Mont St Jean
8e	1776	Rgt d'Austrasie, Rgt Picardie (No. 2)	Rgt de Condé	Légion de Pyrénées-Orientales	*Hanover*, Austerlitz, Halle, **Lübeck**, Danzig, Friedland, Espinosa de los Monteros, Talavera, Chiclana, Vitoria, Villalon, Essling, Wagram, Bar-sur-Aube, Arcis-sur-Aube
9e	1615	Rgt de Normandie, Rgt Picardie (No. 2)	Rgt de Bourbon	Légion de l'Ain	Austerlitz, Venzione, Sacile, R. Piave, Carlsdorf, Wagram, Tyrol, Vitebsk, Moskowa (Borodino), Wiasma, R. Mincio, Parma
10e	1776	Rgt de Neustrie, Rgt Lyonnais (No. 27), Rgt Berwick (No. 88)	Rgt de Colonel-Général	Légion de l'Aude	*Italy*, Castel-Franco, Gayete, Capri, Molins de Rey, *Sicily*, Lützen, Bautzen, Leipzig, Hanau, Caldiero, R. Mincio, Taro, Mont St Jean

Number	Raised	Ancestry & Associations[1]	1814 Bourbon Title	Post '100 days' Formation	Engagements[2] (with at least 1 Bn present) in approx. date order[3]
11e	1635	Rgt La Marine, Rgt Normandie (No. 9), Rgt La Fère (No. 52)	–	Légion du Gard	Ulm, Graz, Sacile, Wagram, Znaïm, *Spain*, Tortosa, Wittenberg, Dresden, Leipzig, Hanau, McDonald's Corps, Mont St Jean
12e	1692	Rgt Auxerrois, Rgt Le Dauphin (No. 29)	–	Légion de la Seine	Mühldorf, La Salza, Austerlitz, Auerstädt, Czarnowo, Pultusk, Eylau, Deppen, Friedland, Eckmühl, Ratisbon, Thann, Abensburg, Engerau, Wagram, *Magdebourg & Hannover*, Vilna, Drissa, Vitebsk, Smolensk, Valoutina, Moskowa, Hamburg, Dresden, Arcis-sur-Aube, St Dizier, Fleurus
13e	1597	Rgt Bourbonnais, Rgt Poitou (No. 25), Rgt Le Dauphin (No. 29), Colonial Rgt Le Cap (No. 106)	–	Légion de la Drôme	Caldiero, *Istria*, Isonzo Pass, Oberlaybach, Wagram, *Tyrol*, Bautzen, Hanau, Hochheim, **Mayence**, **Palma-Nova**
14e (Intré-pide)	1776	Rgt de Forez, Rgt Béarn (No. 15)	–	Légion de la Côte d'Or	Ulm, Austerlitz, Jena, **Thorn**, Eylau, Heilsberg, Zaragoza, Villel, Tarragona, Alcañiz, Valencia, Lützen, Bautzen, Dresden, Wachau, Arcis-sur-Aube, Conflans, L'Hôpital
15e	1597	Rgt de Béarn, Rgt Touraine (No. 33)	–	Légion de Calvados	Friedland, Zaragoza, Medina de Rio Seco(2), Vimeiro, La Coruña, Oporto 1 & 2, Arapiles, Bautzen, Würschen, Sorauren, Leipzig, Nivelle, Vauchamps, Bar-sur-Aube

Number	Raised	Ancestry & Associations[1]	1814 Bourbon Title	Post '100 days' Formation	Engagements[2] (with at least 1 Bn present) in approx. date order[3]
16e	1776	Rgt Agenois, Rgt Condé (No. 55)	–	Légion de Vaucluse	Brisgau, Trafalgar,* Neumark, Ebersberg, Aspern, Essling, Wagram, Znaïm, **Rosas**, **Gerona**, **Fort Olivio**, **Tarragona**, **Saguntum**, San Felipe, Alicante, Lützen, Bautzen, Würschen, Dresden, Leipzig, R. Mincio
17e	1597	Rgt d'Auvergne, Rgt Royal-deux-Ponts (No. 99)	–	Légion de la Côte du Nord	Austerlitz, Auerstädt, Jena, Eylau, Heilsberg, Thann, Eckmühl, Essling, Wagram, Smolensk, Moskowa, Viasma, Krasnoi, Stettin, Külm, Leipzig, **Dresden**, Mont St Jean
18e	1776	Rgt Royal-Auvergne, Rgt Aquitaine (No. 35)	–	Légion de Maine-et-Loire	Austerlitz, Jena, Eylau, Heilsberg, Ebersberg, Vienna, Essling, Wagram, Znaïm, Smolensk, Moskowa, Dresden, Leipzig, Hanau, Magdebourg, La Rothière, Montereau, Suerbourg, Strasbourg
19e	1597	Rgt de Flandres, Gardes Françaises, G. N. de Paris, Rgt Royal (No. 23)	–	5e Légion	**Danzig**, Wagram, **Astorga**, Busaco, Torres-Vedras, Jacobouwo, Borisow, Dresden, Leipzig, Brienne, Montereau, Bar-sur-Aube, Mont St Jean
20e	1776	Rgt de Cambrésis, Gardes Françaises, Rgt Royal-Marine (No. 60), Rgt Bouillon (No. 98)	–	Légion de la Loire	R. Adige, Caldiero, Naples, Tarragona, Valencia, *Spain*, *Italy*

Number	Raised	Ancestry & Associations[1]	1814 Bourbon Title	Post '100 days' Formation	Engagements[2] (with at least 1 Bn present) in approx. date order[3]
21er	1589	Rgt de Guyenne, Rgt Flandre (No. 19), Rgt Marechal de Turenne (No. 37), Rgt Royal Rousillon (No. 54), Rgt Monsieur (No. 75), Rgt Conti (No. 81) Rgt Enghien (No. 93)	–	Légion de l'Ardèche	Auerstädt, Pultusk, Eylau, Eckmühl, Wagram, Smolensk, Valoutina, Moskowa, Dresden, Bergen-op-Zoom, Mont St Jean
22e	1776	Rgt Viennois, Rgt Guyenne (No. 21)	–	Légion du Loiret	**Stralsund**, Heilsberg, Friedland, Astorga, Arapiles, Lützen, Bautzen, Würschen, Katzbach, St Sébastien, Leipzig, Maastricht, Fleurus, Ligny, Wavre, Namur
23e	1656	Rgt Royal, Rgt Bourbonnais (No. 13), Rgt Vintimille (No. 49), Rgt Royal-Marine (No. 60), Rgt Bouillon (No. 98)	–	Légion de l'Yonne	Caldiero, Raguse, Dalmatia, Albania, Sacile, R. Piave, Croatia, Wagram, *Spain*, Lützen, Bautzen, Juterbogk, Hanau, Savoy, Ligny, Wavre
24e	1775	Rgt de Brie, Rgt Piemont (No. 3), Rgt Lorraine (No. 47)	–	Légion du Cher	*Shipboard,* Tyrol*, Jena, Pultusk, Golymin, Eylau, Braunsburg, Friedland, Espinosa de los Monteros(3), Somosierra(3), Madrid(3), Uclés(3), Medellín(3), Talavera(3), Chiclana(3), Fuentes de Oñoro(3), Miranda, Essling(1), Wagram(1), Danzig(1), Vitoria, Sorauren, Dresden(1), Bayonne, Mormant(1), Méry-sur-Seine(1), St Julien(2), Arcis-sur-Aube, Montmélian

Number	Raised	Ancestry & Associations[1]	1814 Bourbon Title	Post '100 days' Formation	Engagements[2] (with at least 1 Bn present) in approx. date order[3]
25e	1616	Rgt de Poitou, Rgt Limousin (No. 42), Rgt La Sarre (No. 51)	–	Légion du Cantal	Austerlitz, Auerstädt, Pultusk, Eylau, Königsberg, Landshut, Eckmühl, Ratisbon, Wagram, Znaïm, *Spain*, Minsk, Smolensk, Moskowa, Malojaroslavetz, Krasnoi, Dresden, Kulm, Leipzig, Mont St Jean
26e	1775	Rgt de Bresse, Rgt Champagne (No. 7), Rgt Marechal de Turenne (No. 37), Rgt Enghien (No. 93), Rgt Le Roi (No. 105)	–	Légion de la Vendée	*Dominique(2)*, *Martinique(2)*, *Guadalupe(2)*, Beja(2), Evora, Obidos,[13] Vimeiro, Oporto, **Ciudad Rodrigo**, **Almeida**, Busaco, Sabugal, Fuentes de Oñoro, Arapiles, Bautzen, Sorauren, St Sébastien, Bidassoa, Rhune, Leipzig, Fère-Champenoise, Châtillon
27e	1616	Rgt de Bresse, Rgt Champagne (No. 7), Rgt Flandre (No. 19)	–	Légion d'Indre-et-Loire	Günzburg, Ulm, Tyrol, Jena, Eylau, Friedland, Tudela, Ebersberg, Essling, Wagram, Tamames, Ciudad Rodrigo, Almeida, Arapiles, Lützen, Würschen, Sorauren, Dresden, Kulm, Nivelle, Orthez, Toulon, Mont St Jean
28e	1775	Rgt de Maine, Gardes Françaises, G. N. de Paris, Rgt Navarre (No. 5)	–	Légion de la Meuse	Ulm, Austerlitz, Jena, **Lübeck**, Bergfried, Eylau, Heilsberg, Königsberg, Talavera, Almonacíd, Busaco, Vitoria, Sorauren, Dresden, Nivelle, Bayonne, Bar-sur-Aube, Arcis-sur-Aube, Fère-Champenoise, Mont St Jean

Number	Raised	Ancestry & Associations[1]	1814 Bourbon Title	Post '100 days' Formation	Engagements[2] (with at least 1 Bn present) in approx. date order[3]
29e	1667	Rgt du Dauphin, Rgt Chartres (No. 90)	–	Légion de la Haut-Garonne	Caldiero, Naples, Calabria, Reggio, Raab, Wagram, Tyrol, Vilna, Königsberg, Danzig, Hamburg, Mont St Jean
30e	1775	Rgt de Perche, Rgt Aquitaine (No. 35)	–	Légion de la Charente	Austerlitz, Jena, Auerstädt, Heilsberg, Eylau, Landshut, Eckmühl, Essling(1), Wagram, Smolensk, Moskowa (Borodino), Viasma, Krasnoi, Beresina, **Hamburg**, Ligny, Namur
31er	1610	Rgt d'Aunis	–	–	*San Domingo (Effectively destroyed by 1804 and men absorbed into 7e and 105e Ligne. Number remained vacant thereafter.)*
32e (Le Brave)	1775	Rgt de Bassigny, Rgt La Marine (No. 11), Rgt Bourgogne (No. 59), Rgt Medoc (No. 70)	–	Légion de l'Aisne	Günzburg, Haslach, Ulm, Halle, Friedland, Vimeiro, Talavera, Almonacíd, *Spain*, Lützen, Würschen, Vitoria, Sorauren, Dresden, Leipzig, Nivelle, Montereau, Orthez, Toulouse, Strasbourg
33e	1625	Rgt de Touraine, Rgt Navarre (No. 5), Rgt La Couronne (No. 45), Rgt Le Port-au-Prince (Col.)	–	Légion de Loire-et-Cher	Austerlitz, Auerstädt, Jena, Eylau, **Zaragoza**, Landshut, Eckmühl, Mt Kita, Wagram, Smolensk, Moskowa (Borodino), Krasnoi, *Spain*, *Saxony*, Dresden, Kulm, Leipzig, Namur

Number	Raised	Ancestry & Associations[1]	1814 Bourbon Title	Post '100 days' Formation	Engagements[2] (with at least 1 Bn present) in approx. date order[3]
34e	1775	Rgt d'Angoulême, Rgt Champagne (No. 7), Rgt Royal des Vaisseaux (No. 43), Rgt Languedoc (No. 67), Rgt Angoumois (No. 80)	–	Légion de Seine-et-Oise	Ulm, Austerlitz, Jena, Pultusk, Friedland(1), **Zaragoza**, Ocaña, Villa Garcia, **Badajoz**(1), Albuera(2), **Burgos**, Lützen, Würschen, **San Sebastien**, Bidassoa, Dresden, Nivelle, Bayonne, Arcis-sur-Aube, Ligny, Wavre, Namur, Rocroi
35e	1625	Rgt d'Aquitaine, Rgt Beauvoisis (No. 57)	–	Légion de Vaucluse	Ulm, Sacile, Raab, Wagram, Moskowa, Malojaroslavetz, Krasnoi, Beresina, Glogau, R. Mincio, Parma, Corsica
36e	1691 (E. Bukhari says 1775)	Rgt d'Anjou, Rgt Chartres (No. 90)	–	Légion d'Indre-et-Loire	Ulm, Austerlitz, Jena, Eylau, Heilsberg, La Coruña, Astorga, Busaco, Arapiles, Vitoria, Dresden, Kulm, Bayonne, Orthez, Laon, Arcis-sur-Aube, Toulouse
37e	1625	Rgt Maréchal-de-Turenne, Rgt Guyenne (No. 21), Rgt Bourbon (No. 56), Rgt Nassau (No. 96)	36e Rgt de Ligne (Napoleon restored the number 37e in 1815)	Légion des Deux-Sèvres	*Shipboard*,* **Stralsund, Gerona,** *Spain (Catalonia)*, Molins de Rey(1), Eckmühl, Essling, Wagram, **Tarragona**, Polotsk, Beresina, Dresden, Leipzig, **Besançon**, Brienne, La Rothière, **Bayonne,** Ligny, Wavre
38e	1629	Rgt Dauphiné	–	–	This number was vacant during the Imperial Napoleonic period.

Number	Raised	Ancestry & Associations[1]	1814 Bourbon Title	Post '100 days' Formation	Engagements[2] (with at least 1 Bn present) in approx. date order[3]
39e	1629	Rgt d'Île-de-France, Rgt Royal (No. 23), Rgt Vermandois (No. 61)	37e Rgt de Ligne (Napoleon restored the number 39e in 1815)	Légion d'Aveyron	Elchingen, Ulm, Austerlitz, Jena, Eylau, Friedland, Ebersberg, Essling, Wagram, Tamames, **Ciudad Rodrigo**, Busaco, Fuentes de Oñoro, Arapiles, **Danzig**(1), Lützen, Sorauren, Dresden, Leipzig, Bayonne, Orthez, Toulouse
40e	1630	Rgt Soisonnais, Gardes Françaises, G. N. de Paris, Rgt Bourbonnais (No. 13)	38e Rgt de Ligne (Napoleon restored the number 40e in 1815)	Légion de Doubs	Ulm, Austerlitz, Jena(3), Pultusk, Somosierra, Ebersberg, Essling(1), Wagram, Arzobispo, Ocaña, **Badajoz**(1), Fuentes de Oñoro(1), Albuera(2), Lützen, Würschen, Irun, Dresden, Kulm, Leipzig, Nivelle, La Rothière, Montmirail, Orthez, Paris, Toulouse
41er	1634	Rgt de la Reine	–	–	This number was vacant during the Imperial Napoleonic period, having been absorbed into the 17e Ligne in 1803
42e	1635	Rgt de Limousin, Rgt Bearne (No. 15)	39e Rgt de Ligne (Napoleon restored the number 42e in 1815)	Légion de la Corèze	Maida, *Calabria*, Raab, Cardadeu(3), Molins de Rey (3), Valls(3), Wagram, **Gerona**, Vich, **Tarragona**, Bautzen, Würschen, Leipzig, Caldiero, *Savoy*

Number	Raised	Ancestry & Associations[1]	1814 Bourbon Title	Post '100 days' Formation	Engagements[2] (with at least 1 Bn present) in approx. date order[3]
43e	1638	Rgt Royal-Vaisseaux, Rgt Auvergne	40e Rgt de Ligne (Napoleon restored the number 43e in 1815)	Légion de l'Eure	Ulm, Austerlitz, Jena, Eylau, Heilsberg, Spain (Alhourin 14/4/12), Lützen, Vitoria, Sorauren, Kulm, Bidassoa, Leipzig, Hanau, Nivelle, Orthez, Laon, Fère-Champenoise, Paris, Toulouse
44e	1642	Rgt d'Orléans, Rgt Orléans (No. 44), Rgt Bretagne (No. 46), Rgt du Roi (No. 105)	41er Rgt de Ligne (Napoleon restored the number 44e in 1815)	Légion de la Dordogne	Jena, Putulsk, Eylau, **Danzig**, Friedland, **Zaragoza**, Tudela, **Tortosa**, Castalla, Beresina, *Spain*, **Hamburg**, Fleurus, Ligny
45e	1643	Rgt de la Couronne, Rgt Hainault (No. 50), Rgt Barrois (No. 91)	42e Rgt de Ligne (Napoleon restored the number 45e in 1815)	Légion de l'Oise	Austerlitz, Jena, Lübeck, Friedland, Essling, Wagram, Talavera, Almonacíd, Flushing, Chiclana, Albuera, *Saxony*, Vitoria, Sorauren, Dresden, Nivelle, Orthez, Tarbes, Toulouse, Mont St Jean (Eagle – Sgt. Ewart)
46e	1644	Rgt de Bretagne, Rgt Normandie (No. 9), Rgt Île-de-France (No. 39), Rgt Royal Rousillon (No. 54)	43e Rgt de Ligne (Napoleon restored the number 46e in 1815)	Disbanded	Ulm, Austerlitz, Jena, Lübeck, Eylau, Heilsberg, Königsberg, Eckmühl, Essling, Wagram, Znaïm, Fuentes de Oñoro, Smolensk, Moskowa, Krasnoi, Beresina, Kulm, Leipzig, Hanau, Magdeburg, Brienne, La Rothière, Montereau, Arcis-sur-Aube, Mont St Jean

Number	Raised	Ancestry & Associations[1]	1814 Bourbon Title	Post '100 days' Formation	Engagements[2] (with at least 1 Bn present) in approx. date order[3]
47e	1644	Rgt de Lorraine, Rgt Walsh (No. 92)	44e Rgt de Ligne (Napoleon restored the number 47e in 1815)	Légion du Finistère	*Shipboard**, *Portugal*, Zaragoza, Medina de Rioseco(2), La Coruña, Oporto, Astorga, Busaco, Arapiles, Lützen, Würschen, Vitoria, Sorauren, Bidassoa, Rhune, Leipzig, Nivelle, Bayonne, Mainz, Orthez, Toulouse
48e	1610	Rgt d'Artois, Rgt Royal (No. 23)	45e Rgt de Ligne (Napoleon restored the number 48e in 1815)	Légion du Lot	Austerlitz, Auerstädt, Jena, Eylau, Thann, Eckmühl, Wagram, **Flushing**, Moskowa, Krasnoi, Beresina, **Stettin**, **Hamburg**, Fère-Champenoise, Ligny
49e	1647	Rgt de Vintimille, Rgt Nassau (No. 96)	?	–	This number was vacant during the Imperial Napoleonic period, having been dissolved in 1803.
50e	1651	Rgt d'Hainault, Rgt Bourbonnais (No. 13), Rgt Martinique (Col.), Rgt La Guadaloupe (Col.)	46e Rgt de Ligne (Napoleon restored the number 50e in 1815)	Légion de Sarthe	Ulm, Scharnitz(2), Jena, Eylau, Friedland, *Spain*, Coa, Fuentes de Oñoro, Arapiles, Lützen, Würschen, Vitoria, Sorauren, Dresden, Leipzig, Hanau, Nivelle, Montmirail, Orthez, Laon, Paris, Toulouse, Ligny, Wavre
51er	1651	Rgt de La Sarre, Rgt Hainault (No. 50), Rgt Alsace (No. 53)	47e Rgt de Ligne (Napoleon restored the number 51er in 1815)	Légion de la Vienne	Austerlitz, Jena, Auerstädt, Eylau, Talavera, Almonacíd, Ocaña, Albuera, Tarifa, Vitoria, Sorauren, Dresden, Kulm, Bidassoa, Leipzig, Bayonne, Orthez, Quatre-Bras, Mont St Jean

Number	Raised	Ancestry & Associations[1]	1814 Bourbon Title	Post '100 days' Formation	Engagements[2] (with at least 1 Bn present) in approx. date order[3]
52e	1654	Rgt La Fère, Rgt Piémont (No. 3), Rgt Penthièvre	48e Rgt de Ligne (Napoleon restored the number 52e in 1815)	Légion de l'Ariège	R. Adige, Caldiero, Naples, Sacile, R. Piave, Raab, Wagram, *Spain*, Würschen, Pamplona, **Torgau**, R. Mincio
53e	1656	Rgt d'Alsace, Rgt Bouillon (No. 98)	49e Rgt de Ligne (Napoleon restored the number 53e in 1815)	–	Sacile, Raab, Wagram, Tyrol, Moskowa, Malojaroslavetz, Viasma, Krasnoi, *Italy*, Caldiero, R. Mincio
54e	1657	Rgt Royal-Rousillon, Rgt Guyenne (No. 21)	50e Rgt de Ligne (Napoleon restored the number 54e in 1815)	Légion de la Creuse	Dürnstein, Austerlitz, Jena, Friedland, Espinosa de los Monteros, Somosierra, Essling, Wagram, Talavera, Chiclana, Fuentes de Oñoro, *Germany*(2), *Spain*(1), Vitoria, Sorauren, Dresden, Leipzig, Bayonne, Bar-sur-Aube, Maastricht, Fère-Champenoise, Mont St Jean
55e	1644	Rgt de Condé, Rgt Flandre (No. 19), Rgt Rouerge (No. 58)	51er Rgt de Ligne (Napoleon restored the number 55e in 1815)	Légion de la Marne	Ulm, Austerlitz, Jena, Eylau, Heilsberg, Ocaña, Albuera, Vitoria, Sorauren, Kulm, Nivelle, Orthez, Toulouse, Quatre-Bras, Mont St Jean
56e	1657	Rgt Royal-Rousillon, Gardes Françaises, Rgt Touraine (No. 33), Rgt Dauphine (No. 38)	52e Rgt de Ligne (Napoleon restored the number 56e in 1815)	Légion du Nord	Caldiero, **Stralsund, Rosas, Gerona,** Molins de Rey(1), Eckmühl, Essling, Wagram, Polotsk, Beresina, Dresden, Leipzig, Hanau, Brienne, La Rothière, Magdeburg, Troyes, Ligny, Wavre, Namur

Number	Raised	Ancestry & Associations[1]	1814 Bourbon Title	Post '100 days' Formation	Engagements[2] (with at least 1 Bn present) in approx. date order[3]
57e (Le Terrible)	1667	Rgt Beauvoisis, Rgt Limousin (No. 42), Rgt Vermandois (No. 61)	53e Rgt de Ligne (Napoleon restored the number 57e in 1815)	Légion du Haut-Rhin	Ulm, Austerlitz, Jena, Eylau, Heilsberg, Thann, Landshut, Eckmühl, Essling, Ratisbon, Wagram, *Spain*, Moskowa, Malojaroslavetz, Viasma, Krasnoi, Kulm, Dresden, Danzig, Hanau, Bar-sur-Aube, Kehl, Landau
58e	1667	Rgt de Rouerge, Rgt Touraine (No. 33), Rgt Walsh (No. 92), Rgt Île Bourbon (Col.)	54e Rgt de Ligne (Napoleon restored the number 58e in 1815)	Légion des Vosges	Ulm, Austerlitz, Friedland, Vimeiro, Talavera, Almonacíd, Albuera, Badajoz, Lützen, Würschen, Vitoria, Sorauren, Dresden, Leipzig, Hanau, Bayonne, Montereau, Orthez, Paris, Magdeburg, Ligny, Wavre
59e	1668	Rgt de Bourgogne	55e Rgt de Ligne (Napoleon restored the number 59e in 1815)	Disbanded 1815	Günzburg, Ulm, Jena, Eylau, Friedland, Somosierra, Ebersberg, Essling, Wagram, Tudela, Tamames, **Ciudad Rodrigo**, Fuentes de Oñoro, Arapiles, Stettin, Saxony, Lützen, Würschen, **Danzig**, Vitoria, Sorauren, Dresden, Leipzig, Orthez, Toulouse, Ligny, Wavre
60e	1669	Rgt Royal-Marine, Rgt Royal (No. 23)	56e Rgt de Ligne (Napoleon restored the number 60e in 1815)	Disbanded 1815	Caldiero, R. Piave, Raab, Wagram, Dresden, Toulouse

Number	Raised	Ancestry & Associations[1]	1814 Bourbon Title	Post '100 days' Formation	Engagements[2] (with at least 1 Bn present) in approx. date order[3]
61er	1669	Rgt Vermandois, Rgt La Marine(No. 11), Rgt Beaujolais (No. 74)	57e Rgt de Ligne (Napoleon restored the number 61er in 1815)	Légion de la Manche	Austerlitz, Auerstädt, Jena, Eylau, Friedland, Landshut, Eckmühl, Wagram, Viasma, Moskowa, Krasnoi, Quatre Bras, Mont St Jean
62e	1667	Rgt Salm-Salm, Rgt d'Artois (No. 48), Rgt de Salm-Salm (No. 62), Rgt du Monsieur (No. 75), Rgt R-H-Darmstadt (No. 94)	58e Rgt de Ligne (Napoleon restored the number 62e in 1815)	Légion de l'Hérault	Caldiero, Gaëte, R. Piave, Raab, Wagram, Arapiles, Logroño, Lutzen, Bautzen, San Sebastien, Leipzig, Brienne, R. Mincio
63e	1672	Rgt d'Ernest, Rgt Champagne (No. 7), Rgt La Marine (No. 11), Rgt Bresse (No. 26)	59e Rgt de Ligne (Napoleon restored the number 63e in 1815)	Légion d'Allier	Jena, Eylau, Friedland, Espinosa de los Monteros, Essling, Wagram, Talavera, Fuentes de Oñoro, Albuera, Vitoria, Sorauren, Kulm, Bidassoa, Leipzig, Nivelle, Bayonne, Ligny
64e	1672	Rgt Salis-Samande, Various battalions of line rgts	60e Rgt de Ligne (Napoleon restored the number 64e in 1815)	Disbanded 1815	Ulm, Austerlitz, Jena, Pultusk, Friedland(1), Zaragoza, Alcañiz, Maria, Belchite, Essling, Wagram, Ocaña, Badajoz, Albuera(3), Sorauren, Dresden, Bayonne(1er & 2e), Ligny, Wavre
65e	1672	Rgt Sonnenberg	61er Rgt de Ligne (Napoleon restored the number 65e in 1815)	Disbanded 1815	**Stralsund**, Heilsberg, Eckmühl, Essling, Wagram, Ratisbon, **Flushing**, Astorga, **Badajoz**, Fuentes de Oñoro, Arapiles, Lützen, Würschen, Dresden, Leipzig, **Torgau**, Bayonne, Laon, Fère-Champenoise, Paris, Namur

Number	Raised	Ancestry & Associations[1]	1814 Bourbon Title	Post '100 days' Formation	Engagements[2] (with at least 1 Bn present) in approx. date order[3]
66e	1672	Rgt Castella, Vol. du Finistère, Vol. de la Marne	62e Rgt de Ligne (Napoleon restored the number 66e in 1815)	Disbanded 1815	*Portugal*, Guadeloupe, La Coruña, Oporto, Ciudad Rodrigo, Busaco, Torres Vedras, Coa, Fuentes de Oñoro, Arapiles, Lützen, Sorauren, Leipzig, Hanau, Craonne, Laon
67e	1672	Rgt Languedoc, Rgt La Marine (No. 11), Rgt de Beaujolais (No. 74)	63e Rgt de Ligne (Napoleon restored the number 67e in 1815)	Légion de la Haute Loire	Trafalgar,* **Stralsund**, Essling, Cardadeu(1), Valls(1), Wagram, Gerona, Lützen, Bautzen, Würschen, R. Mincio(1)
68e	1673	Rgt Beauce	Vacant after 1802	–	*San Domingo – destroyed in 1802.*
69e	1673	Rgt Vigier, Rgt de Normandie (No. 9), Rgt de la Sarre (No. 51), Rgt de Barrois (No. 91)	64e Rgt de Ligne (Napoleon restored the number 69e in 1815)	Légion des Basses Alpes	Elchingen, Ulm, Jena, Eylau, Friedland, Ebersberg, Essling, Wagram, Tamames, Busaco, Fuentes de Oñoro, Arapiles, Lützen, Würschen, Dresden, Leipzig, Nivelle, Bayonne, Orthez, Toulouse, Ligny
70e	1674	Rgt Medoc, Rgt de Poitu (No. 25), Rgt de Vexin (No. 72), Rgt de Beaujolais (No. 74), Rgt de Dillon (No. 87)	65e Rgt de Ligne (Napoleon restored the number 70e in 1815)	Légion de Morbihan	Trafalgar,* Zaragoza, Obidos, Vimeiro, La Coruña, Oporto, Busaco, Sabugal, Arapiles, Sahagún, Bautzen, Sorauren, Leipzig, Nivelle, La Rothière, Orthez, Fère-Champenoise, Paris, Ligny, Wavre
71er	1674	Rgt Vivarais	Vacant after 1801	Vacant	*1801: 3e Bn. to San Domingo (absorbed by 86e Rgt); 1er & 2e Bns. absorbed by 35e Rgt*

Number	Raised	Ancestry & Associations[1]	1814 Bourbon Title	Post '100 days' Formation	Engagements[2] (with at least 1 Bn present) in approx. date order[3]
72e	1674	Rgt Vexin, D-Brig. des Lombards, 199e D-Brig.	66e Rgt de Ligne (Napoleon restored the number 72e in 1815)	Disbanded 1815	Friedland, **Thann**, Eckmühl, Essling, Wagram, Flushing, Smolensk, Valutina Gora, La Moskowa, Krasnoi, Beresina, Kulm, Leipzig, Hanau, La Rothière, Montereau, Bar-sur-Aube, Troyes, Paris, Quatre Bras, Mont St Jean
73e	1674	Rgt Royal-Comtois, Rgt de Vintimile (No. 49)	Vacant after 1801	Vacant	Absorbed into 23e Rgt in 1801
74e	1674	Rgt Beaujolais	Vacant after 1803	Vacant	Disbanded 1803
75e	1674	Rgt Monsieur, Rgt d'Aquitaine (No. 35), Rgt de Bourgogne (No. 59), Rgt de Saintonge (No. 82)	67e Rgt de Ligne (Napoleon restored the number 75e in 1815)	Légion de Morbihan	Ulm, Hollabrünn, Austerlitz, Jena, Heilsberg, Eylau (2), Heilsburg, Talavera, Almonacíd, Würschen, Vitoria, Sorauren, Dresden, Bidassoa, Dresden, Orthez, Toulouse, Namur
76e	1677	Rgt Châteauvieux, Rgt d'Aunis (No. 31), Rgt de la Dauphine (No. 38)	68e Rgt de Ligne (Napoleon restored the number 76e in 1815)	Légion de la Nièvre	Elchingen, Ulm, Jena, Pultusk, Eylau, Friedland, Ebersberg, Essling, Wagram, Tamames, **Ciudad Rodrigo**, Busaco, Fuentes de Oñoro, Sorauren, Kulm, **Dresden**, Nivelle, Bayonne, Toulouse, Ligny, Wavre
77e	1680	Rgt La Marck	Vacant after 1801	Vacant	*San Domingo – destroyed in 1803.*
78e	1684	Rgt Penthièvre	Vacant after 1803	Vacant	*Incorporated into 2e Rgt 1803*

Number	Raised	Ancestry & Associations[1]	1814 Bourbon Title	Post '100 days' Formation	Engagements[2] (with at least 1 Bn present) in approx. date order[3]
79e	1684	Rgt Boulonnais, Rgt Soissonnais (No. 40), Rgt de la Couronne (No. 45)	69e Rgt de Ligne (Napoleon restored the number 79e in 1815)	Légion de la Haute-Garonne	Trafalgar,* Caldiero, *Italy*, *Albania*, *Dalmatia*, Mt Kita, Wagram, Znaïm, *Spain (Catalonia)*, **Figueras**, Lützen, Bautzen, **Dresden**
80e	1684	Rgt Angoumois	Vacant after 1803	Vacant	*Incorporated into 34e Rgt 1803*
81er	1684	Rgt Conti, Rgt de Navarre (No. 5), Rgt d'Aunis (No. 31), Rgt de Saintonge (No. 82)	70e Rgt de Ligne (Napoleon restored the number 81er in 1815)	Légion de l'Aude	Hollabrünn, *Dalmatia*, Mt Kita, Wagram, Znaïm, *Spain*, Dresden, Orthez, Toulouse
82e	1684	Rgt Saintonge	71er Rgt de Ligne (Napoleon restored the number 82e in 1815)	Disbanded	*Martinique, Guadaloupe (Destroyed); Another 82e raised in France 1803 & 2Btns sent to W. Indies:* 1808: Vimeiro (3e Bn), Almeida, Busaco, Fuentes de Oñoro, Arapiles, Bautzen, Würschen, Vitoria, Sorauren, Leipzig, **Barcelona**, Ligny
83e	1684	Rgt Foix	Vacant after 1803	Vacant	*1er & 2e absorbed into 3e Rgt; 3e Bn to San Domingo, absorbed into 89e Rgt*
84e (Un contre Dix[5])	1684	Rgt Rohan, Rgt de Picardie (No. 2), Rgt d'Auvergne (No. 17), Rgt Lyonnais (No. 27), Rgt de Rouergue (No. 58)	72e Rgt de Ligne (Napoleon restored the number 84e in 1815)	Légion du Var	Ulm, Sacile, Graz (St Leonard)[5], Wagram, Malojaroslavetz, Krasnoi, Caldiero, R. Mincio, Mont St Jean

Number	Raised	Ancestry & Associations[1]	1814 Bourbon Title	Post '100 days' Formation	Engagements[2] (with at least 1 Bn present) in approx. date order[3]
85e	1690	Rgt Diesbach, Rgt Lyonnais (No. 27), Rgt de La Fère (No. 52), Rgt Beauvoisis (No. 57)	73e Rgt de Ligne (Napoleon restored the number 85e in 1815)	Légion de Seine-et-Marne	Austerlitz, Auerstädt, Jena, Pultusk, Eylau, Eckmühl, Essling, Wagram, Hollabrünn, Moskowa, Smolensk, Krasnoi, Vilna, Kulm, **Dresden**, **Magdeburg**, Laon, Fère-Champenoise, Paris, Mont St Jean
86e	1689	Rgt Courten, Rgt de La Reine (No. 41), Rgt de La Mark (No. 77)	74e Rgt de Ligne (Napoleon restored the number 86e in 1815)	Disbanded	Evora, Vimeiro, La Coruña, Oporto, Busaco, Arapiles, Lützen, Vitoria, Sorauren, Leipzig, Hanau, Bayonne, Orthez, Tarbes, Paris, Toulouse, Ligny, Namur
87e	1690	Rgt Dillon	Disbanded 1803	Vacant	*Incorporated into 5e Rgt 1803*
88e	1698	Rgt Berwick, Rgt de Bourbon (No. 56)	75e Rgt de Ligne (Napoleon restored the number 88e in 1815)	Disbanded	Ulm, Austerlitz, Jena, Pultusk, Ebersberg, Essling, Wagram, Ocaña, Villa Garcia, **Badajoz**, Fuentes de Oñoro (1 Bn), Albuera (2e & 3e Bns), **Badajoz**, Lützen, Würschen, Vitoria, Sorauren, Bidassoa, **Dresden**, Leipzig, **Danzig**, La Rothière, Laon, Paris, Ligny, Wavre
89e	1690	Rgt Royal-Suédois	Vacant	Vacant	*Raised in W. Indies. Fought there until 1809 under naval command and captured there in 1809*[6]
90e	1691	Rgt Chartres	Vacant	Vacant	*Sent to San Domingo, 1802. Virtually destroyed 1803*
91er	1692	Rgt Barrois	Vacant	Vacant	*Disbanded 1803*

Number	Raised	Ancestry & Associations[1]	1814 Bourbon Title	Post '100 days' Formation	Engagements[2] (with at least 1 Bn present) in approx. date order[3]
92e	1698	Rgt Walsh, Rgt d'Aquitaine (No. 35)	76e Rgt de Ligne[7] (Napoleon restored the number 92e in 1815)	Légion de la Charente-Inférieure	Ulm, Sacile, Graz (St Leonard), Wagram, La Moskowa, Malojaroslavetz, Krasnoi, Beresina, Glogau, Trieste Castle, R. Mincio, Quatre Bras, Mont St Jean
93e	1706	Rgt Enghien, Rgt de Guyenne (No. 21)	77e Rgt de Ligne (Napoleon restored the number 93e in 1815)	Légion de la Lozère	Trafalgar,* **Montserrat**, Molins de Rey(1), Eckmühl, Essling, Wagram, *Catalonia*, Valutina Gora, La Moskowa, Krasnoi, Beresina, Vilna, Lützen, Dresden, Leipzig, Hanau, Brienne, Bar-sur-Aube, Magdeburg, Quatre Bras, Mont St Jean
94e	1709	Rgt Royal-Hesse-Darmstadt, Rgt de Salm-Salm (No. 62), Rgt R-H-Darmstadt (No. 94)	78e Rgt de Ligne (Napoleon restored the number 94e in 1815)	Légion des Basses-Alpes	Austerlitz, Jena, Lübeck, Friedland, Espinosa de los Monteros, Madrid, Essling, Wagram, Talavera, Chiclana, Fuentes de Oñoro, Tarifa, Saxony, Vitoria, Sorauren, Dresden, Bayonne, Toulouse
95e	1734	Rgt Salis-Grisons	79e Rgt de Ligne (Napoleon restored the number 95e in 1815)	?	Austerlitz, Jena, Lübeck, Friedland, Espinosa de los Monteros, Madrid, Medellín, Essling, Wagram, **Cádiz**, Albuera, Tarifa, Vitoria, Sorauren, Dresden, Bayonne, Mont St Jean

Number	Raised	Ancestry & Associations[1]	1814 Bourbon Title	Post '100 days' Formation	Engagements[2] (with at least 1 Bn present) in approx. date order[3]
96e	1745	Rgt Nassau, Rgt de Touraine (No. 33)	80e Rgt de Ligne (Napoleon restored the number 96e in 1815)	Légion de la Moselle	Ulm, Halle, Braunsberg, Friedland, Somosierra, Essling, Wagram, Talavera, **Cádiz**, Chiclana, *Saxony*, Vitoria, Kulm, Leipzig, Nivelle, Bayonne, Orthez, Paris, Ligny, Namur,
97e	1752	Rgt Steiner	Disbanded 1803	Vacant	*Incorporated into 60e Rgt 1803*
98e	1757	Rgt Bouillon	Disbanded 1803	Vacant	*1802: 3e Bn to San Domingo; 1803: Disbanded*[8]
99e	1757	Rgt Royal-Deux-Ponts	Disbanded 1803	Vacant	*Incorporated into 62e Rgt 1803*
100e	1758	Rgt Rheinbach, Rgt de Piémont (No. 3)	81er Rgt de Ligne (Napoleon restored the number 100e in 1815)	Légion de Haute-Marne	Ulm, Jena, Pultusk, **Zaragoza**, **Badajoz**, Albuera, Miranda, Vitoria, Dresden, Bayonne, Toulouse, Quatre Bras, Mont St Jean
101er	1787	Rgt Royal-Liégeois	82e Rgt de Ligne (Napoleon restored the number 101er in 1815)	Disbanded 1815	Caldiero, Gaëte, Calabria, Arapiles, Würschen, Juterbogk, Hanau, *Italy*, Bayonne, Bar-sur-Aube, Arcis-sur-Aube, **Strasbourg**
102e	?	Rgt du Dauphin (No. 29), Rgt Royal-Deux-Ponts (No. 99)	83e Rgt de Ligne (Napoleon restored the number 102e in 1815)	Légion des Landes	Caldiero, Naples, Sacile, R. Piave, Raab, Wagram, *Spain (Catalonia)*, Leipzig, R. Mincio

Number	Raised	Ancestry & Associations[1]	1814 Bourbon Title	Post '100 days' Formation	Engagements[2] (with at least 1 Bn present) in approx. date order[3]
103e	?	Rgt Royal des Vasseaux (No. 43), Rgt Royal-Suédois (No. 89)	84e Rgt de Ligne (Napoleon restored the number 103e in 1815)	Disbanded 1815	Ulm, Jena, Zaragoza, Essling, Wagram, Ocaña, Badajoz, Fuentes de Oñoro, Albuera, Lützen, Würschen, Vitoria, Dresden, Leipzig, Hanau, Toulouse
104e	?	Various free companies	85e Rgt de Ligne (Napoleon restored the number 104e in 1815)	Disbanded 1815	*1803: Incorporated into 11e. 1814: Reformed using remnants of 17e, 52e and 101er.* **Strasbourg.**
105e	1663	Rgt Le Roi, Rgt de Navarre (No. 5)	86e Rgt de Ligne (Napoleon restored the number 105e in 1815)	Légion de la Haute-Vienne	Jena, Eylau, Heilsberg, Friedland, **Thann**, Eckmühl, Essling, Wagram, *Spain*, Sorauren, Bidassoa, Bayonne, **Hamburg**, Arcis-sur-Aube, Mont St Jean
106e	1772	Colonial Rgt Du Cap, Rgt de l'Auvergne (No. 17)	87e Rgt de Ligne (Napoleon restored the number 106e in 1815)	Légion des Côtes du Nord	R. Adige, Sacile, Raab, Wagram, Moskowa, Malojaroslavetz, Krasnoi, R. Mincio
107e	1772	Colonial Rgt de Pondichéry	88e Rgt de Ligne (Napoleon restored the number 107e in 1815)	Disbanded	*1793: India (1er Btn captured & taken into British service), 1799: 2e Btn. joined 6e D-Brig. in France where new 107e raised & went to Italy. 1802: 2e Bn to San Domingo, 1803: disbanded. New 107e raised 1814.* Ligny, Quatre-Bras, Mont St Jean

Number	Raised	Ancestry & Associations[1]	1814 Bourbon Title	Post '100 days' Formation	Engagements[2] (with at least 1 Bn present) in approx. date order[3]
108e	1772	Colonial Rgt de l'Île de France, Rgt Bourbonnais (No. 13), Rgt Vivavrais (No. 71)	89e Rgt de Ligne (Napoleon restored the number 108e in 1815)	Disbanded	Austerlitz, Auerstädt, Jena, Eylau, Landshut, Eckmühl, Wagram, Moskowa, Krasnoi, Beresina, **Thorn**, **Hamburg**, **Antwerp**, Quatre Bras, Mont St Jean
109e	1772	Colonial Rgt de la Martinique, Colonial Rgt de la Guadeloupe	Disbanded 1803	Vacant	*1803: 1er & 2e Bns to 21e Rgt and 3e to India – absorbed into Rgt de l'Île de France 1804.*
110e	1773	Colonial Rgt du Port-au-Prince, Colonial Rgt de l'Île de Ré, Colonial Rgt de Cachaix	Disbanded 1803	Vacant	*1803: 1er Bn to 55e Rgt, 2e and 3e Bns to 86e.*
111e	1793	Several colonial and regular regiments were used at various times to raise four different 111e regiments.	90e Rgt de Ligne (Napoleon restored the number 111e in 1815)	Disbanded	Austerlitz, Auerstädt, Jena, Eylau, *Spain*, Eckmühl, Essling (1), Wagram, Znaïm, Moskowa, Malojaroslavetz, Viasma, Krasnoi, Vilna, Ligny, Wavre
112e	1801[9]	2e Piémontaise D-Brig.	Disbanded 1803	Disbanded	*1803: Re-raised from Belgian recruits. 1809[10]: Italy*, Raab, Wagram, *Saxony*, Bautzen, Würschen, Katzen, Leipzig, Hanau, Fère-Champenoise
113e	1802	3e D-Big. Polonaise, 1808: re-raised from Tuscan L.I.	Disbanded 1814	Vacant	*1803: San Domingo (destroyed). 1808:* **Figueras, Gerona, Ciudad Rodrigo**, Arapiles, Danzig, Paris
114e	1801	2e D-Big. Polonaise, Re-raised from 1er & 2e Prov. 1808	Disbanded 1814	Vacant	**Valencia**, **Zaragoza**, Alcañiz, Maria, Belchite, **Tortosa**, Saguntum

Number	Raised	Ancestry & Associations[1]	1814 Bourbon Title	Post '100 days' Formation	Engagements[2] (with at least 1 Bn present) in approx. date order[3]
115e	1808	3e & 4e Rgts Provisoires	Disbanded 1814	Vacant	**Valencia**, **Zaragoza**, Alcañiz, Maria, Belchite, **Tortosa**, **Tarragona**, Toulouse
116e	1808	5e & 6e Rgts Provisoires, Chass. des Montagnes (1er Bn)	Disbanded 1814	Vacant	Bailén (6e Rgt Provisoire 1808), Tudela, **Zaragoza**, Alcañiz, Maria, Belchite, **Tortosa**, **Tarragona**, Saguntum, Orthez, Tarbes, Toulouse
117e	1808	9e & 10e Rgts Provisoires	Disbanded 1814	Vacant	Tudela, **Zaragoza**, **Tarragona**, Saguntum, **Valencia**, Orthez, Toulouse, **Barcelona** (surr.)
118e	1808	11e Rgt Provisoire	Disbanded 1814	Vacant	**Zaragoza**, Arapiles, Vitoria, Sorauren, Bidassoa, Bayonne, Orthez, Arcis-sur-Aube, Toulouse
119e	1808	13e & 14e Rgts Provisoires	Disbanded 1814	Vacant	**Zaragoza**, Medina de Rioseco, Arapiles, Vitoria, **San Sébastien**, Sorauren, Bidassoa, Bayonne, Orthez, Toulouse
120e	1808	17e & 18e Rgts Provisoires	Disbanded 1814	Vacant	Medina de Rioseco, Arapiles, **Burgos**, Vitoria, Sorauren, Bidassoa, **Bayonne**, Orthez, Toulouse
121er	1809	1er Rgt Supplémentaire, 3e, 4e, 5e Légions de Réserve	Disbanded 1814	Vacant	Bailén (1er Rgt Suppl., 3e, 4e & 5e Légions de Res.1808), **Zaragoza**, **Lérida**, **Tarragona**, Saguntum, Castalla, Würschen, Molins de Rey, Leipzig, La Rothière, Arcis-sur-Aube, Fère-Champenoise, Paris

Number	Raised	Ancestry & Associations[1]	1814 Bourbon Title	Post '100 days' Formation	Engagements[2] (with at least 1 Bn present) in approx. date order[3]
122e	1809	2e Rgt Supplémentaire, 1er & 2e Légions de Réserve	Disbanded 1814	Vacant	Bailén (2e Rgt Suppl., 1er & 2e Légions de Res.1808), 1st Oporto, **Astorga**, Arapiles, Lützen, Würschen, Vitoria, Sorauren, Dresden, Bidassoa, Leipzig, Bayonne, Bar-sur-Aube, Craonne, Laon, Arcis-sur-Aube
123e	1810	Various Dutch Rgts which fought from 1803 to 1810 in that guise.	Disbanded 1814	Vacant	As Dutch: **Hameln**, Nienberg, **Colberg**, **Stralsund**, Talavera, Almonacíd, Ocaña. As 123e: Polotsk, Beresina, **Wittenberg**, **Wesel**
124e	1810	Various Dutch Rgts (inc. Oranje-Nassau) which fought from 1803 to 1810 in that guise.	Disbanded 1814	Vacant	As Dutch: **Hameln**, **Nienberg**, **Colberg**, **Stralsund**. As 124e: Polotsk, Beresina, **Stettin**, **Wittenberg**
125e	1810	Various Dutch Rgts which fought from 1803 to 1810 in that guise.	Disbanded 1814	Vacant	As Dutch: **Hameln**, **Nienberg**, **Colberg**, **Stralsund**, Eylau. As 125e: **Magdeburg**
126e	1810	Various Dutch Rgts which fought from 1803 to 1810 in that guise.	Disbanded 1814	Vacant	As Dutch: **Stralsund**. As 126e: Combats in Russian Campaign of 1812.
127e	1811	Légion Hanovrienne, Rgt de Westphalie	Disbanded 1814	Vacant	Smolensk, Valutina Gora, Krasnoi, Beresina, **Wesel**
128e	1811	Légion Hanovrienne, Rgt de Westphalie	Disbanded 1814	Vacant	Polotsk, Beresina, Vilna, **Küstrin**, **Kehl**

Number	Raised	Ancestry & Associations[1]	1814 Bourbon Title	Post '100 days' Formation	Engagements[2] (with at least 1 Bn present) in approx. date order[3]
129e	1811	Légion Hanovrienne, Oldenburg Inf. Rgt	Disbanded 1814	Vacant	Krasnoi, Beresina
130e	1811	1er, 3e & 6e Bns Auxiliaires	Disbanded 1814	Vacant	*Spain*, **Pamplona**, Bayonne
131er	1811[11]	Various Dutch Rgts which had amalgamated to form the van Walcheren Rgt and which fought from 1803 to 1811 in that guise.	Disbanded 1814	Vacant	As Dutch: No important actions. As 124e: Saxony & Italy, Gross-Beeren, Juterbogk, Leipzig, R. Mincio
132e (Un contre huit[12])	1812	Rgt Île de Ré	Disbanded 1814	Vacant	*Italy, Saxony,* Lützen, Gross-Beeren, Juterbogk, Leipzig, La Rothière, R. Mincio, Paris, Rosnay
133e	1812	2e Rgt de la Méditerranée	Disbanded 1814	Vacant	*Italy*, *Saxony*, Gross-Beeren, Juterbogk, Leipzig, **Landau**
134e	1813	Garde Municipale de Paris, 125e Rgt (4e & 5e Bns)	Disbanded 1814	Vacant	Würschen, **Magdeburg**
135e	1813	Levied from eligible citizens	Disbanded 1814	Vacant	Halle, Leipzig, Hanau
136e	1813	Levied from eligible citizens	Disbanded 1814	Vacant	Lützen, Würschen, Leipzig, Montmirail, Arcis-sur-Aube, Paris
137e	1813	Levied from eligible citizens	Disbanded 1814	Vacant	Würschen, Gross-Beeren, Juterbogk, Leipzig, Hanau, Mainz
138e	1813	Levied from eligible citizens	Disbanded 1814	Vacant	Lützen, Bautzen, Würschen, Katzbach, Kulm, Leipzig, Montmirail, Paris, **Glogau**

Number	Raised	Ancestry & Associations[1]	1814 Bourbon Title	Post '100 days' Formation	Engagements[2] (with at least 1 Bn present) in approx. date order[3]
139e	1813	Levied from eligible citizens	Disbanded 1814	Vacant	Lützen, Würschen, Katzbach, Leipzig, Hanau, *France*
140e	1813	Levied from eligible citizens	Disbanded 1814	Vacant	Lützen, Würschen, Katzbach, Leipzig, Hanau
141er	1813	Levied from eligible citizens	Disbanded 1814	Vacant	Lützen, Würschen, Katzbach, Leipzig, Paris
142e	1813	Levied from eligible citizens	Disbanded 1814	Vacant	Lützen, Würschen, Leipzig, Hanau, Troyes
143e	1813	Levied from eligible citizens	Disbanded 1814	Vacant	*Catalonia*
144e	1813	Levied from eligible citizens	Disbanded 1814	Vacant	Lützen, Würschen, Katzbach, Leipzig, Hanau, La Rothière
145e	1813	Levied from eligible citizens	Disbanded 1814	Vacant	Lützen, Würschen, Leipzig
146e	1813	Levied from eligible citizens	Disbanded 1814	Vacant	*Rheinbund*
147e	1813	Levied from eligible citizens	Disbanded 1814	Vacant	Lützen
148e	1813	Levied from eligible citizens	Disbanded 1814	Vacant	Lützen, Würschen, Leipzig
149e	1813	Levied from eligible citizens	Disbanded 1814	Vacant	Katzbach, Arcis-sur-Aube, Fère-Champenoise
150e	1813	Levied from eligible citizens	Disbanded 1814	Vacant	Katzbach, Leipzig, **Maastricht**
151er	1813	Levied from eligible citizens	Disbanded 1814	Vacant	Würschen, **Glogau**, *France*

Number	Raised	Ancestry & Associations[1]	1814 Bourbon Title	Post '100 days' Formation	Engagements[2] (with at least 1 Bn present) in approx. date order[3]
152e	1813	Levied from eligible citizens	Disbanded 1814	Vacant	**Hamburg, Harburg,** Katzbach, Leipzig, *France*
153e	1813	Levied from eligible citizens	Disbanded 1814	Vacant	Katzbach, Leipzig, **Châlons,** Montereau
154e	1813	Levied from eligible citizens	Disbanded 1814	Vacant	Katzbach, Leipzig, *France*
155e	1813	Levied from eligible citizens	Disbanded 1814	Vacant	Würschen, Katzbach, Leipzig, Hanau, Brienne
156e	1813	Levied from eligible citizens	Disbanded 1814	Vacant	Würschen, Juterbogk, Hanau, Paris, Mainz
157e	Vacant throughout the Napoleonic Wars				
158e	Vacant throughout the Napoleonic Wars				
159e	Vacant throughout the Napoleonic Wars				
160e	Vacant throughout the Napoleonic Wars				
161e	Vacant throughout the Napoleonic Wars				
162e	Vacant throughout the Napoleonic Wars				
163e	Vacant throughout the Napoleonic Wars				

* Indicates secondment to naval duties, usually on board ship on marine infantry duty.

** Italic type indicates a general location, over a protracted period with no significant engagements. Bold type indicates a city defence or siege (in which the unit either defended or laid siege).

[1] The Ancestry and Associations column indicates, with the first entry, the original, usually Royal, parent regiment. The entries thereafter indicate the titles and numbers of the regiments in the period from 1775/76, when many regiments were split, to 1792 and the first of the two amalgamations. 'Col.' indicates a colonial regiment.

[2] Certain regiments had elite cos. with Oudinot at Friedland. These are not indicated.

[3] Only those engagements considered significant by the authors have been included.

[4] The battle honour 'Jena' was awarded to a number of units who fought at Auerstädt. It is not certain that all of these were actually present at Jena itself but we have included it if the unit received the honour.

[5] The 84e fought so well at Graz that Napoleon awarded them the sobriquet 'One against Ten' to be engraved on their eagle.

[6] Smith, D. (*Napoleon's Regiments*, Greenhill Books, 2000). However, Bukhari, E. (*French Napoleonic Line Infantry*, Almark Publishing Co., 1973) says they were dissolved in 1803.

[7] Nafziger, G.F. (*The French Army* Vol. 2, self published, 1997). Smith, D. op. cit. only says the regiment was 'disbanded on 12 May 1814 but re-raised at once, then disbanded and re-raised on 13 March 1815'. He mentions nothing of its 1814 numbering or designation.

[8] Smith, D. op. cit. However, Bukhari, E. op. cit. says they were incorporated into 92e.

[9] Smith, D. op. cit. However, Bukhari, E. op. cit., says 1794 as 112e D-Brig.

[10] Smith, D. op. cit. and Bukhari, E. op. cit. give this regiment as having a presence at the Battle of Valls (Catalonia 25 Feb. 1808). However, Smith, in his book *The Greenhill Napoleonic Wars Databook* (Greenhill Books, 1998), makes no mention of this regiment as present at that battle and Oman, Sir C. op. cit. does not show them as part of any of the divisions present with St Cyr's VII Corps at the time.

[11] Bukhari, E. op. cit. says 1812.

[12] Sobriquet awarded for the action at Rosnay in 1814 when, numbering only a few hundred, they defeated a force at least eight-fold stronger.

[13] The French name for the Roliça battle(s).

FRENCH LIGHT INFANTRY REGIMENTS

Number	Raised	Ancestry & Associations	1814 Bourbon Title	Post '100 days' Formation	Engagements** (with at least 1 Bn present) in approx. date order
1er	1563	Gardes Françaises, G. N. de Paris	Rgt du Roi	Légion des Basses-Alpes	*Calabria*, *Italy*, *Catalonia*, Raab, **Tarragona**, *Spain*, *Illyria*, Lützen, Bautzen, Juterbogk, Leipzig, Mincio, Bar-sur-Aube, Quatre-Bras, Mont St Jean
2e	1793	1er Bn Franc de Muller	2e Rgt du Dauphin	Légion de la Reine	Austerlitz, **Danzig**, Heilsberg, Friedland, Obidos(3e), Vimeiro(3e), La Coruña(3), 1st Oporto, Busaco, Sabugal, Arapiles, Lützen, Würschen, Vitoria, Bidassoa, Katzbach, Leipzig, **Danzig**, Nivelle, Bayonne, Montmirail, Vauchamps, Arcis-sur-Aube, Fère-Champenoise, Paris, Quatre-Bras, Mont St Jean
3e	1778	Chasseurs-à-Cheval des Pyrénées,[1] Chasseurs d'Auvergne (No. 7)	3e Rgt du Dauphin	Légion des Basses-Pyrénées	Hollabrünn, **Colberg**, Valls, Eckmühl, Essling, Wagram, *Tyrol*, **Tarragona**, **Figueras**, Castalla, Würschen, Leipzig, **Tortosa**
4e	1616	Rgt Poitu (No. 25), Chasseurs des Vosges (No. 8)	Rgt de Monsieur	Légion de la Gironde	Ulm, Friedland, Medina de Rioseco (1er, 2e, 4e), Roliça(3e), Vimeiro(3e), La Coruña(4), 1st & 2nd Oporto, Busaco, Sabugal, **Badajoz**, Arapiles, **Danzig**, Lützen, Würschen, Vitoria, Dresden, Kulm, Leipzig, Bayonne, Montmirail, Vauchamps, Montereau, Orthez, Paris, Toulouse, Quatre-Bras, Mont St Jean

Footnotes on p. 95.

Number	Raised	Ancestry & Associations	1814 Bourbon Title	Post '100 days' Formation	Engagements (with at least 1 Bn present) in approx. date order
5e	1616	Chasseurs Bretons, Rgt Lyonnais (No. 27)	Rgt d' Angoulême	Légion du Jura	*San Domingo*, **Stralsund**, **Zaragoza**, Alcañiz, Maria, Belchite, Wagram, *Shipboard*,* **Tortosa**, **Tarragona**, Lützen, Würschen, Sorauren, Bidassoa, Bautzen, Leipzig, **Tortosa**, **Bayonne**, Vauchamps, Montereau, Mont St Jean
6e	1793	1er Bn Chasseurs	Rgt de Berri	Unknown	Elchingen, Ulm, Jena, Eylau, Friedland, *Spain*, Essling, Wagram, Tamames, **Ciudad Rodrigo**, Busaco, Arapiles, **Dresden**, Leipzig, Vauchamps, Ligny
7e	1788	Chasseurs du Gevaudan (No. 10)	Rgt de Colonel-Général	7e Léger	Jena, Eylau, Eckmühl, Essling, Wagram, Smolensk, Valutina Gora, Borodino, Malojaroslavetz, Krasnoi, Beresina, Kulm, Dresden, Magdeburg
8e	1793	Légion Franche Étrangère	8e Léger	8e Léger	*Italy, Dalmatia*, Sacile, R. Piave, Mt Kita, Wagram, Znaïm, **Figueras**, *Spain*, Malojaroslavetz, Krasnoi, Beresina, Dresden, Juterbogk, Leipzig, Hanau, Torgau, Wavre
9e (L'Incomparable)	1788	Chasseurs des Cevennes (No. 9)	?	Légion des Ardennes	Ulm, Eylau, Friedland, Espinosa de los Monteros, Somosierra, Essling, Wagram, **Badajoz**, Lützen, Bautzen, Würschen, Vitoria, Sorauren, Dresden, Kulm, Bidassoa, Leipzig, **Torgau**, **Bayonne**, Montmirail, Orthez, Paris, Toulouse, Ligny

Number	Raised	Ancestry & Associations	1814 Bourbon Title	Post '100 days' Formation	Engagements (with at least 1 Bn present) in approx. date order
10e	1684	Chasseurs des Ardennes, Rgt Foix (No. 83)	Disbanded	Légion de Bas-Rhin	Ulm, Austerlitz, Jena, Eylau, Heilsberg, Friedland, Eckmühl, Essling, Wagram, *Spain*, *Russia*, Lützen, Vitoria, Dresden, Leipzig, Hanau, Vauchamps, Bar-sur-Aube, Arcis-sur-Aube, **Strasbourg**
11e	1788	Chasseurs Royaux-Corses (No. 3), Bataillon Valaisan, Tirailleurs du Po	Disbanded & re-raised 1815	Légion de Bas-Rhin	*The 11e went through various phases of disbandment and re-raising, including destruction in San Domingo. The three units listed as their ancestors were formed into a new 11e in 1811.* **Gerona**, Hollabrünn, Austerlitz, **Lübeck**, Eylau, Heilsberg, Essling, Wagram, Polotsk, Beresina, Dresden, Leipzig, Brienne, Montereau, Paris, Ligny
12e	1671	Rgt Royal-Italien, Chass. Royaux de Dauphine (No. 2)	Disbanded	Légion de Bas-Rhin	**Danzig**, Heilsberg, Friedland, Vimeiro, Almonacid, Albuera, Lützen, Würschen, Vitoria, Sorauren, Kulm, Leipzig, **Bayonne**, Orthez, Toulouse, Ligny
13e	1684	Rgt de Rohan (No. 84)	Disbanded & re-raised 1815	Unknown	Austerlitz, Auerstädt, Jena, Eylau, Thann, Eckmühl, Wagram, Smolensk, Borodino, Viasma, Dresden, Kulm, **Dresden**, **Antwerp**, Mont St Jean

Number	Raised	Ancestry & Associations	1814 Bourbon Title	Post '100 days' Formation	Engagements (with at least 1 Bn present) in approx. date order
14e	1796	108e D-Brig, 139e D-Brig, 1er Légion des Francs	Disbanded	Unknown	Caldiero, Naples, Calabria, Ionian Islands, Lützen, Bautzen, Katzbach, Trieste, Leipzig, Hanau, Mincio, Kehl
15e	1794	D-Brig. des Tirailleurs	Disbanded & re-raised 1815	Unknown	Austerlitz, Vimeiro, La Coruña, Thann, Landshut, Eckmühl, Wagram, **Ciudad Rodrigo**, Smolensk, Borodino, Krasnoi, Dresden, **Hamburg**, Montereau, Ligny, Wavre, Namur
16e	1788	Rgt Royal-Italien, Rgt Royal-Corse	Disbanded	Vacant	Jena, Eylau, Friedland, **Valencia**, **Gerona**, Espinosa de los Monteros, Essling, Wagram, Talavera, **Cadiz**, Barossa, Fuentes de Oñoro, Albuera, **Tarifa**, Lützen, Würschen, Vitoria, Sorauren, Dresden, Bidassoa, Leipzig, R. Nive, Montmirail, Vauchamps, Montereau, Bar-sur-Aube, Arcis-sur-Aube, Paris
17e	1671	Rgt Royal-Italien (1er Bn)	Disbanded	Vacant	Ulm, Hollabrünn, Austerlitz, Jena, Pultusk, Eylau, Friedland, 1st Oporto, Amarante, 2nd Oporto, Thann, Essling, Wagram, Znaïm, Busaco, Sabugal, Salamanca, Arapiles, **Danzig**, Sorauren, Bidassoa, Leipzig, Hanau, Bayonne, Bar-sur-Aube, Arcis-sur-Aube, **Strasbourg**

Number	Raised	Ancestry & Associations	1814 Bourbon Title	Post '100 days' Formation	Engagements (with at least 1 Bn present) in approx. date order
18e	1795	102e Rgt de Ligne, Vol. de la Haute-Saône, 2e Rgt de Lot-et-Garonne	Disbanded	Vacant	Ulm, *Dalmatia*, Sacile, Mt Kita, *Croatia*, R. Piave, Wagram, Znaïm, *Catalonia*, Vitebsk, **Montserrat**, Borodino, Malojaroslavetz, Viasma, Krasnoi, *Spain*, Würschen, Dresden, Juterbogk, Leipzig, *Catalonia*
19e	1799	3e D-Brig. Légère, 6e D-Brig. Légère, 141e D-Brig., 31e Gend. à Pied, Vol. de l'Aisne	Vacant	Vacant	*Destroyed in San Domingo, 1802. Survivors re-absorbed by 3e D-Brig. Légère.*
20e	Vacant		Vacant	Vacant	
21er	1739	Rgt Royal-Corse	Disbanded	Vacant	Ulm, Jena, Pultusk, Friedland, **Zaragoza**, Ebersberg, Essling, Wagram, **Badajoz**, Fuentes de Oñoro, Albuera, Lützen, Vitoria, Bidassoa, **Dresden**, Leipzig, **Danzig**, **Bayonne**, Orthez, Toulouse
22e	1795	Chasseurs Corses, Vol. de l'Aveyron, Rgt de l'Isère	Disbanded	Vacant	Caldiero, Naples, *Calabria*, R. Piave, Lützen, Bautzen, Pirna, Katzbach, Leipzig, Hanau
23e	1792	Légion des Alpes	Disbanded	Vacant	Caldiero, Maida, *Calabria*, R. Piave, Raab, Wagram, *Catalonia*, **Figueras**, Lützen, Bautzen, Leipzig, Paris

Number	Raised	Ancestry & Associations	1814 Bourbon Title	Post '100 days' Formation	Engagements (with at least 1 Bn present) in approx. date order
24e	1778	Rgt de Montréal (No. 106)	Disbanded	Vacant	Ulm, Austerlitz, Jena, Eylau, Heilsberg, Friedland, *Spain*, Eckmühl, Essling, Wagram, Znaïm, Smolensk, Valutina Gora, Borodino, Viasma, Krasnoi, Beresina, Bautzen, Pirna, Dresden, Leipzig, Brienne, La Rothière, Montereau, Bar-sur-Aube, Arcis-sur-Aube
25e	1791	Gardes Françaises, G. N. de Paris	Disbanded	Vacant	Günzburg, Ulm, Jena, Eylau, Friedland, **Zaragoza**, Essling, Wagram, Tamames, **Ciudad Rodrigo**, Fuentes de Oñoro, Arapiles, Lützen, Würschen, Sorauren, **Dresden**, Leipzig, **Danzig**, **Bayonne**, Toulouse
26e	1795	Chasseurs Vol. de la Meuse, Chasseurs du Rhin, Chasseurs du Nord, Légion des Alpes, Vol. de l'Allier, Rgt de l'Ain	Disbanded	Vacant	Ulm, Austerlitz, Jena, Heilsberg, Eckmühl, Ebersberg, Essling, Wagram, Hollabrünn, Znaïm, Polotsk, Beresina, Dresden, Leipzig, Brienne
27e	1794	Chasseurs Corses, Vol. des Bosches-du-Rhône, Rgt de Lille	Disbanded	Vacant	Austerlitz, Jena, Halle, Friedland, Espinosa de la Monteros, Uclés, Essling, Wagram, Talavera, Barossa, Fuentes de Oñoro, Arapiles, Lützen, Würschen, Dresden, Bidassoa, **Dresden**, Nivelle, **Bayonne**, *N. France*

Number	Raised	Ancestry & Associations	1814 Bourbon Title	Post '100 days' Formation	Engagements (with at least 1 Bn present) in approx. date order
28e	1795	Various units possessing only remnants of their original formations	Disbanded	Vacant	Hollabrünn, Friedland, **Zaragoza**, Ebersberg, Essling, Wagram, **Badajoz**, Fuentes de Oñoro, Albuera, **Badajoz**, **Salamanca**, **Danzig**, Lützen, Würschen, Vitoria, Sorauren, Dresden, Kulm, Leipzig, **Bayonne**, Toulouse
29e	1797	6e D-Brig. Légère, 8e D-Brig. Légère, D-Brig. de la Haute-Saône	Disbanded	Vacant	*Russia*, Lützen, Würschen, Pirna, Dresden, Leipzig, La Rothière, Vauchamps, Montereau, Troyes
30e	1797	Various volunteer battalions	Vacant	Vacant	
31er	1801	1ère D-Brig. Légère Piémontaise	Disbanded	Vacant	Friedland, La Coruña, 1st Oporto, 2nd Oporto, Busaco, Fuentes de Oñoro, Arapiles, Sorauren, Bidassoa, R. Nive, Bayonne, Orthez, Toulouse
32e	1805	Various Ligurian troops	Disbanded	Vacant	**Zaragoza**, *Catalonia*, 1st Oporto, 2nd Oporto, **Gerona**, Busaco, Lützen, Bautzen, Würschen, Pirna, **Dresden**, Leipzig, Lyons
33e	1809 1810	1st raising: 7e & 8e Rgts Suppl., 2nd Raising: 3e Dutch Jäger, 6th Dutch Line	Disbanded	Vacant	**Colberg**, **Stralsund**, Krasnoi, **Hamburg**
34e	1811	2e, 4e, 5e & 7e Rgts Auxilliaires	Disbanded	Vacant	**Ciudad Rodrigo**, Sorauren, Orthez, Toulouse

Number	Raised	Ancestry & Associations	1814 Bourbon Title	Post '100 days' Formation	Engagements (with at least 1 Bn present) in approx. date order
35e	1812	1er Rgt de la Méditerranée	Disbanded	Vacant	Würschen, Gross-Beeren, Juterbogk, Leipzig, Hanau, *Italy*
36e	1812	Rgt de Belle Île	Disbanded	Vacant	Gross-Beeren, Juterbogk, Leipzig, Hanau, Parma
37e	1813	Gardes Municipales	Disbanded	Vacant	Lützen, Bautzen, Dresden, Pirna, Leipzig, Hanau, La Rothière, Vauchamps, Paris

* Indicates secondment to naval duties, usually on board ship on marine infantry duty.

** Italic type indicates a general location, over a protracted period with no significant engagements. Bold type indicates a city defence or siege (in which the unit either defended or laid siege.

[1] Attached infantry regiments.

OTHER FRENCH INFANTRY REGIMENTS

Title	Raised	Constituent troops & Associations	Engagements* (with at least 1 Bn present) in approx. date order
Fusiliers Vétérans			*Italy, Hamburg, France*
1er & 2e Garde de Paris	1802		**Danzig**, Friedland, Bailén. Disbanded 1812.
Légion Corse	1802		**Gaëte**, *Calabria*
Pionniers Blancs	1806	Austrian prisoners	Bailén, **Gerona**. Disbanded 1810.
Bn de Chasseurs Rentrés	1809		**Flushing**
Chasseurs d'Orient	1802	Légions Coptes, Grecques, & Syriennes, Corps Turcs, Guides d'Omar	Trafalgar,** *Italy*, *Dalmatia, Corfu*
Chasseurs Coloniaux	1802	West Indian recruits from Marseilles and Bordeaux	*Hispaniola*, **San Domingo, Guadeloupe.** Disbanded 1810.
Chasseurs des Montagnes	1808	Bns des Hautes Pyrenées, Pyrenées Orientales & Haute Garonne	*Spain*, **San Sebastien**

* Italic type indicates a general location, over a protracted period with no significant engagements. Bold type indicates a city defence or siege (in which the unit either defended or laid siege).

** Indicates secondment to naval duties, usually on board ship on marine infantry duty.

SWISS INFANTRY (Excluding those in Spanish service at the start of the Peninsular War)

Regiment & Uniform	Raised	Constituent troops & Associations	Engagements* (with at least 1 Bn present) in approx. date order
1er (Red Coat, facings Yellow, turnbacks white)	1805	1er, 2e & 3e Demi-Brigades Suisses	Trafalgar,** Maida, *Calabria*, **Capri**, Polotsk, Beresina
2e (Red Coat, facings Royal Blue, turnbacks white)	1806		**Rosas**, *Portugal*, La Coruña
3e (Red Coat, facings Black, turnbacks white)	1806		Bailén, Polotsk, Beresina
4e (Red Coat, facings Sky Blue, turnbacks white)	1806		Heilsberg, Friedland, Bailén, Obidos, Vimeiro, 1st Oporto, Polotsk, Beresina

* Italic type indicates a general location, over a protracted period with no significant engagements. Bold type indicates a city defence or siege (in which the unit either defended or laid siege).

** Indicates secondment to naval duties, usually on board ship on marine infantry duty.

POLISH INFANTRY (VISTULA LEGION)

Regiment	Raised	Constituent troops & Associations	Engagements* (with at least 1 Bn present) in approx. date order
1er Rgt (Légion de la Vistule)	1808	Originally formed from the Légion Polacco-Italienne (Polish/Italian Legion) in 1801, which operated as part of, first, the Italian army and, next, that of Naples. In 1813, the Legion was formed into a Regiment of two battalions.	Maida, *Silesia*, **Zaragoza**, Tudela, Alcañiz, Maria, Belchite, Saguntum, **Valencia**, Beresina
2e Rgt (Légion de la Vistule)	1808		**Zaragoza**, Tudela, Maria, Beresina, **Wittenberg**
3e Rgt (Légion de la Vistule)	1808		**Zaragoza**, Alcañiz, Krasnoi, Beresina
4e Rgt (Légion de la Vistule)	1809		*Spain*, *Poland*
Rgt de la Vistule	1813		**Soissons**, Arcis-sur-Aube
1er Rgt Lanciers (Légion de la Vistule)	1805		**Zaragoza**, Tudela, Talavera, Almonacíd

* Italic type indicates a general location, over a protracted period with no significant engagements. Bold type indicates a city defence or siege (in which the unit either defended or laid siege).

SPANISH INFANTRY

Regiment	No. of Bns	Raised	Constituent troops & Associations	Engagements* (with at least 1 Bn present) in approx. date order
Régiment Espagnol Joséph Napoléon	To 1813: 4, then 2	1809	Captured troops from Rgts Guadalajara & Asturias in Denmark	Borodino, Krasnoi, Beresina, Lützen, Bautzen, Leipzig, Hanau, Glogau. 1813: Converted to Pionniers.
1er Bataillon de Pionniers	1	1811	Spanish sappers (some from Denmark)	**Danzig**
Rgt Catalonien	1	1811	Spanish prisoners	Disbanded after a few months, following British victory at Salamanca (Arapiles)

* Italic type indicates a general location, over a protracted period with no significant engagements. Bold type indicates a city defence or siege (in which the unit either defended or laid siege).

KING JOSEPH'S ARMY (INFANTRY)

Regiment	No. of Bns	Raised	Constituent troops & Associations	Engagements (with at least 1 Bn present) in approx. date order
Grenadiers de la Garde	2 x 6 Cos	1808	French officers and men	
Voltigeurs de la Garde	2 x 6 Cos	1809	French officers and men	
Fusiliers de la Garde	2 x 6 Cos	1809	French officers and men	
Rgt Royal-Étranger	4 + Depot	1808	German, Austrian & Italian troops	
Rgt Royal-Irlandais	2	1809	A few Irish the rest probably Spanish	
1er Rgt Légère de Castilla	2	1809	Probably a mixture of nationalities	

Regiment	No. of Bns	Raised	Constituent troops & Associations	Engagements (with at least 1 Bn present) in approx. date order
2e Rgt Légère de Murcia	2?	1809	Probably a mixture of nationalities	
1er - Madrid	2 + Depot	1809	Largely Spanish	
2e - Toledo	2 + Depot	1809	Largely Spanish	
3e - Sevilla	2 + Depot	1810	Largely Spanish	
4e - Soria	2 + Depot	1810	Largely Spanish	
5e - Granada	2 + Depot	1810	Largely Spanish	
6e - Málaga	2 + Depot	1810	Largely Spanish	
7e - Córdoba	2 + Depot	1810	Largely Spanish	
1ère Cavallerie	6 Rgts	–	Never a physical reality – a few recruits only	
Cazadores a Caballo	4 Rgts	1809/10	Spanish – never reached full strength	Guadalajara, Albuera
Lanceros de Sevilla	2 Sqns	1810	Poles and Andalucians	*1812*: With Soult in Andalucía – mustered only a few score sabres.
Husares de Guadalajara	1 Sqn	1812	Raised by ex guerrillero Saturno Abuín	

PORTUGUESE INFANTRY[1] (LÉGION PORTUGAISE)

Regiment & Uniform	Raised	Constituent troops & Associations	Engagements* (with at least 1 Bn present) in approx. date order
1er (Brown Coat & trousers, facings Red, turnbacks white)	1808	13e D-Brig. D'Élite	Wagram, Smolensk, Valutina Gora, Borodino, Krasnoi
2e (Brown Coat & trousers, facings Red, turnbacks white)	1808		Smolensk, Valutina Gora, Borodino, Krasnoi
3e (Brown Coat & trousers, facings Red, turnbacks white)	1808		Beresina
Chasseurs à Cheval	1808		*Portugal*, Wagram, Krasnoi, Beresina

* Italic type indicates a general location, over a protracted period with no significant engagements. Bold type indicates a city defence or siege (in which the unit either defended or laid siege).

[1] Originally scheduled to comprise five regiments – only three were raised

OTHER FOREIGN INFANTRY

Regiment & Uniform (where known)	**Raised**	**Constituent troops & Associations**	**Engagements* (with at least 1 Bn present) in approx. date order**
Bn de Neuchâtel (Dk Yellow coat, Scarlet collar/cuffs)	1807		Wagram, *Spain*, Borodino, Krasnoi, Dresden, Leipzig, Hanau
Bn Valaisan	1805		**Gerona**
1811: 1er Étranger (Dk Green coat & trousers. Red collar, cuffs, t/backs)	1805/ 1811	Germans (1805: Rgt Tour d'Auvergne)	*Calabria, Spain, Tyrol*, R. Mincio
1811: 2e Étranger (Sky Blue coat & trousers. Yellow collar)	1805/ 1811	Germans (1805: Rgt d'Isembourg)	
1811: 2e Étranger (Suisse) – as for Swiss Uniforms	1815	Survivors of the four Swiss regiments	Ligny, Wavre
1811: 3e Étranger (Dk Green coat & trousers, Red t/backs, Yellow collar)	1803/ 1811	Irish emigrants (1803: Légion Irlandais)	L. Irlandais: **Flushing, Astorga.** 3e Étranger: **Antwerp**
1811: 4e Étranger (Dk Green coat & trousers. Red collar & t/backs)	1806/ 1811	Prussian prisoners (1806: Rgt Prusse)	Rgt Prusse: **Flushing, Astorga.** 4e Étranger: **Wörden**
Rgt d'Illyrie (Dalmatien)	1810	Dalmatian recruits	Krasnoi, Beresina, Juterbogk, Leipzig, Hanau
Légion du Midi (Piémontaise)	1803	Piedmontese recruits	*Portugal*, La Coruña, Busaco, Fuentes de Oñoro. Disbanded 1811.
Rgt de Westphalie (or Westphalien)	1806	Prussian prisoners (1806: Rgt Prusse)	*Spain*, **Valencia**. Merged into the Légion Hanovrienne in 1808.

Regiment & Uniform (where known)	**Raised**	**Constituent troops & Associations**	**Engagements* (with at least 1 Bn present) in approx. date order**
Légion Hanovrienne	1804	Included a Chasseurs à Cheval regt	1st Oporto, **Ciudad Rodrigo**, Busaco, Fuentes de Oñoro. Disbanded 1811.
Rgt d'Albanie (or Albanaise)	1809	Greek, Albanian, Italian and Dalmatian recruits – Ionian Islands	**Corfu**
Bn Septinsulaire	1807	Venetian and Dalmatian recruits + prisoners. Cavalry & artillery units existed.	**Corfu, Ste Maure** (Ionia). Disbanded 1813.
Bn de Pionniers Noirs	1803	W. Indians & mulattos	**Fiume, Gaëte.** 1806: Transferred to Neapolitan army.
1er Légion du Nord	1806	Recruited in Hagenau	**Thorn, Danzig,** Heilsberg. In 1808 became part of Grand Duchy of Warsaw (5th Rgt)
2e Légion du Nord	1806	Recruited in Nuremberg	
1er Prov. Infanterie Croate (Dk Green coats & breeches, facings Yellow)	1809	Austrian Grenzers (1st & 2nd)	Malojaroslavetz, Krasnoi, Beresina, **Glogau**
2e Prov. Infanterie Croate (Dk Green coats & breeches, facings Yellow)	1809	Austrian Grenzers (3rd & 4th)	Würschen
3e Prov. Infanterie Croate (Dk Green coats & breeches, facings Yellow, collar piped Lt. Blue)	1809	Austrian Grenzers (10th & 11th)	Polotsk, Beresina
4e Prov. Infanterie Croate	1812	Austrian Grenzers (10th & 11th, 2nd Bns)	*Italy*

* Italic type indicates a general location, over a protracted period with no significant engagements. Bold type indicates a city defence or siege (in which the unit either defended or laid siege).

FRENCH CARABINIER REGIMENTS

Number	**Raised**	**Ancestry & Associations**	**1814 Bourbon Title**	**Post '100 days' Formation**	**Engagements (with at least 1 Sqn present) in approx. date order**
1er Rgt	1693	Royal-Carabiniers	Carabiniers de Monsieur	Carabiniers de Monsieur	Austerlitz, Jena, Eylau, Bailén,[1] Friedland, Eckmühl, Wagram, Moskowa, Dresden, Leipzig, Hanau, Montmirail, Paris, Mont St Jean
2e Rgt	1776	Royal-Carabiniers	Carabiniers de Monsieur	Carabiniers de Monsieur	Austerlitz, Jena, Eylau, Bailén,[1] Heilsberg, Friedland, Tudela, Eckmühl, Essling, Wagram, Moskowa, Leipzig, Hanau, Montmirail, Mont St Jean

[1] Smith, D. op.cit., p. 234 indicates this. Bukhari, E. op. cit., p. 32, says that 'one squadron was on service in Spain' in 1808. Oman, Sir C. op. cit., Vol. I, p. 183, only shows the 1er and 2e Cuirassiers Provisoire as present at Bailén; these later formed the 13e Cuirassiers. We have found no other reference to their presence here. There were members of the regiment (from the depots – esp. officers) forming the provisional units who would have been killed, injured or captured at Bailén, thus suggesting, from records of *tués et blessés,* the presence of the regiments themselves.

FRENCH CUIRASSIER REGIMENTS

Number	Raised	Ancestry & Associations	1814 Bourbon Title[1]	Post '100 days' Formation[2]	Engagements[*] (with at least 1 Sqn present) in approx. date order
1er	1657	Rgt Colonel-Général	Cuirassiers du Roi	Cuirassiers du Roi (No. 1)	Ulm, Austerlitz, Jena, Königsberg, Eckmühl, Essling, Wagram, Hollabrünn, Znaïm, Krasnoi, Moskowa, Leipzig, Hanau, Paris, Mont St Jean
2e	1635	Rgt Cardinal-Duc, Royal-Cavalerie	Cuirassiers de la Reine	Cuirassiers de la Reine	Austerlitz, Jena, Eylau, Friedland, Eckmühl, Essling, Wagram, Moskowa, Lützen, Dresden, Wachau, Leipzig, La Rothière, Vauchamps, Mont St Jean
3e	1654	Rgt Commissaire Général	Cuirassiers du Dauphin	Disbanded Nov. 1815	Austerlitz, Jena, Eylau, Friedland, Eckmühl, Essling, Wagram, Moskowa, Beresina, Würschen, Dresden, Danzig, Wachau, Leipzig, La Rothière, Champaubert, Fère-Champenoise, Mont St Jean
4e	1643	Comps. Vol. La Reine-Mère, Rgt de la Reine	Cuirassiers d'Angoulême	Cuirassiers d'Angoulême	*Italy*, Heilsberg, Friedland, Essling, Wagram, Beresina, Dresden, Wachau, Leipzig, Vauchamps, **Hamburg**, Fère-Champenoise, Mont St Jean

Footnotes on p. 107.

Number	Raised	Ancestry & Associations	1814 Bourbon Title[1]	Post '100 days' Formation[2]	Engagements[*] (with at least 1 Sqn present) in approx. date order
5e	1653	Rgt Nogent-Cavalerie, Rgt Stanislaus Roi, Rgt Royal-Pologne	Cuirassiers de Berry	Cuirassiers de Berry	Ulm, Austerlitz, Jena, Eylau, Bailén,[3] Eckmühl, Essling, Wagram, Hollabrünn, Moskowa, Leipzig, Hanau, Champeaubert, Troyes, Fère-Champenoise, Ligny, Mont St Jean
6e	1635	Dragons du Cardinal, Fus. à Cheval de son Eminence, Fusiliers à Cheval du Roi, Rgt du Roi	Cuirassiers Colonel-Général	Cuirassiers d'Orléans	Heilsberg, Essling, Wagram, Moskowa, Wachau, Leipzig, Champaubert, Paris, Ligny, Mont St Jean
7e	1659	Rgt Royal-Étranger	Cuirassiers de Berry	Disbanded Dec. 1815	Heilsberg, **Zaragoza**,[4] Essling, Wagram, Moskowa, Wachau, Leipzig, Champaubert, Paris, Ligny, Mont St Jean
8e	1638	Rgt de Villequier (Comp. Mestre-de-Camp), Cuirassiers du Roi	–	Disbanded Dec. 1815	Heilsberg, Catalonia, Essling, Wagram, Moskowa, Viasma, Krasnoi, Wachau, Leipzig, Hanau, Vauchamps, Paris, Ligny, Mont St Jean
9e	1665	Rgt de Villars, Rgt d'Anjou, Rgt d'Aquitaine, Rgt d'Artois	–	Disbanded Dec. 1815	Austerlitz, Jena, Friedland, Bailén,[3] Eckmühl, Wagram, Moskowa, Beresina, Dresden, Wachau, Leipzig, Ligny, Mont St Jean
10e	1643	Various Croatian Rgts, Rgt Royal-Cravates	–	Disbanded Dec. 1815	Ulm, Austerlitz, Jena, Eylau, Bailén,[3] Eckmühl, Essling, Wagram, Znaïm, Moskowa, Leipzig, Hanau, Paris, Ligny, Mont St Jean

Number	Raised	Ancestry & Associations	1814 Bourbon Title[1]	Post '100 days' Formation[2]	Engagements* (with at least 1 Sqn present) in approx. date order
11e	1665	Rgt de Montclar (Comp. Mestre-de-Camp), Rgt Royal-Rousillon	–	Cuirassiers d'Orléans	Ulm, Austerlitz, Jena, Eylau, Friedland, Bailén,[3] Eckmühl, Essling, Wagram, Znaïm, Moskowa, Dresden, Wachau, Leipzig, Laon, Quatre-Bras, Mont St Jean
12e	1668	Chev. Lég. du Dauphin	–	Cuirassiers du Roi (No. 2)	Ulm, Austerlitz, Jena, Eylau, Friedland, Eckmühl, Essling, Wagram, Znaïm, Moskowa, Krasnoi, Dresden, Wachau, Leipzig, Mont St Jean
13e 'l'Intré-pide'	1808	1er & 2e Cuirassiers Prov.	Cuirassiers de la Reine	–	Tudela, Saguntum, *Catalonia*, Leipzig, *France*
14e	1810	2nd Dutch Cuirassiers	Disbanded	–	Friedland, *Germany*, **Stralsund**, Polotsk, Beresina, Leipzig

* Italic type indicates a general location, over a protracted period with no significant engagements. Bold type indicates a city defence or siege (in which the unit either defended or laid siege).

1 Three of the main sources we have used for the data in these tables (Nafziger, G. *The French Army Royal, Republican, Imperial*, Vol. III; Smith, D., (*Napoleon's Regiments*, Greenhill Books, 2000); and Bukhari, E., (*Napoleon's Cavalry*, Osprey, 1979) are somewhat at variance on this aspect. The fourth: Bucquoy, E.L. (*Les Uniformes du Premier Empire* [Les Cuirassiers], Grancher, Paris, 1978) is silent on Bourbon naming.

2 As stated above, there are inconsistencies both between and within the stated sources. This is even more evident for post-Napoleonic naming. The names we give are our best assessment based on the sources and our own logic.

3 Smith, D. op.cit., p. 234 indicates this. Bukhari, E. op. cit., p. 32, says that 'one squadron was on service in Spain' in 1808. Oman, Sir C. op. cit., Vol. I, p. 183, only shows the 1er and 2e Cuirassiers Provisoire as present at Bailén; these later formed the 13e Cuirassiers. We have found no other reference to their presence here. There were members of the regiment (from the depots – esp. officers) forming the provisional units who would have been killed, injured or captured at Bailén, thus suggesting, from records of *tués et blessés*, the presence of the regiments themselves.

4 The only Cuirassier unit we can find listed as potentially available from the parent Corps (Bessière's), is 5e *Escadron de Marche* of 329 sabres – part of the Pamplona garrison – (Oman, Sir C. op. cit., p. 614). We can not be certain whether this may later have joined 7e Cuirassiers.

FRENCH DRAGOON REGIMENTS

Number	Raised	Ancestry & Associations	1814 Bourbon Title	Post '100 days' Formation	Engagements* (with at least 1 Sqn present) in approx. date order[1]
1er	1656	Drag. Étranger du Roi, Royal-Dragons, 1811: 1er Chev.-Lég. Lanciers	Rgt de Lanciers du Roi (Restored to 1er Chev.-Lég. Lanciers by Napoleon 1815)	Disbanded	Ulm, Austerlitz, Jena, Eylau, Heilsberg, Friedland, Vimeiro, Talavera, Barossa
2e	1635	Enghien-Cavalerie, Rgt de Condé	Rgt de Drag. du Roi (No. 1)	2e Rgt Dragons du Doub	Ulm, Jena, Eylau, Heilsberg, Friedland, **Zaragoza**, Tudela, Uclés, Talavera, Barossa, *Saxony*, Königsberg, Wachau, **Maastricht**, Mont St Jean
3e	1649	Rgt Enghien, Rgt Bourbon, 1811: 2e Chev.-Lég. Lanciers	Restored to 2e Chev.-Lég. Lanciers by Napoleon 1815	–	Ulm, Austerlitz, Jena, Eylau, Friedland, Obidos, Vimeiro, Alba de Tormes
4e	1667	Chartres-Cavalerie, Rgt Clermont, Rgt La Marche, Conti-Dragons	Rgt de Drag. de la Reine (No. 2) (Restored to 4e Dragons by Napoleon 1815)	Disbanded	Ulm, Austerlitz, Jena, Eylau, Heilsberg, Friedland, Vimeiro, Talavera, Albuera, Wachau, Bar-sur-Aube, Laon, Arcis-sur-Aube, Fère-Champenoise, Ligny
5e	1668	Colonel-Général Drag. Rgt, Rgt Royal-Dragons	Rgt de Drag. du Dauphin (No. 3) (Restored to 5e Dragons by Napoleon 1815)	3e Rgt Drag. de la Garonne	Ulm, Austerlitz, Jena, Eylau, Medellín, Ocaña, **Danzig**, Vitoria, Bayonne, Brienne, Vauchamps, Craonne, Laon, Fère-Champenoise, Paris, Ligny, Wavre

Footnotes on p. 113.

Number	Raised	Ancestry & Associations	1814 Bourbon Title	Post '100 days' Formation	Engagements* (with at least 1 Sqn present) in approx. date order[1]
6e	1673	Dragons La Reine	Rgt de Drag. de Monsieur (No. 4) (Restored to 6e Dragons by Napoleon 1815)	1er Rgt Drag. du Calvados	Ulm, Austerlitz, Jena, Eylau, Friedland, Medina de Rioseco, **Zaragoza**, Fuentes de Oñoro, Arapiles, Vitoria, Gross-Beeren, Leipzig, Craonne, Fère-Champenoise, Paris, Ligny
7e	1673	Dragons Le Dauphin	Rgt de Drag. de Monsieur (No. 5) (Restored to 7e Dragons by Napoleon 1815)	7e Rgt Drag. de la Manche	*Calabria*, R. Piave, Raab, Wagram, Znaïm, Moskowa, Vinkovo, Viasma, Dresden, Wachau, Leipzig, La Rothière, Magdeburg, Vauchamps, Fère-Champenoise, Paris, Mont St Jean
8e	1674	Rgt Toulouse, Rgt Drag. de Penthièvre, 1811: 3e Chev.-Lég. Lanciers	Rgt de Lanciers du Dauphin (Restored to 3e Chev.-Lég. Lanciers by Napoleon 1815)	–	Ulm, Austerlitz, Jena, *Poland*, Eylau, Heilsberg, Friedland, Sahagun, Ocaña, Busaco
9e	1673	Rgt Lorraine, 1811: 4e Chev.-Lég. Lanciers	Rgt de Lanciers de Monsieur (Restored to 4e Chev.-Lég. Lanciers by Napoleon 1815)	–	Ulm, Austerlitz, Jena, Eylau, Heilsberg, Friedland, Talavera, *Andalucía*
10e	1674	Rgt Mestre-de-Camp-Général, 1811: 5e Chev.-Lég. Lanciers	Rgt de Lanciers d'Angoulême (Restored to 5e Chev.-Lég. Lanciers by Napoleon 1815)	–	Ulm, Austerlitz, Jena, Eylau, Friedland, *Portugal*, Alba de Tormes, Fuentes de Oñoro

Number	Raised	Ancestry & Associations	1814 Bourbon Title	Post '100 days' Formation	Engagements* (with at least 1 Sqn present) in approx. date order[1]
11e	1674	Rgt Dragons d'Angoulême	Rgt de Drag. de Berry (No. 6) (Restored to 11e Dragons by Napoleon 1815)	6e Rgt Drag. de la Loire	Ulm, Hollabrünn, Austerlitz, Jena, Eylau, Friedland, Fuentes de Oñoro, Arapiles, Vitoria, Gross-Beeren, **Strasbourg**
12e	1675	Rgt Dragons d'Artois	Rgt de Drag. D'Orléans (No. 7) (Restored to 12e Dragons by Napoleon 1815)	10e Rgt Drag. de la Seine	Günzburg, Ulm, Austerlitz, Jena, Eylau, Königsberg, *Spain & Portugal*, Almonacíd, Ocaña, Vitoria, Juterbogk, **Bayonne**, Craonne, Laon, Paris, Ligny
13e	1676	Rgt Dragons de Condé, Rgt Comte-de-Provence, Rgt Drag. de Monsieur	Rgt de Drag. de Condé (No. 8) (Restored to 13e Dragons by Napoleon 1815)	Disbanded	Ulm, Hollabrünn, Austerlitz, Jena, Pultusk, Eylau, 1st Oporto, **Astorga**, Vitoria, Gross-Beeren, **Hamburg**, Wavre
14e	1672	Rgt Drag. de Chartres	9e Rgt de Dragons (No. 9) (Restored to 14e Dragons by Napoleon 1815)	Uncertain	Ulm, Austerlitz, Jena, Heilsberg, Friedland, Medellin, Talavera, R. Gebora, Albuera, Bar-sur-Aube, Arcis-sur-Aube, Paris, Ligny
15e	1688	Rgt Drag. de Noailles	10e Rgt de Dragons (No. 10) (Restored to 15e Dragons by Napoleon 1815)	4e Rgt Drag. de la Gironde (uncertain)	Ulm, Austerlitz, Jena, Pultusk, Eylau, *Spain & Portugal*, Tamames, Alba de Tormes, Arapiles, Vitoria, Pirna, Wachau, Leipzig, Brienne, La Rothière

Number	Raised	Ancestry & Associations	1814 Bourbon Title	Post '100 days' Formation	Engagements* (with at least 1 Sqn present) in approx. date order[1]
16e	1718	Rgt Drag. d'Orléans	11e Rgt de Dragons (No. 11) (Restored to 16e Dragons by Napoleon 1815)	Disbanded	Ulm, Austerlitz, Jena, Eylau, Ocaña, Vitoria, Wachau, Arcis-sur-Aube, Ligny
17e	1743	Vol. de Saxe, Rgt Drag. Schönberg	12e Rgt de Dragons (No. 12) (Restored to 17e Dragons by Napoleon 1815)	5e Rgt Drag. de l'Herault (uncertain)	Ulm, Austerlitz, Jena, **Danzig**, Friedland, La Coruña, 1st Oporto, Albuera, Wachau, **Magdeburg**, Troyes, Arcis-sur-Aube, Ligny
18e	1744	Rgt Drag. du Roi	13e Rgt de Dragons (No. 13) (Restored to 18e Dragons by Napoleon 1815)	Disbanded	Elchingen, Ulm, Austerlitz, Jena, **Graudenz**, Friedland, *Spain*, Pirna, Leipzig, Brienne, Montereau, Paris
19e	1793	Vol. d'Angers	14e Rgt de Dragons (No. 14) (Restored to 19e Dragons by Napoleon 1815)	Disbanded	Ulm, Austerlitz, Jena, Friedland, *Spain & Portugal*, Pirna, Dresden, Wachau, Hanau, Brienne, Strasbourg
20e	1793	Rgt Drag. de Hainault	15e Rgt de Dragons (No. 15) (Restored to 20e Dragons by Napoleon 1815)	Disbanded	Ulm, Austerlitz, Jena, Eylau, Heilsberg, Friedland, Albuera, Leipzig, Hanau, Brienne, Namur

Number	Raised	Ancestry & Associations	1814 Bourbon Title	Post '100 days' Formation	Engagements* (with at least 1 Sqn present) in approx. date order[1]
21er	1793	Rgt Drag. de la Manche, Légion de la Police, 1er Drag. Rgt Piémontaise	Disbanded[2]	Vacant	Ulm, Austerlitz, Jena, Eylau, Almonacíd, Alba de Tormes, Vitoria, Juterbogk, Wachau, **Bayonne**, Troyes, Craonne, Laon, Fère-Champenoise
22e	1635	Piedmontese Rgt d'Orléans, Rgt d'Anjou	Disbanded[2]	Vacant	Ulm, Austerlitz, Jena, Eylau, *Spain*, Wachau, Brienne
23e	1670	Rgt Royal Piémont, Rgt Prince-de-Piémont	Disbanded[2]	Vacant	R. Tagliamento, R. Piave, Graz, Raab, Wagram, Moskowa, Malojaroslavetz, Krasnoi, Beresina, Dresden, Leipzig, Hanau, Paris
24e	1761	Rgt Royal-Lorraine	Disbanded[2]	Vacant	Valls, Raab, Wagram, Vich, Saguntum, Castalla, Juterbogk
25e	1665	Rgt de Bourgogne, Rgt de Bretagne, Rgt Royal-Bourgogne	Disbanded[2]	Vacant	Ulm, Austerlitz, Jena, Eylau, **Lugo**, Alba de Tormes, Fuentes de Oñoro, Arapiles, Vitoria, Dresden, Wachau, Leipzig, **Dresden**, Montereau, Fère-Champenoise
26e	1671	Rgt Drag. de Rousillon, Rgt Drag. de Berry	Disbanded[2]	Vacant	Ulm, Austerlitz, Jena, Eylau, Heilsberg, Friedland, Tudela, Medellín, Talavera, Ocaña, Albuera, Juterbogk, Leipzig, Craonne, Laon, Fère-Champenoise, Paris

Number	Raised	Ancestry & Associations	1814 Bourbon Title	Post '100 days' Formation	Engagements* (with at least 1 Sqn present) in approx. date order[1]
27e	1674	Rgt Royal-Normandie	11e Rgt de Dragons (No. 11)	Vacant	Ulm, Austerlitz, Jena, Friedland, 1st Oporto, Albuera, Arapiles, **Wittenberg**, Arcis-sur-Aube
28e	1803	1er Corps des Hussards (bis), 7e Rgt Hussards	Disbanded[2]	Vacant	Medina de Rioseco, R. Piave, Wagram, Moskowa, Beresina, Dresden, Leipzig, Vauchamps, Laon, Paris
29e	1802	11e Rgt Hussards, 1811: 6e Chev.-Lég. Lanciers	Disbanded but restored to 6e Chev.-Lég. Lanciers by Napoleon 1815	Vacant	Caldiero, *Naples*, R. Piave, Wagram
30e	1802	12e Rgt Hussards	Disbanded[2]	Vacant	R. Tagliamento, *Naples*, Wagram, Moskowa, Krasnoi, Beresina, Lützen, Bautzen, Dresden, Leipzig, Paris

* Italic type indicates a general location, over a protracted period with no significant engagements. Bold type indicates a city defence or siege (in which the unit either defended or laid siege).

[1] Some regiments are recorded as fighting at Bailén. These are men of 6e *Dragons Provisoires* to whom these regiments provided drafts. We have not included Bailén.

[2] Various squadrons of these regiments were used to form the 15 Bourbon Dragoon regiments.

FRENCH CHEVAU-LÉGER LANCIERS REGIMENTS

Number	Raised	Ancestry & Associations	1814 Bourbon Title	Post '100 days' Formation	Engagements* (with at least 1 Sqn present) in approx. date order
1er	1811	1er Dragons	1er Lanciers du Roi	Lanciers du Roi	Smolensk, Moskowa, Beresina, Lützen, Dresden, Kulm, Wachau, Leipzig, Hanau, Laon, Fère-Champenoise,[1] Paris, Ligny, Mont St Jean
2e	1811	3e Dragons	2e Lanciers de la Reine	Disbanded	*Spain*, Moskowa, Beresina, Katzbach, Leipzig, Hanau, La Rothière, Montmirail, Bar-sur-Aube, Craonne, Fère-Champenoise, Mont St Jean
3e	1811	8e Dragons	3e Lanciers du Dauphin	Lanciers du Dauphin[2]	Polotsk, Krasnoi, Beresina, Pirna, Kulm, Leipzig, Hanau, Champaubert, Troyes, Mont St Jean
4e	1811	9e Dragons	Légion de Monsieur	Disbanded	Portugal, Moskowa, Krasnoi, Beresina, Katzbach, Leipzig, Champaubert, Troyes, Mont St Jean
5e	1811	10e Dragons	Légion d'Angoulême	Disbanded	*Spain*, Moskowa, Beresina, Kulm, Wachau, Hanau, Montmirail, Laon, Quatre-Bras, Mont St Jean

Footnotes on p. 115.

Number	Raised	Ancestry & Associations	1814 Bourbon Title	Post '100 days' Formation	Engagements* (with at least 1 Sqn present) in approx. date order
6e	1811	29e Dragons	Disbanded but re-raised by Napoleon	Lanciers de Berry	Krasnoi, Moskowa, Katzbach, Wachau, Laipzig, Hanau, Montmirail, Quatre-Bras, Mont St Jean
7e	1811	1er Lanciers (Légion de la Vistule)	Disbanded	Vacant	*Spain*, Katzbach, Dresden, Hanau, Montereau
8e	1811	2e Lanciers (Légion de la Vistule)	Disbanded	Vacant	Polotsk, Beresina, Lützen, Würschen, Dresden, Wachau, Leipzig
9e	1811	31er Chass. à Chev., Légion Hanovrienne	Disbanded	Vacant	Valutina Gora, Moskọwa, Beresina, **Danzig**, Kulm, Vauchamps, Fère-Champenoise

* Italic type indicates a general location, over a protracted period with no significant engagements. Bold type indicates a city defence or siege (in which the unit either defended or laid siege).

[1] Smith, D. op. cit., p. 257 states their presence also at the 'B[attle of] Champenoise' on 10 Feb. 1814. There was no Champenoise battle on that date to our knowledge. It is possible that he intended to indicate the battle of Champaubert, which did take place on that day; however, Smith does not give this unit as present in the order of battle in his book *The Greenhill Napoleonic Wars Data Book*.

[2] Smith, D. op. cit., p. 259. Nafziger, G. op. cit., p. 37, uses '*Dauphine*' (King's eldest daughter) rather than '*Dauphin*' (King's eldest son).

FRENCH CHASSEURS À CHEVAL REGIMENTS

Number	Raised	Ancestry & Associations	1814 Bourbon Title	Post '100 days' Formation	Engagements* (with at least 1 Sqn present) in approx. date order
1er [1]	1651	Conti Chasseurs, Rgt Drag. de Boufflers (No. 1), Chasseurs d'Alsace	Rgt de Chasseurs du Roi	Chasseurs du Roi	Austerlitz, Auerstädt, Jena, Eylau, Eckmühl, Raab, Wagram, Hollabrünn, Znaïm, Moskowa, Viasma, Lützen, Bautzen, Würschen, Kulm, Leipzig, Hanau, Maubeuge, Fère-Champenoise, Charleroi, Quatre-Bras, Mont St Jean
2e	1673	Chevalier de Fimarçon Drag., Drag. de Montmorency, Chasseurs des Evêches (No. 2)	Rgt de Chasseurs de la Reine	Disbanded	Austerlitz, Auerstädt, Jena, Eylau, Eckmühl, Ebersberg, Wagram, *Spain*, Lithuania, Smolensk, Moskowa, Krasnoi, Würschen, Pirna, Wachau, Leipzig, Hanau, Paris, Magdeburg, Strasbourg
3e	1675	Drag. de Deux-Ponts (No. 3), Chass. de Flandres (No. 3)	Rgt de Chasseurs du Dauphin	Disbanded	Caldiero, Heilsberg, Friedland, Eckmühl, Croatia, Essling, Mt Kita, Wagram, Hollabrünn, Moskowa, Beresina, Dresden, Wachau, Leipzig, Hanau, Fère-Champenoise, Mont St Jean
4e	1675	Drag. de Durfort, Chass. de Franche-Comté (No. 4)	Rgt de Chasseurs de Monsieur	Disbanded	*Martinique*, R. Adige, Gaëte, Moskowa, Krasnoi, Beresina, Bautzen, Katzbach, Wachau, Leipzig, Charleroi, Mont St Jean

Footnotes on p. 121.

Number	Raised	Ancestry & Associations	1814 Bourbon Title	Post '100 days' Formation	Engagements* (with at least 1 Sqn present) in approx. date order
5e	1675	Drag. de Segur, Chass. du Hainault (No. 5)	Rgt de Chasseurs d'Angoulême	Disbanded	Austerlitz, Jena, Pultusk, Eylau, Friedland, Medellín, Talavera, *Spain*, Vitoria, Juterbogk, Leipzig, Bar-sur-Aube, Orthez, Arcis-sur-Aube, Toulouse
6e	1676	Drag. de Languedoc, Chass. de Languedoc (No. 6)	Rgt de Chasseurs de Berry	Chasseurs du Cantal	*Calabria*, Sacile, R. Piave, Wagram, Moskowa, Dresden, Wachau, Leipzig, Ligny, Mont St Jean
7e	1745	Volontaires Royaux, Légion Royale, Chass. des Alpes, Chass. de Picardie (No. 7)	Rgt de Chasseurs d'Orléans	Disbanded	Jena, Eylau, Heilsberg, Friedland, *Spain*, *Italy*, *Austria*, Essling, Raab, Wagram, Hollabrünn, Fuentes de Oñoro, Polotsk, Danzig, Dresden, Juterbogk, Wachau, Leipzig, Hanau, **Strasbourg**
8e	1749	Arquebusiers de Grassin, Fusiliers de la Morlière, Volontaires Bretons, Vol. de Flandre, Vol. de Hainault, Légion de Flandre, Chass. de Pyrénées (No. 2), Chass. de Guyenne (No. 8)	Rgt de Chasseurs de Bourbon	Disbanded	Ulm, Sacile, R. Piave, Raab, Wagram, Tyrol, Smolensk, Moskowa, Lützen, Hanau, Fère-Champenoise, Paris, Wavre
9e	1757	Vol. de Hainault, Légion de Hainault, Chass. des Vosges (No. 3), Chass. de Lorraine (No. 9)	Rgt de Chasseurs du Colonel-Général	Disbanded	Maida, *Calabria*, R. Piave, Wagram, Hollabrünn, Moskowa, Viasma, Wachau, Leipzig, Ligny, Mont St Jean

Number	Raised	Ancestry & Associations	1814 Bourbon Title	Post '100 days' Formation	Engagements* (with at least 1 Sqn present) in approx. date order
10e	1758	Vol. de Clermont-Prince, Légion de Condé, Chass. de Cévennes (No. 4), Chass. de Bretagne (No. 10)	10e Chass. à Cheval	Disbanded	Elchingen, Ulm, Jena, Eylau, Friedland, Medina de Rioseco, Medellín, Talavera, Ocaña, Wachau, Bar-sur-Aube, Craonne, Paris, Toulouse, **Magdeburg, Langres**
11e	1762	Vol. Étrangers de Würmser, Légion de Soubise, Chass. de Géraudan (No. 5), Chass. de Normandie (No. 11)	11e Chass. à Cheval de l'Isère	Disbanded	Ulm, Austerlitz, Jena, Eylau, Heilsberg, Friedland, Eckmühl, Wagram, Hollabrünn, *Portugal*, Fuentes de Oñoro, Moskowa, Katzbach, Wachau, Leipzig, Hanau, Mont St Jean, Mézières
12e	1769	Légion Corse, Chass. des Ardennes (No. 6), Chass. de Champagne (No. 12)	12e Chass. à Cheval de la Marne	Disbanded	Austerlitz, Auerstädt, Jena, Eylau, Friedland, Ebersberg, Wagram, Hollabrünn, Fuentes de Oñoro, Moskowa, Beresina, Katzbach, Wachau, Leipzig, Bar-sur-Aube, Craonne, Ligny, Mont St Jean
13e	1792	Légion Américaine; Légion du Nord; Compagnie Noir; Drags. de la Manche, de la Seine Inférieure & du Calvados	13e Chass. à Cheval de la Meuse	Disbanded	Austerlitz, Jena, Eylau, Friedland, Essling, Wagram, Fuentes de Oñoro, Arapiles, Sorauren, Juterbogk, **Bayonne**, Troyes, Bar-sur-Aube, Toulouse
14e	1793	Hussards des Alpes, d'Égalité & de la Mort	14e Chass. à Cheval du Morbidan	Disbanded	Caldiero, Naples, *Calabria*, Heilsberg, Eckmühl, Essling, Wagram, Hollabrünn, Arapiles, Vitoria, Gross-Beeren, Wachau, Leipzig, Hanau, Brienne, Belfort

Number	Raised	Ancestry & Associations	1814 Bourbon Title	Post '100 days' Formation	Engagements* (with at least 1 Sqn present) in approx. date order
15e	1793	Chass. Bretons (de Beysser), Chass. Bourgignons (de la Côte-d'Or)	15e Chass. à Cheval de l'Oise	Disbanded	*Italy*, Eylau, Friedland, *Galicia*, Tamames, Alba de Tormes, *Portugal*, *Saxony*, Sorauren, Wachau, Leipzig, Orthez, Arcis-sur-Aube, Toulouse
16e	1793	Chass. Normands (de la Bertèche)	Disbanded	Vacant	Austerlitz, Jena, Halle, Eylau, Eckmühl, Essling, Wagram, Znaïm, Moskowa, Krasnoi, Würschen, Kulm, Dresden, Wachau, Leipzig, Hanau, Fère-Champenoise
17e	1793	Chev.-Lég. de Ouest-Flandre	Vacant	Vacant	Disbanded 1795 (see 26e)
18e	1793	Chev.-Lég. Belges, Drag. de Bruxelles	Vacant	Vacant	Disbanded 1795
19e	1793	Légion de Rosenthal Chass.	Disbanded	Vacant	*Italy*, **Danzig**, Eckmühl, Ebersberg, Essling, Wagram, Hollabrünn, Moskowa, Krasnoi, Beresina, **Dresden**, Leipzig, R. Mincio
20e	1793	Légion de la Moselle, Légion du Centre (du Luckner)	Disbanded	Vacant	Jena, Eylau, Heilsberg, Friedland, *Italy*, *Austria*, Essling, Raab, Wagram, Fuentes de Oñoro, Polotsk, Beresina, Katzbach, Wachau, Leipzig, *France*
21er	1793	Hussards Braconniers	Disbanded	Vacant	Ulm, Pultusk, Friedland, Talavera, Ocaña, Albuera, Juterbogk, Wachau, Vitoria, Orthez, Toulouse

Number	Raised	Ancestry & Associations	1814 Bourbon Title	Post '100 days' Formation	Engagements* (with at least 1 Sqn present) in approx. date order
22e [2]	1793	Légion des Pyrénées-Orientales	Disbanded	Vacant	Ulm, Austerlitz, Jena, Eylau, Heilsberg, Friedland, Medina de Rioseco, Sabugal(1), Arapiles, Vitoria, Gross-Beeren, Juterbogk, Wachau, Montereau, Toulouse
23e	1793	Légion des Ardennes	Disbanded	Vacant	*Italy*, Eckmühl, Wagram, Polotsk, Beresina, **Danzig**, Katzbach, Wachau, Leipzig, Vauchamps, Fère-Champenoise
24e	1793	Chasseurs Voluntaires	Disbanded	Vacant	Caldiero, Friedland, *Spain*(3), Mt Kita(1), Essling, Wagram, Fuentes de Oñoro, Polotsk, Beresina, Danzig, Wachau, Leipzig, Hanau, Troyes
25e	1795	Légion des Montagnes	Disbanded	Vacant	Caldiero, *Calabria*, Sacile, R. Piave, Smolensk, Moskowa, Beresina, Hanau, Gross-Beeren, Wachau, Leipzig, Besançon, Magdeburg, Hamburg
26e	1802	17e Chass. à Chev., Hussards Piémontaises	Disbanded	Vacant	Ulm, Austerlitz, **Stralsund**, Obidos, Vimeiro, Medellín, Talavera, Almonacíd, Arapiles, Dresden, Wachau, Leipzig, Bar-sur-Aube
27e	1808	Chev.-Lég. d'Arenburg (Belg.)	Disbanded	Vacant	*Spain*, Albuera, Dresden, Wachau, Hanau, La Rothière, Bar-sur-Aube

Number	Raised	Ancestry & Associations	1814 Bourbon Title	Post '100 days' Formation	Engagements* (with at least 1 Sqn present) in approx. date order
28e	1808	Raised from Tuscan Dragoons	Disbanded	Vacant	Fuentes de Oñoro, Arapiles, Moskowa, Viasma, Krasnoi, Beresina, **Hamburg**
29e	1808	3e Regt. Prov. de Cav. Lég.	Disbanded	Vacant	Vich, Gross-Beeren, Juterbogk, Wachau, Leipzig
30e	1811		Vacant	Vacant	*Became Chev. Lég. Lanciers immediately on forming.*
31er	1811	1er & 2e Regts Prov. de C. L., Drag. de Hamburg, Légion Hanovrienne	Disbanded	Vacant	Fuentes de Oñoro, Arapiles, Würschen, Gross-Beeren, Wachau, Leipzig, Caldiero, R. Mincio, **Magdeburg**

* Italic type indicates a general location, over a protracted period with no significant engagements. Bold type indicates a city defence or siege (in which the unit either defended or laid siege).

[1] Smith, D. op. cit. indicates the presence of various Chasseur regiments at Bailén (& elsewhere in Spain). These were detachments from those regiments forming *Régiments Provisoires*.

[2] Bukhari, E. op. cit. p. 137, says regimental histories for 22e to 26e are not given in French Ministry lists, since, although formed as Chasseurs, they were assigned as *guides* to Corps commanders' staffs. He is silent on Regts 27e to 31er inclusive, except to say when, where and from whom they were formed (p. 107).

FRENCH HUSSAR REGIMENTS

Number	Raised	Ancestry & Associations	1814 Bourbon Title	Post '100 days' Formation[1]	Engagements* (with at least 1 Sqn present) in approx. date order
1er	1720	Hussards de Bercheny	Hussards du Roi	Disbanded	Ulm, Jena, Eylau, Friedland, *Portugal*, Busaco, Sabugal(1), Juterbogk, Leipzig, R. Mincio, Namur
2e 'Noblesse Oblige'	1735	Hussards de Chamborant	Hussards de la Reine	Disbanded	Austerlitz, Jena, Halle, Friedland, Medellín, Talavera, Gebora, Albuera, Lützen, Vitoria, Wachau, Leipzig, Montereau, **Belfort**
3e	1764	Hussards de Esterhazy, Huss. de Bercheny, Huss. de Chamborant, Huss. de Nassau	Hussards du Dauphin	Disbanded	Elchingen, Ulm, Jena, Eylau, Friedland, Alba de Tormes, Arapiles, Vitoria, Sorauren, Kulm, Wachau, Leipzig, Brienne, Montereau, **Belfort**
4e	1783	Huss. de Colonel-Général, Huss. de Esterhazy, Huss. de Bercheny, Huss. de Chamborant, Huss. de Conflans	Hussards de Monsieur	3e Hussards de la Moselle	Austerlitz, Jena, Halle, Friedland, **Zaragoza**, Medellín, Barossa, Saguntum, Gross-Beeren, **Magdeburg**, Ligny
5e	1783	Huss. de Lauzun	Hussards d'Angoulême	5e Hussards	Austerlitz, Jena, Eylau, Heilsberg, Eckmühl, Wagram, Hollabrünn, Znaïm, Fuentes de Oñoro, Moskowa, Beresina, Würschen, Katzbach, Wachau, Leipzig, Hanau, Hamburg, Ligny

Footnotes on p. 124.

Number	Raised	Ancestry & Associations	1814 Bourbon Title	Post '100 days' Formation[1]	Engagements* (with at least 1 Sqn present) in approx. date order
6e	1792	Troupes Lég. à Chev. de Boyer	Hussards de Berry	6e Hussards	Ulm, R. Piave, Wagram, Moskowa, Dresden, Wachau, Leipzig, Montmirail, **Schlestadt**, Wavre
7e	1792	Huss. de Lamothe	Hussards d'Orléans	7e Hussards	
8e 'Hussards Gentil-hommes'	1793	Légion d'Éclaireurs	Disbanded	Vacant	Ulm, Austerlitz, Jena, Eylau, Heilsberg, Essling, Wagram, Hollabrünn, Moskowa, Beresina, **Danzig**, Kulm, Wachau, Leipzig, **Magdeburg, Strasbourg, Kehl**
9e	1793	2e Corps de Huss. de la Liberté	Disbanded	Vacant	Ulm, Austerlitz, Jena, Pultusk, Eylau, Danzig, Heilsberg, Friedland, Ebersberg, Essling, Raab, Wagram, *Spain*(3)[2], Moskowa, Gross-Beeren, Katzbach, Wachau, Laipzig, Hanau, Schlestadt
10e	1793	Huss. de Jemappes (Huss. Noirs/Huss de la Mort)	Disbanded	Vacant	Ulm, Austerlitz, Jena, Pultusk, **Zaragoza**, Wagram, Gebora, Albuera, Lützen, Katzbach, Wachau, Hanau, Torgau
11e	1810	Van Heeken Huzars (Dutch), Timmermans Huzars (Dutch)	Disbanded	Vacant	*Pre 1810*: **Colberg, Stralsund.** *1810 onwards*: Valutina Gora, Moskowa, Beresina, Katzbach

Number	Raised	Ancestry & Associations	1814 Bourbon Title	Post '100 days' Formation[1]	Engagements* (with at least 1 Sqn present) in approx. date order
12e	1813	9e(bis) Hussards (1812–1813)	Disbanded	Vacant	Saguntum, **Valencia**, Gross-Beeren, Leipzig, *France*
13e	1813	13e(bis) Hussards	Re-formed from Huss. Jérôme Napoléon	Disbanded	**Magdeburg**, Leipzig
14e	1813	Raised from Genoese and Piedmontese	Disbanded	Vacant	Dresden, **Dresden**. Re-raised Feb. 1814 – *Italy*

* Italic type indicates a general location, over a protracted period with no significant engagements. Bold type indicates a city defence or siege (in which the unit either defended or laid siege).

[1] The 5e, 6e and 7e Hussards are given by Smith, D. op. cit., p. 285–87, as '…disbanded on 12 May 1814 and re-raised.'

[2] These squadrons were formed into the 9e(bis) Hussards and fought at Saguntum and the siege of Valencia under that name. They later formed the 12e Hussards.

NOTE: The cavalry of the foreign legions attached to the French Army are dealt with in the appropriate infantry tables.

ARTILLERIE À PIED

Number	Raised	Ancestry & Associations	Engagements* in approx. date order[1]
1er	1720		Pultusk, Eylau, **Danzig**, Friedland, Medina de Rioseco, **Zaragoza**, Essling, Wagram, Talavera, **Flushing**, **Cadiz**, Fuentes de Oñoro, **Badajoz**, **Ciudad Rodrigo**, Arapiles, Polotsk, Smolensk, Moskowa, Krasnoi, Beresina, Lützen, Bautzen, Würschen, Vitoria, Dresden, Juterbogk, Wachau, Leipzig, **Torgau**, La Rothière, Paris, Toulouse
2e	1720		Caldiero, **Gaëte**, Friedland, Raab, Wagram, Znaïm, **Gerona**, **Capri**, **Salamanca**, **Corfu**, Moskowa, Malojaroslavetz, Viasma, Krasnoi, Beresina, Lützen, Bautzen, Würschen, Dresden, Juterbogk, Wachau, Leipzig, La Rothière, Ligny, Namur
3e	1720		Austerlitz, Eylau, Bailén, **Zaragoza**, Vimeiro, Wagram, **Gerona**, **Lérida**, **Ciudad Rodrigo**, **Almeida**, **Tortosa**, **Tarragona**, **Badajoz**, Arapiles, **Burgos**, Kulm, **San Sebastien**, Wachau, Leipzig, Hanau, **Tortosa**, Paris, Toulouse
4e	1720		**Gaëte**, Sacile, Thann, Essling, Raab, Wagram, **Gerona**, **Cadiz**, Moskowa, Malojaroslavetz, Krasnoi, Beresina, Lützen, Würschen, Dresden, Juterbogk, Wachau, Leipzig, Hanau, Paris, Mont St Jean
5e	1720		Austerlitz, Eylau, **Danzig**, **Graudenz**, **Stralsund**, **Zaragoza**, Essling, Wagram, Ocaña, **Ciudad Rodrigo**, **Tortosa**, **Badajoz**, **Almeida**, **Tarragona**, Smolensk, Moskowa, Krasnoi, Lützen, Dresden, Katzbach, Wachau, Leipzig, Bar-sur-Aube, **Pensicola**, Arcis-sur-Aube, Paris,
6e	1757		**Neisse**, Vimeiro, **Zaragoza**, **Astorga**, **Cadiz**, **Ciudad Rodrigo**, **Almeida**, **Badajoz**, Fuentes de Oñoro, Albuera, **Tarragona**, **Pensicola**, Moskowa, Krasnoi, Lützen, Würschen, **San Sebastien**, Dresden, Kulm, Leipzig, **Bayonne**, **Bergen-op-Zoom**, Fère-Champenoise, Paris, Ligny, Mont St Jean

Footnotes on p. 126.

Number	Raised	Ancestry & Associations	Engagements* in approx. date order[1]
7e	1762		Austerlitz, Jena, **Danzig**, Friedland, **Reggio**, Espinosa, Essling, Wagram, **Gerona, Cadiz, Astorga, Tarragona**, Arapiles, Smolensk, Moskowa, Polotsk, Beresina, Würschen, Vitoria, Dresden, Kulm, **San Sebastien**, Juterbogk, Wachau, Leipzig, **Bayonne, Wittenberg**, Craonne, Toulouse
8e	1784	Rgt du Corps Royal de l'Artillerie des Colonies	**San Domingo, Zaragoza**, Essling, Wagram, Znaïm, Almonacíd, **Antwerp, Ciudad Rodrigo**, Barossa, **Tarragona**, Moskowa, Krasnoi, Beresina, Lützen, Würschen, Gross-Beeren, Kulm, **San Sebastien**, Wachau, Leipzig, **Hamburg**, Laon, Paris, Mont St Jean
9e	1810	Dutch Artillery	*pre-1810:* **Colberg, Stralsund.** *1810 onwards:* Smolensk, Polotsk, Moskowa, Krasnoi, Beresina, Lützen, Kulm, Wachau, Leipzig, Hanau, La Rothière, Bar-sur-Aube

* Italic type indicates a general location, over a protracted period with no significant engagements. Bold type indicates a city defence or siege (in which the unit either defended or laid siege).

[1] The 'Engagements' list indicates those engagements at which the regiment had a substantial part of a company, or more, present. It is not exhaustive.

ARTILLERIE À CHEVAL

Number	Raised	Ancestry & Associations	Engagements* in approx. date order
1er	1795		*Calabria*, Wagram, **Valencia**, Moskowa, Beresina, Dresden, Kulm, Wachau, Leipzig, La Rothière, Paris
2e	1795		Austerlitz, Friedland, **Zaragoza**, R. Piave, Essling, Vich, **Ciudad Rodrigo**, Moskowa, Beresina, Vitoria, Dresden, Wachau, Leipzig, Fère-Champenoise, Paris, Mont St Jean
3e	1795		Heilsberg, Friedland, Medellín, Essling, Wagram, Ocaña, **Badajoz**, Barossa, Sabugal, Albuera, Arapiles, Smolensk, Moskowa, Polotsk, Viasma, Krasnoi, Lützen, Vitoria, Kulm, Wachau, Hanau, La Rothière, Craonne, Paris
4e	1795		R. Piave, Wagram, Moskowa, Malojaroslavetz, Beresina, Bautzen, Würschen, Dresden, Katzbach, Kulm, Juterbogk, Wachau, **Dresden**, **Strasbourg**, R. Mincio, Mont St Jean
5e	1795		Jena, Eylau, **Neisse**, Heilsberg, **Valencia**, Vimeiro, Wagram, Talavera, Belchite, **Lérida**, Albuera, Smolensk, Moskowa, Bautzen, Würschen, Juterbogk, Wachau, Leipzig, Hanau, Hamburg, Laon, Fère-Champenoise
6e	1795		Jena, Eylau, **Neisse**, Heilsberg, Friedland, Essling, Wagram, Talavera, **Badajoz**, Smolensk, Krasnoi, Lützen, Dresden, Juterbogk, Wachau, Leipzig, Hanau, Fère-Champenoise
7e	1795	Dutch Artillery (1810)	*pre-1810:* **Colberg**, **Stralsund**, Ocaña. *1810 onwards:* Disbanded 1811
8e	1795		*Disbanded 1801*

* Italic type indicates a general location, over a protracted period with no significant engagements. Bold type indicates a city defence or siege (in which the unit either defended or laid siege).

ARTILLERIE DE LA MARINE

In 1812, the regiments were converted to service on land following the blockading of the French Navy in port.

Number	Raised	Ancestry & Associations	Engagements* in approx. date order
1er	1812		Valutina Gora, Beresina, Lützen, Würschen, Dresden, Leipzig, Hanau, Brienne, La Rothière, Vauchamps, Paris
2e	1812		Beresina, Lützen, Bautzen, Leipzig, Hanau, Vauchamps, Paris
3e	1812		Lützen, Würschen, Leipzig, Hanau, Brienne, Paris
4e	1812		Barossa, Beresina, Bautzen, Würschen, Dresden, Leipzig, **Bergen-op-Zoom**, Paris

* Italic type indicates a general location, over a protracted period with no significant engagements. Bold type indicates a city defence or siege (in which the unit either defended or laid siege).

5. FIGHTING METHODS

There are some mistaken perceptions about how the French went about their (frequently successful) activities on the battlefield.

Among these are the 'clouds of skirmishers' and 'attack in column' concepts. It is true that many French Line Infantry units were theoretically capable of breaking out into skirmish order and engaging the enemy with musketry thus deployed. However, in reality the skirmish 'cloud' was a very open order line, with deployment as paired infantrymen (one of whom usually loaded the musket, the other firing), whose members took advantage of whatever cover presented itself. Its main purpose was to deflect the enemy's attention from the activities of the formed units to the rear of the skirmish line and to inflict not heavy, but damaging casualties particularly in terms of morale effect. Consequently, officers – both commissioned and non-commissioned – were specifically targeted, thereby affecting the ability of the formed enemy unit's command to exercise proper control when manoeuvring and to prevent desertion.

Some Continental armies (e.g. Spanish and early Prussians) did not have light companies in their line battalions, boasting only a few (eight, in the case of the Spanish) light troops in each company, whose main task was to act as advanced scouts during a march. Thus they were unable to mount effective countermeasures. British battalions, however, had such light companies and, furthermore, independent light infantry (e.g. 5/60th Rifles) units were attached to their brigades and divisions. The British line was less open in its order and thus was able to form an effective counter to French skirmishing. It is probably this, rather than any inherent superiority of line over column, that lead to the formed British line units meeting French attacks in column and defeating them with often a single volley of musketry and controlled charge. There is evidence that the French columns believed the British skirmish line to have been the main defensive line, because of its relatively closer order and were thus a little discomfited at the sight of a steady line of battalions awaiting their attack when they believed they had already seen off the main defensive line.

The theory regarding superiority of line over column, probably arose from the assertions of Professor Sir Charles Oman and was strengthened by many authors writing books – particularly about the Peninsular War – which were influenced by Oman's very thorough research. In more recent years, this theory has come under greater scrutiny and is losing much credibility. Certainly French drill manuals do not call for attempting to close with the enemy in column.

We looked, earlier, at the intended effect of French skirmish lines. Certainly, Napoleon believed that the key to defeating an enemy on the field was to sap his morale and boost that of one's own troops. To this end, the formation of 'grand batteries' of artillery was also a French tactic that proved effective. Indeed, as a former artillery officer, the Emperor was well-placed to appreciate the effect of this arm. He endeavoured to achieve a ratio of artillery to infantry far higher than that of most of his enemies. The introduction of battalion guns referred to earlier reinforces this view. The main importance of artillery was, again, to establish a moral superiority. Before mounting an attack, the French infantry would witness the 'preparation' of their intended targets by a sustained artillery bombardment. Once more, casualties from this would not have been enormous; however, the morale effect was significant. To experience (even only aurally) one's immediate neighbour being disembowelled or decapitated by a six-pound ball of cast iron did not make for the steadiest of nerves. Consequently, the French columns (the most expeditious formation for a rapid advance) would approach their task with confidence bolstered, whilst their targets would be endeavouring to come to terms with the artillery barrage and, shortly thereafter, the commencement of a galling fire from hidden skirmishers. As the columns approached, blood curdling yells of '*En avant; vive l'Empereur!*' would assail their ears and, at the first appearance of the French, many would let off a ragged and ineffectual volley of musketry and take to their heels. As a result, the French '*colonnes d'attaque*' would have no need to deploy into line for a fire fight, as their drill manuals prescribed.

The formations employed by the infantry included the three-deep line; the column of *pelotons* (effectively companies) usually used to move about the battlefield when not close to the enemy; the column of divisions (two companies wide) which could form up with various intervals between them: full interval to facilitate deployment into line, half interval to keep options open or *serré* (fully closed up) to provide a mass for attack. Additionally, there was the *ordre mixte* which comprised a line formed from one or more battalions, with a column at either end which could rapidly be formed into squares if threatened by cavalry. This had the benefit of providing substantial firepower if and when required. Finally, the square was available when cavalry threatened. A number of march speeds were in use, usually the *pas-*

ordinaire (about eighty paces per minute) was used to move about the battlefield, *pas-de-charge* (about 120 paces per minute) being used to deliver a shock attack.

The French approach to mounting an attack was not universally successful. The French were defeated by more than one Continental army on more than one occasion. However, usually this was because some aspect of the formula could not be or was not employed for whatever reason. In the case of the British – pretty well alone – their own defensive tactics helped foil the French. As well as the skirmishing factor, Wellington would employ a simple means of negating the artillery bombardment. He would instruct his infantry either to retire behind the military crest defining his defensive position, or to lie down in their ranks, thereby offering a much reduced target. Amazingly, continental commanders did not adopt this ruse, preferring, as one Prussian General put it, 'to see their enemy'.

Cavalry was generally used in its traditional role. Light cavalry acted as the armies' eyes and ears, collecting intelligence and seeking out the enemy's location. It would additionally harass a retreat or form part of a rearguard. However, it could be and, indeed, was employed in the battlefield charge. Dragoons performed their originally intended role as mounted infantry (witness the action at La Coruña in 1809) and also acted as shock troops if battlefield opportunities presented themselves and heavier cavalry were unavailable. The heavier cavalry were held to exploit signs of wavering in the enemy by launching a devastating charge. On those occasions when the signs of wavering were not observed or mistaken, the charge could end in disaster and, generally, cavalry attacks were not made in isolation, being much better mounted as part of a combined arms action. On one famous occasion (Mont St Jean), the massed regiments of cuirassiers were led to attack British squares unsupported by infantry or artillery and were destroyed in great numbers.

In defence, the French behaved much as any other nation. Infantry would be deployed in line or as a skirmish screen; artillery would be positioned at key points to cover enemy attacks, preferably in enfilading positions, whilst cavalry would be held in reserve, frequently concealed behind ground features to exploit enemy reverses.

Probably the greatest asset the French Army possessed, aside from its confidence, was Napoleon's strategic genius. His use of the system of Army Corps and divisions in independent roles to keep his enemy guessing and reacting rather than taking the initiative was supreme.

The ploy of tempting an enemy to divide his forces and then attacking each portion separately to ensure superior numbers was legendary.

6. GENERAL OFFICERS

To convey the nature of French general officers in such a small space is impracticable. The names ring through history – so many, it would be impossible to do them all justice. So we have decided to take a 'snapshot' by looking at one commander who progressed through the ranks to the highest position. With the Revolution having opened opportunities for the citizenry, as Napoleon later commented, every soldier potentially 'had a Marshal's baton in his knapsack' – very different from the British system. The man we have chosen fought in almost every theatre, became, in 1814, Minister of War to Louis XVIII, returned to Napoleon's side as Chief of Staff in the 'Hundred Days' and, at the Coronation of Queen Victoria in 1838, enjoyed adulation from the British public as the personal Ambassador of King Louis. Variously known to the British soldier in Spain and Portugal as 'Marshal Salt' and 'The Duke of Damnation', Jean de Dieu Soult was Wellington's most implacable foe in war and yet, in 1838, they greeted each other as old comrades. There are those who have criticized Soult's opportunism but he must have enjoyed the confidence of both the Emperor and King Louis, to have been accepted back into senior positions more than once by both rulers. Furthermore he was seen by the common soldier of his homeland and his enemy alike as a commander of professional ability and humanity.

Born in the same year as both Arthur Wellesley and Napoleon Bonaparte (1769), Soult had aristocratic blood but his own family were artisans – glass makers – and were certainly not wealthy. His Christian name probably reflects the pious Catholic belief of his mother but, in many histories, he is called by the name 'Nicholas'. This is a not uncommon nickname that was used for those who were perceived to have committed some serious error or 'crime' (and was applied to Napoleon after the Hundred Days). It was certainly uncomplimentary and may have resulted from the allegations that he attempted to form a Portuguese Kingdom, with himself wearing the crown. He and Marshal Ney were fierce rivals and Ney's troops used the term 'King Nicholas' when referring to Soult.

Soult was hard to control as a boy and, whilst he was making several abortive attempts to find a career in the area surrounding his family home in the Black Mountains, his mother fell on seriously hard times. The young Soult immediately volunteered for the army, giving his mother the money he obtained thereby and so started on the path that was to produce one of France's most competent soldiers.

In 1785, he joined his first regiment – the Royal Regiment of Infantry – in which he served for two years, achieving the exalted rank of corporal. Since his noble blood was not of a colour sufficiently blue to obtain a commission, disillusionment started to set in: Soult was ambitious and wanted advancement. The frustration that this caused got him into some serious trouble and he was lucky not to be cashiered. However, he attempted to leave of his own accord and go into the baking business but the attempt was not successful and he had to buckle down in his chosen career. This lead to advancement to the rank of sergeant. Eventually, when the year 1792 arrived and with it the invasion of France by Prussia and Austria, Soult had already espoused the Revolutionary cause and was able to take advantage of a unique opportunity that only the Revolution could have brought.

The new volunteer or *fédérés* units elected their officers – all, that is, except for the adjutant. The rank was filled by existing army officers (including non-commissioned men) and it was this position that Soult was to fill in the National Guard (Bataillon de l'Haut Rhin). In this position, it was not long before Soult assumed effective command of the unit; his commanding officer had little experience of command and was elderly. Soult achieved great popularity with his men and with several influential figures in the army. His military exploits showed him to be an excellent leader: brave and resolute, with great initiative and determination. By 1793, Soult's exploits gained him a staff position with one of General Hoche's subordinates and an immediate command that provided an excellent opportunity to shine. In an action close to Niederbronn, Soult's force of infantry, cavalry and artillery attacked the Austrians and comprehensively defeated them. This was followed by a command under General Lefebvre when the division was under severe pressure. Soult dealt with a highly excited and desperate General Marceau and prevented him from showing himself up in Lefebvre's presence. From this point on, Soult enjoyed and deserved rapid promotion; by 1795, he was in command of a demi-brigade.

In 1799, the Second Coalition – a partnership between Russia, Britain and Austria – had declared war on France. Bonaparte was in Egypt and Soult had been mouldering as a *chef-de-brigade* in the 'Army of England' (a vain attempt by the French Directory to threaten Britain with invasion). The new conflict provided Soult with the perfect opportunity to take a major role. Most of France's best generals were in Egypt and she sought for able young commanders to act as replacements. Soult was given command of the advance guard of Jourdan's army (Jourdan was not a competent commander as he was later to prove as Joseph Bonaparte's Chief of Staff in Spain ten years later). The battle of Stockach was something of a disaster for Jourdan, although not for Soult, who took command of the rearguard division in the well-organized retreat.

This event led directly to the offer to Soult of a division in the Army of Switzerland. Commanded by André Masséna, whom Soult much admired – and with reason – the army was charged with restoring peace to the quarrelling southern Swiss cantons. Soult realized that there was more than a military job to be done. The Helvetic Republic, as Switzerland had come to be known, was of great strategic importance as a barrier between France and Austria. Both nations were disliked or even hated by the Swiss, whose cantons could not get on with each other. Soult realized that if he could both quell the riotous cantons where several French citizens had been murdered and act in a restrained manner, he might gain their respect and confidence. He fought a battle with two of the districts and entered into a compact with a third; finally, he visited the shrine to William Tell, committing himself to the charge of Swiss boatmen who could have dealt with him much as their neighbours had dealt with other Frenchmen all too recently. This struck a chord with the Swiss and Soult had achieved his objective. The year was still 1799!

This experience must have contributed considerably to Soult's later activities in the Peninsula when he was frequently called upon to display diplomacy as well as military acumen, which he invariably did with much success. There were other opportunities in Switzerland for Soult to display his talents and he took them all with great relish, receiving the high praise of his hero Masséna in so doing.

The next move for the future Marshal was, at the age of thirty-one, and once more with Masséna, to the Army of Italy, in command of the right wing. It was in this post that he suffered his first major setback. Honoré Gazan, one of Soult's divisional commanders (as he was later to be at Albuera in Spain) was commanded to create a diversion during an attack to relieve pressure on the city of Genoa. A terrible storm completely ruined the diversion and Soult's small force was overwhelmed and he was severely wounded and captured. After carrying out an operation on himself to remove a musket ball from his leg,

Soult received medical help from Masséna's personal doctor, who had been allowed through the lines for the purpose. Despite these attentions, the wound worsened until Soult was forced to offer his parole. This was accepted and Soult was able to take proper exercise, thereby accelerating the healing process.

Although Soult could not take further part in hostilities, he was allowed to employ his administrative talents and used conciliation to effect a similar result in Piedmont to the one he had achieved in Switzerland. Prisoner exchange followed soon after and Soult could return to France and resume his military career.

Once Napoleon had become Consul, Soult's reputation came to his ears from the likes of Masséna and, in typical fashion, Bonaparte made him colonel-general of the Chasseurs of the Consular Guard. There rapidly followed, in 1803, his appointment as Commander of the military camp at St-Omer, from where the intended invasion of Britain was to take place – echoes of the experience in another 'Army of England' four years earlier. Within a year, he had been made a Marshal of France.

There followed one of the most successful military careers in the history of the Empire. Soult led his IVe Corps de l'Armée to victory at Landsberg, they were involved at both Memmingen and Hollabrünn and then, at Austerlitz in December 1805, came the event that probably made Soult's name something to be conjured with. He had been held in position by the Emperor for most of the early part of the battle, which was fought before dawn. The Russians occupying the Pratzen Plateau had begun to move off to commence a massive attack on the French centre. Napoleon realized this would leave his enemy vulnerable to a counter-attack. Soult was asked if he could take the plateau with IV Corps and his reply was that this could be done in twenty minutes. As the sun rose, Soult moved his troops out, climbed the slope and appeared, to the dismay of the Russians, almost in their midst. Rapid orders were sent out for troops to re-take the position and these men began to climb the slopes. Pratzen village was occupied, and immediately attacked and cleared by Soult's advancing battalions. Marching steadily on with fixed bayonets, the French sent battalion after battalion of Russians streaming away. Counter-attacks were mounted but these were met with resolution and élan by the unstoppable IV Corps. Within the allotted time, Soult's promise had been fulfilled; it was a brilliant tactical feat. As Napoleon had earlier remarked, 'one sharp blow and the war is over': it was Soult who had struck that blow.

Awarded the sobriquet '*le premier manoeuvrier d'Europe*' by the Emperor, for the way he had moved, deployed and controlled his men, it was a glittering moment in Soult's life. There followed, less than a year later, yet another glowing tribute: 'Marshal Soult is the best of all the generals of Europe, the most capable of manoeuvring great masses, of taking the major role on a field of battle, of doing wonders at the head of a French army.' This latter was made, following the victory at Jena and the taking of Lübeck in 1806. Bergfried, Eylau, Heilsberg and Königsberg followed and, in June 1808, after being named Governor of Old Prussia, he was awarded the title Duke of Dalmatia.

There followed what must have been one of the most dogged displays of military persistence in the history of warfare. Soult went to Spain to replace Bessières as commander of 2ᵉ Corps. This campaign surely ranked high amongst Soult's most frustrating experiences. Nevertheless, although ultimately unsuccessful, it included two battles that historians still argue over in terms of who won: Soult or his British adversaries. It also ended with a battle that need never have been fought and that accounted for the deaths of many brave men. The three battles of which we speak are La Coruña in 1809, Albuera in 1811, and Toulouse in 1814.

At La Coruña, Soult had pursued Sir John Moore's disintegrating army for weeks in the bitterly cold, inhospitable mountains of Galicia. Moore was trying to save as much as he could of Britain's only field army. Soult had been charged by the Emperor with preventing this or 'throwing the British leopard [*sic*] back into the sea'. It is a moot point whether, by this, Napoleon intended to indicate that he wanted the British Army destroyed (which he almost certainly did) or sent packing in their ships away from Spain. At the end of the battle of La Coruña, Soult remained in possession of the field, the British having managed to hold him off long enough for the bulk of their troops to board waiting naval vessels and sail away. Soult had severely mauled them in the process, killing one of their best generals, Sir John Moore. The British rightly claim it was always Moore's intention that the French should be held whilst successive formations boarded the ships. Despite the different points of view, Soult emerges from the argument as a general of substance.

Albuera saw Soult's army attempting the relief of Badajoz fortress. William Beresford had been instructed by Wellington to halt Soult at the Albuera Bridge by occupying a ridge behind the town. Beresford had two divisions of British, one and a half of Portuguese and the

King's German Legion to deploy. During the night he was joined by the Spanish forces of Generals Ballesteros and Castaños. There is considerable debate over whether Beresford occupied the ground intended by Wellington or not. Suffice it to say that there is scarcely a position to occupy. The river can be forded and the 'position' can be outflanked. Which is precisely what Soult attemped. Just in time, the Spaniards of José Zayas' Division of only four battalions formed to refuse the allied right flank and one of the most deadly firefights of the entire war commenced. Troops of both sides were sucked into the maelstrom. The Spanish stood their ground nobly; the French attempted to deploy and became disordered; British reinforcements arrived; French reinforcements also arrived; cannon thundered from both lines. Eventually, a thunderstorm erupted and, in the darkness, rain and confusion, Polish lancers smashed into the flank of the British second division, giving no quarter, and caused great slaughter until they were, in turn, attacked and driven off by British Dragoons. Eventually, the intervention of a young aide-de-camp, Henry Hardinge, who encouraged his divisional commander, Lowry Cole, to advance and attack the enemy, turned the tide and the French retired. The allied army was spent – as, indeed was that of the French. Some maintain that Soult could have sent in his final reserves which might have been enough or might have been nullified by Beresford's remaining men so far unengaged. Soult felt that the enormous damage he had inflicted on Beresford's army represented a victory. Beresford claimed the victory because he had frustrated the French Marshal's designs to relieve Badajoz. The truth is probably that neither and both had reason to claim victory; the carnage on both sides was appalling[42] and, as Wellington remarked in a letter to Beresford three days after the battle 'We must make up our minds to affairs of this kind sometimes, or give up the game.'

Soult had conceived his attack with the cleverness he always displayed in such circumstances but, for some reason, seemed to lose his certainty of touch part way through the battle. He claims that he was unaware of the presence of Blake's army; the Spanish general had arrived the previous night and so one has to accept Soult's statement but there had been little evidence of French respect for Spanish armies previously.

[42] The French suffered almost 8,000 casualties, whilst the less numerous allies had 6,000 killed, wounded and missing.

Finally, after a masterful campaign through the Pyrenees, in which Soult inflicted checks and retreats on his enemies, and a difficult retreat thereafter, once the allies had invaded France, the two armies fought their last battle roughly a week after Napoleon's signature was applied to the deed of abdication. Toulouse was not quite a siege but Soult's positions in front of the town were behind entrenchments and were supported by guns of position. It was a hard nut to crack and the armies paid a heavy price, Soult losing 3,250 men and Wellington 4,500. However, Soult realized, towards the end, that he could not prevail and took his army away on the evening of 11 April 1814.

There is a fairly substantial postscript to the story of Marshal Soult, who had joined the revolutionary army as a headstrong and turbulent youth and ended as one of his country's most respected marshals. When the Bourbon king Louis XVIII ascended the French throne, he appointed Soult as his Minister of War. Despite this, and Soult's description of the erstwhile Emperor as a 'usurper and adventurer' (perhaps 'opportunist' would be a better translation), on his return, Napoleon felt certain enough of him to reinstate Soult and make him Chief of Staff for the Hundred Days campaign. The Marshal, as ever, discharged his duties with skill and faithfulness but the days of the domination of Europe by Napoleonic France came to an end with the defeat at Mont St Jean. Not to an end, however, for the career of Jean de Dieu Soult. After three years of banishment and disgrace, he returned to the service of King Louis and again became a Marshal in 1820. He was the Bourbon's Minister of War from 1830 to 1832, holding several government positions (including Minister for Foreign Affairs) thereafter, attending the coronation of Queen Victoria as the French representative and simultaneously renewing his acquaintance with a certain Arthur Wellesley. The two erstwhile enemies greeted each other with great cordiality and were soon to be seen reminiscing almost like old comrades. War is, indeed, a strange pastime.

CHAPTER 2

The Army of the Grand Duchy of Baden, 1805–15

1. INTRODUCTION

THE DUCHY OF Baden is located in the south-western part of Germany in the bend of the Rhine where it turns north after leaving Lake Constance. The Duchy was formed in 1771 by the merging of Baden-Baden and Baden-Durlach, which had been split during the Reformation, with Karl Friedrich as margrave.

The two provinces were part of the Swabian Kreis, one of the 'Circles' into which Germany was divided during the time of Holy Roman Empire of the German Nation. As such, not only did these duchies have their own small armed forces, they also provided additional forces to any army formed under the auspices of the Holy Roman Empire.

Baden-Baden provided two battalions, and Baden-Durlach one, to the *Reichsarmee* formed as a counter to Frederick of Prussia in 1757. This army served along the southern front, mainly against Prince Henry's covering force, and acted as a link between the French forces in Westphalia and the main Austrian forces in Bohemia and Silesia.

During the early campaigns of the French Revolution the Baden forces continued to provide troops to the Empire, but the pace of the war, and its heavy demands, meant that Baden was soon weary. When Prussia sought release through the Treaty of Basle in May 1795, the French could concentrate on driving Austria and the Empire out of the war. Baden was crossed and re-crossed by both invading and defending armies until, in July 1796, it entered into an armistice, under which it paid two million livres, extending it to a full treaty shortly afterwards.

This desire of the small German states to seek an accommodation with the French was an indication that the Holy Roman Empire had come close to the end of its utility. The war itself dragged on for another year until the Peace of Leoben on 18 April 1797 was followed by the Treaty of Campo Formio in October. Effectively this gave the French the left bank of the Rhine. Those rulers who lost territory were recompensed through the setting up of a Reichsdeputation by the Imperial Diet to discuss secularization of some of the Episcopal states. Although the final resolution was not made until spring 1803, Austria had suffered further defeat at Marengo and had been forced into the Treaty of Luneville in 1801.

Baden's territorial expansion meant that Karl Friedrich (1728–1811) was raised to an Elector in the enlarged Reichstag, but he now leant more towards France rather than Austria. Even the seizure of the Duc d'Enghien from Baden in March 1804 and his subsequent trial and execution failed to change this, and Baden signed a treaty of alliance with the new French Empire in October 1805, just in time to contribute a contingent of troops for the Austerlitz campaign. Indeed, the Black Forest, located in Baden, provided the Grande Armée with flank defence during its march from the Channel to the Danube.

2. BACKGROUND

Austerlitz (2 December 1805) led to yet more loss of territory for Austria through the Treaty of Pressburg. Baden again became the recipient of some of the Swabian lands, and cemented its growing relationship with France through the marriage in 1806 of Karl Ludwig Friedrich, grandson and heir of Karl Friedrich, to Stephanie de Beauharnais, who was the cousin of the Empress Josephine. In July 1806, Napoleon created the Confederation of the Rhine. Karl von Dalberg was Prince Primate, but Napoleon named himself as Protector.

Baden was one of the founder members of the Confederation and Karl Friedrich took the title of Grand Duke. Francis of Austria, who had already proclaimed himself Emperor of Austria as a reaction to Napoleon's assumption of the purple, wrote *finis* to the Holy Roman Empire when he abdicated on 6 August.

From then on, until 1813, Baden troops would be found with French comrades. They formed part of Marshal Brune's Observation Corps in the winter of 1806/07, and then moved into Poland for the Friedland campaign, although as they were with Massena they missed the battle.

In spring 1808, Baden was called on to provide a regiment and supporting artillery for the Spanish campaign and these joined Marshal Lefebvre's IV Corps as part of the German Division. The division fought at Medellín, Talavera and the autumn 1809 campaign, but from 1810, the division was effectively split up as it was used for anti-guerrilla sweeps.

By the autumn of 1813, the French Army in Spain had been forced back north of the Pyrenees. News was coming through that the Eastern Allies had cleared active French forces from central Europe, and that the satellite kingdoms were coming to an accommodation with the victors. To this end, moves were afoot for the remaining German units to cross into the British lines in the hope of repatriation. Unfortunately, whilst the Nassauers and the Frankfurt battalion were successful, the Badeners were not and were disarmed by their late comrades in arms to await Napoleon's first abdication.

The remaining units were mobilized for the Austrian campaign of 1809 where they formed part of Massena's IV Corps before being sent to reinforce the Viceroy of Italy, Eugene, and took part in the battles of Raab and Wagram.

In 1812, the troops were allocated to Marshal Victor's IX Corps. This reserve formation was originally tasked with protecting Napoleon's lines of communication, but with catastrophe facing the main army, was called forward to protect the retreat. As a consequence it fought around the Beresina bridges and only some 1,500 men found their way back to Baden.

In the spring of 1813, the Grand Duchy was called upon to again build up its forces, using its Russian and Spanish veterans as a cadre. Part were assigned to Marshal Ney's III Corps, whilst a second contingent was part of the Leipzig garrison. Napoleon's defeat, and the subsequent retreat behind the Rhine, led to a scramble as the German rulers sought to make peace with the Russians, Austrians and Prussians as quickly as they could.

They were to find that this did not stop them from having to continue to pay a blood tax, however, and the Grand Duke was forced to provide additional Landwehr units in addition to bringing his regular forces up to strength. In the event, however, these forces were used to blockade Strasburg.

When Napoleon returned to France in March 1815 the Baden army contributed a division to serve in the Austrian II Corps in Schwarzenberg's army. The Badeners again spent the campaign besieging Strasburg before Napoleon abdicated for a second, and final, time.

3. COMMAND STRUCTURE

Karl Friedrich was influenced by the Enlightenment and had already made some attempts at reform (such as freedom of the serfs) before the French Revolution and the export of the Rights of Man. The quadrupling of Baden's size as a result of her closer links with France required large scale rationalization of the mechanism of government. Karl Friedrich's advancing years meant that he was not fully able to manage this change, but a number of highly proficient bureaucrats more than made the difference.

The gradual introduction of the Code Napoléon led to the relaxation of guild laws, the loss of noble privileges and the removal of ecclesiastical preferments. In their place came the idea of careers open to talent and a professional bureaucracy. Laws were rationalized, a standard tax system brought in and a system of French-style departments (here called kreis) and prefects instituted.

One reason for this was that Baden had to support a vastly more numerous army, part of the price it had to pay for its French alliance. The population of 924,000 was expected to support an army of 8,000. A more efficient tax system was needed to pay for it, whilst better record keeping allowed a more systematized conscription.

4. THE ARMY

Baden's army at the turn of the century was very small, sufficient for its needs under the old Reich. The expansion necessary meant that it had to offer an opportunity to both the old nobility and the previously untried middle classes. In addition, service in the army had to be attractive not just to the usual cannon fodder, the shiftless, feckless and unemployable, but also to the ambitious, the educated peasant and the career minded.

In the event, they succeeded. The army gained a reputation for hardihood and efficiency. During the retreat from Moscow, the Baden brigade was one of the few that brought its guns with it.

5. THE MILITARY ESTABLISHMENT

Organization

The size of the Baden Army increased in line with its territorial holdings. The organization originally mirrored the Prussian Army, but on the formation of the Confederation of the Rhine, the need was more to operate with French forces, so units were reorganized.

Infantry

TYPE OF UNIT	1805–08	1808–15
Line units	2 battalions per regt 4 cos of 150 men each, per battalion	2 battalions per regt 6 cos (incl. 2 elite cos) per battalion, with 150 men per co.
Grenadier Battalion	1 battalion of 5 cos, of 150 men each	Became Leibgrenadier Garde
Light unit	Originally 1 battalion of 2 cos, increased to 5 in 1806. Co. strength was 150 men	1 battalion of 6 cos (incl. 2 elite cos) with approx. 120 men per company

Leib Regiment Kurfurst became Leib Regiment Grossherzog in 1806 and von Stockhorn in 1811.

Markgraf Ludwig became Erbgrossherzog in 1809 and von Hochberg in 1811.

Kurprince became Grossherzog Erblich in 1806, von Hochberg in 1809 and Grossherzog in 1811.

Von Harrant was formed in 1806, was vacant in 1809 and became von Neuenstein by 1813.

The line units lost their regimental titles in 1813 and were known only by their numbers.

The jäger battalion was von Lingg.

In addition to these regular units, Baden was forced to form an additional eight Landwehr battalions once she renounced her French alliance in 1813.

Cavalry

TYPE OF UNIT	1805–08	1808–15
Hussars	1 Squadron, increased to a 4, 2 co., squadron regiment in 1806. Co. strength was 100 all ranks	1, 4 squadrons (each of 2 co.) regiment with 100 all ranks per company. The unit was not reformed after 1812.
Dragoons	1, 4 squadrons (each of 2 co) regiment with co. strength of 100 all ranks	No change. A second regiment was formed in 1813.
Garde du Corps	1, 2 co., squadron of 100 all ranks	No change

Artillery

In 1805 the artillery battalion consisted of two foot artillery companies equipped with six 6-pounder guns and two howitzers. These were joined by a horse artillery company in 1806 and a third foot company in 1809. The line units that served in Russia also formed regimental artillery companies.

6. UNIFORMS

INFANTRY

Originally the line units wore a Prussian-style bicorne, but this was replaced in 1806 with a raupenhelm of Bavarian style. When formed, the grenadier companies had a white plume and the voltigeurs a green one. In 1813, Austrian shakos were adopted.

The coat was dark blue, with scarlet facings (collar, cuffs and turnbacks) for all units until 1806 when individual collar and cuff colours were allocated. Turnbacks remained scarlet. In 1810 all units reverted again to scarlet facings. The grenadiers had scarlet epaulettes and the voltigeurs green. Regimental facings were re-adopted in 1813.

Up to 1810 breeches were white, but blue overalls were issued in 1810.

REGIMENT	COLLAR, CUFFS AND LAPELS	METAL
1. Leibregiment	Scarlet; white lace batons on collar and three on cuffs. 1813: Rose Pink	White
2. Grossherzog Erblich	Deep Yellow. 1813: White	Brass
3. Markgraf Ludwig	White. 1813: Deep Yellow	Brass. 1813: white
4. Von Harrant	Poppy Red. 1813: White	Brass

When the Baden Army was asked to supply a unit for Spain Infantry Regiment (IR)4 von Harrant was re-formed by exchanging its first battalion for the second Battalion of IR3. There were therefore two units in which one battalion had white facings and another with poppy red.

In 1810 IR4 was re-equipped from French stores with a habit-coat.[1] Collar, cuffs, lapels and turnbacks were scarlet, and the elite companies continued to wear their distinctives.

The jäger battalion wore a Bavarian kasket from its formation, but the raupe was mid-green instead of the line unit's black and there was a green plume. The coat was dark green with black, piped white, collar, cuffs and turnbacks. In 1813 the turnbacks were changed to scarlet. The epaulettes were mid-green, and the breeches were dark grey, changed to dark green in 1813.

The Garde Grenadier battalion (which saw little action) wore a French-style bearskin with a white metal front plate and scarlet and white flounders. The scarlet back patch carried a white grenade. The blue single-breasted coat had white lace batons and the cuffs, collar and turnbacks were scarlet with white piping. Breeches were white with black gaiters.

[1] A habit-coat was a long-tailed uniform coat worn by the French Army until 1812.

CAVALRY

In 1805 the hussar regiment had worn a mirliton but adopted a shako in 1806. The flounders were yellow. For parade the plume was green, but yellow pom-pons were worn on campaign. The dolman was green with a scarlet collar and cuffs and the braiding was yellow. The pelisse was dark green with black-brown fur, and the parade breeches were scarlet with dark grey overalls for campaign. Dark green overalls were adopted in 1810.

Officers wore gold metal and the pelisse fur was either white or light grey.

Horse furniture was green with yellow edging. The sheepskins were white for ORs and black for trumpeters and officers.

The original dragoon regiment wore an infantry-style raupenhelm with a white plume for troopers and a white over red for officers. The light blue coat had scarlet collar, cuffs, lapels and turnbacks. White breeches and black cavalry boots were worn for parade, but light blue overalls were issued for campaign. Officers were distinguished by silver epaulettes.

Horse furniture was light blue trimmed with white lace. Sheepskins were white for troopers and black for trumpeters and officers.

The two dragoon regiments wore essentially the same uniform. Brass buttons and yellow lace, where applicable, differentiated the second one, formed in 1813.

The Garde du Corps wore Austrian heavy cavalry helmets but with a white raupe. The tunic was white with red collar, cuffs and turnbacks. Officers wore silver epaulettes. The horse furniture was scarlet with white or silver edging.

ARTILLERY

Both foot and horse companies wore the raupenhelm with a black crest, the horse company having a white plume. The coats were dark blue with scarlet turnbacks and black collar, cuffs and lapels. The foot companies had scarlet piping.

Breeches were white, with grey overalls for campaign. The foot companies also had dark blue overalls from 1813. The horse company had white pouchbelts and light cavalry sabres.

LANDWEHR

Possibly blue coat, white trousers and shakos. It is unknown if the individual battalions were differentiated by facings.

7. BATTLE HISTORY

(Roman numerals indicate original Corps affiliation; these often changed during the campaign.)

1806–07

D	Siege of Danzig, 10 March–24 May 1807
S	Siege of Stralsund, 15 January–20 August 1807 (from July only)

Spain

Al	Almonacíd, 11 August 1809
Ba	Operations around Bayonne, 9–13 December 1813
M	Medellín, 29 March 1809
N	Nivelle, 10 November 1813
O	Ocaña, 18–19 November 1809
SM	San Marcial, 31 August–1 September 1813
T	Talavera, 27–28 July 1809
Vi	Vitoria, 21 June 1813
Z	Zornoza, 30 October 1808

1809

A	Aspern–Essling, 21–22 May 1809
E	Ebelsberg, 3 May 1809
R	Raab – 14 June 1809; siege of Raab, 15–22 June 1809
V	Voralberg, May–October 1809
W	Wagram, 5–6 July 1809 (IR3 was detached to Lobau Island during the battle)
Zn	Znaim, 10–11 July 1809

1812

Be	Beresina, 26–28 November 1812
Bo	Borodino, 7 September 1812

1813–14

Ag	Altenburg, 28 September 1813

B Bautzen, 20–21 May 1813
K Katzbach, 26 August 1813
L Lutzen, 2 May 1813
Le Leipzig, 16–19 October 1813 (IR2 and Jägers were in garrison)
St 1 Blockade of Strasburg

1815
H Hausbergen, 9 July 1815
St 2 Blockade of Strasburg, 28 June–30 July 1815 (also includes siege of Neu-Briesach, 2 July–10 August 1815)

UNIT	1806–7	SPAIN	1809	1812	1813–14	1815
Leib-garde			V			H, St 2
IR 1	D, S		IV: E, R, W, Zn	I: Bo	III: L, B, K, Le, St 1	St 2
IR 2	D, S		IV: E, R, W, Zn	IX: Be	Ag, Le, St 1	St 2
IR 3	D, S		IV: A	IX: Be	III: L, B, K, Le, St 1	H, St 2
IR 4	D	Z, M, T, Al, O, Vi, SM, N, Ba				St 2
Jägers			IV: E, R W, Zn	IX: Be	Ag, Le	H, St 2
Hussars	D, S		V	IX: Be		
1st Lt Dragoons	D		IV: E, A, W, Zn		III: L, B, K, Le, St 1	H, St 2
2nd Lt Dragoons					St 1	H, St 2

8. TACTICS

In 1805 the army operated using the Prussian system but once Baden joined the Confederation of the Rhine it began reorganizing the army along French lines. Accordingly, it adopted the 1791 regulations to enable it to work alongside its French allies.

In 1806 the Baden troops were not well regarded by their French generals. By 1809, however, the army's re-organization had taken effect and during the Austrian campaign of that year the improvement had been noted.

In 1812, the self sacrifice of the Baden dragoon regiment's charges kept the Beresina bridges clear from the attacking Russians.

CHAPTER 3

The Army of the Kingdom of Bavaria, 1805–15

1. INTRODUCTION

THE ELECTORATE OF Bavaria was one of the biggest of the German states within the Holy Roman Empire, but the single-mindedness of the Hohenzollerns meant that Prussia was soon the leading light. Earlier in the century, the Wittelsbachs had caused Austria very serious headaches through alliances with the French. In 1704 Marlborough's victory at Blenheim had stopped an advance down the Danube against Vienna, whilst between 1742 and 1745 Carl Albrecht was crowned Emperor as Carl VII as a reaction to Maria Theresa. His early death, and the failure of Frederick the Great to support his French and Bavarian allies erased what could have been a substantial threat to Austrian supremacy.

Bavaria proper was part of the Bavarian Kreis of the Holy Roman Empire, which apart from Bavaria proper also included a series of smaller secular and ecclesiastical states. In 1777, Max III Joseph died and the succession fell to Carl Theodor of the (Upper Rhenish) Palatinate, (roughly the area between the Moselle and the Rhine). The Wittelsbachs were to rule Bavaria until the overthrow of the monarchy in 1918.

For all its size, Bavaria put far fewer troops into the field than Prussia. Whilst it supported Austria in opposing the French Revolution, the drawn out struggle drained her of men and treasure. The war was not leisurely like the earlier wars, fought to distinct rules and at particular times of the year. Rather, armies swept backwards and forwards, devastating whole areas and dislocating trade and commerce.

The seat of war shifted to the south once Prussia withdrew from the war in the Treaty of Basle. Although Erzherzog Karl won some victories along the Rhine, the main Austrian effort went into defending Italy. In an acknowledgement that things would change, Austria and the Reich agreed to a truce under the Peace of Leoben (18 April 1797).

It was, however, clear that France expected to retain her captured territories on the left (west) bank of the Rhine. This meant that any disposed German states would require restitution from elsewhere, especially through the absorption of the free Imperial cities. The conference was held at Rastatt and was held between the Reich and France; by this artifice, Austria could protect herself from any ill tidings. Before it finished, however, war broke out again until the victories of Marengo and Hohenlinden forced Austria to concede the political victory to the new First Consul, Napoleon Bonaparte. Negotiations could then recommence, as the Treaty of Luneville, with France in a position of great strength.

As the Reich feared, it was expected to give up most of the left bank of the Rhine, but it took until 1803 for any decision to be made regarding arrangements for those rulers so dispossessed. In particular, Bavaria gained Wurzburg (later given up) and the bishoprics of Bamberg and Augsburg; it was apparent that France wanted to build up Bavaria as a creditable threat to Vienna.

2. BACKGROUND

The increasing marginalization of the Holy Roman Empire, and the hollow claims of the Habsburgs to rule it led to Franz II to take the title of Emperor Franz I of Austria in 1804. On 24 August 1805 Bavaria signed a defensive alliance with the newly imperial France, followed on 23 September by one specifically against Austria. These actions followed the Austrian accession to the Third Coalition with Britain and Russia. Austria mobilized at the beginning of September 1805 and the army moved forward into Bavaria taking up a position at Ulm. Encircled by the French Grande Armée, it was forced to surrender.

The few survivors, reinforced by depot troops and a Russian army under Kutusov, were finally defeated at Austerlitz (2 December 1805). The resulting Treaty of Pressburg raised Bavaria to a kingdom and rewarded her with increased territory at the expense of Austria; the Tyrol and Voralberg in particular giving access to Italy. Bavaria was further linked to the French orbit by the marriage of the Princess Augusta to Eugène de Beauharnais, the Emperor Napoleon's stepson and soon to be his Viceroy of Italy. Bavaria was one of the first adherents to the Confederation of the Rhine when it was set up in July 1806.

From this time, Bavarian troops served as part of the imperial armies in all theatres except for Spain. In 1809, they contributed a significant part of the initial force in the Army of Germany, and in 1812 fought as a corps in Russia. In 1813, a new army was raised for the spring campaign in Germany but Maximilian I Joseph (the first King of Bavaria) saw the writing on the wall for Napoleon and renounced his allegiance early enough to save most of his gains.

3. COMMAND STRUCTURE

As a member of the Confederation of the Rhine, Bavaria was expected to modernize her system of government, mimicking as much as possible that operating in France, itself a *non plus ultra*, of course.

One major reason for doing so was to ensure that the states' finances were robust enough to support an increased army and to keep it up to strength. Instead of a dependence on impressed soldiers from the ranks of the poor and dispossessed, service had to made attractive enough to both encourage enlistment and to discourage avoidance of conscription. The administration had to ensure that these conscription rolls were kept up to date to make sure that no time was wasted in getting men into uniform.

The constitution of 1808 was supposed to allow a form of national representation, but this was largely a dead letter. A council of state replaced the *kabinett* system, and departments (or *kreis*) under *generalkomissars* governed at local level.

One way to increase tax revenues was to either ameliorate or to completely remove some of the restrictions associated with the last vestiges of feudalism. Church lands were expropriated and sold off, whilst some of the more overt examples of 'superstition', such as way-side calvaries and shrines, were suppressed or destroyed.

Just as the army was opened to talent, so too was the economic life of the country. The suppression of guilds meant that entrepreneurs could start new businesses, although these 'trade unions' were never abolished. Whilst the state took over the judicial function from both the local magnates and the ecclesiastical courts, the nobility fought a rearguard action to protect their ancient rights.

One reason that there was not a full social revolution was that there was not a ready made bureaucracy able to take on the responsibility of forcing one through. Maximilian von Montgelas had been reform minded since 1799, but without schools and colleges there was no depth of trained support. Those that were in place, however, were Bavarians first and Germans second; nationalism, if it existed at all, was felt to be a conservative doctrine.

4. OFFICER CORPS

Previous to the Napoleonic period, the officer corps had been open only to the nobility and aristocracy. Constitutional changes, actively encouraged by the reform-minded King and his chief minister, Montgelas, offered the opportunity for the sons of the mercantile class to serve in the army, an opening made more necessary in order to ensure that the Bavarian Army could fulfil its treaty requirements.

5. OTHER RANKS

Hand in hand with these changes, reforms were made by dissolving guild privileges, secularizing the church and, finally, abolishing serfdom. All of this meant that the number of men available to join the army increased, lists of those eligible being maintained by the bureaucracy of the centralizing government.

By these means, the army could be kept up to strength, reserves maintained and replacements identified. In all, some 110,000 men served in Bavaria's army during this period.

6. THE MILITARY ESTABLISHMENT

Organization

TYPE	1803–11	1811–15
Line Infantry Approx. 2,400 all ranks	1 Regt = 2 Bns 1 Bn = 1 Grenadier Co. & 4 Fusilier Cos; 1 Co. per bn in depot	1 Regt = 2 Bns 1 Bn = 1 Grenadier, 1 Schutzen and 4 Fusilier Cos; 1 Co. per bn in depot. In 1814 grenadier cos replaced by 5th Fusilier co.
Light Infantry Approx. 1,200 all ranks	Bns = 4 Fusilier Cos; 1 Co. in depot	Bns = 1 Karabinier, 1 Schutzen and 4 Fusilier Cos; 1 Co. in depot
Grenadier-Garde (raised in 1814 from grenadier cos)		1 Regt = 3 Bns 1 Bn = 6 Cos
Landwehr & National Guard		1 Bn = 4 Cos
Kuirassier Regt (converted in 1804 to dragoons) All cavalry approx. 600 all ranks	1 Regt = 6 Sqns; 2 in depot	From 1815: 2 Regts = 4 Sqns
Dragoon Regts (converted in 1811 to chevau-léger)	2 Regts = 6 Sqns; 2 in depot	
Chevau-léger Regts	4 Regts = 6 Sqns; 2 in depot	6 (7 in 1813) Regts = 6 Sqns; 2 in depot
Hussar Regts (from 1813)		1 Regt = 8 Sqns, then 2 Regts
Uhlan Regt (from 1813)		1 Regt = 6 Sqns
Artillery Each battery approx. 6 guns and howitzers	(1805) 3 bns totalling 11 mixed cos (1809) 3 divisions each of 4 cos	(1812) 4 bns each of 5 cos

7. UNIFORMS

GUARD GRENADIERS

For almost all of the Napoleonic period, the Bavarian Army functioned with only purely ceremonial household units. In 1814 it was decided to raise a new unit that would also serve in the field if required. The uniform colour was cornflower-blue with scarlet collar, cuffs and lapels with white buttonhole lacing.

The headdress was a black bearskin with brass front plate, red rear patch with white cross, and a white top, blue base plume.

LINE INFANTRY

The background colour of the Bavarian infantry was of a cornflower blue. This was a relatively new introduction, as during the eighteenth century it had been a dark, almost Prussian, blue, then at the turn of the century it was briefly white.

The headgear was a distinctive helmet called the raupenhelm, which carried a black woollen caterpillar crest.

Each regiment carried different coloured facings at the collar, cuffs and lapels and piping, with all turnbacks red. Units with the same colour facings were differentiated by their button colour, as follows:

LINE INFANTRY

REGIMENTAL NO.	REGIMENTAL TITLES	FACINGS	BUTTONS
1	Leib-Regiment 1811 – Konig	Black 1802 – Red with white lace buttonholes	White
2	Kurprinz 1806 – Kronprinz	Black 1802 – Red with yellow buttonhole lace	Yellow
3	Herzog Karl 1806 – Prinz Karl	Red, white piping from 1806	Yellow
4	vacant Von Weichs 1804 – Salern 1811 – Sachsen-Hildburghausen	Sulphur yellow, red piping from 1806	White

REGIMENTAL NO.	REGIMENTAL TITLES	FACINGS	BUTTONS
5	Graugeben 1800 – von Preysing	Pink (red edging)	White
6	Herzog Wilhelm	Red, white piping from 1806	White
7	Zedtwitz-Stengel 1804 – von Morawitsky 1806 – Lowenstein-Wertheim	White Pink from 1806	Yellow
8	Herzog Pius	Sulphur yellow, red piping from 1806	Yellow
9	Graf von Ysenburg	Scarlet, poppy red collar with yellow lapels and cuffs from 1806	Yellow
10	von Junker 1800 – Pompei-Dalwigk 1804 Junker	Crimson, poppy red collar with yellow lapels and cuffs from 1806	White
11 1806 – to Wurzberg Re-raised 1807 Disbanded 1811	Schlossberg 1801 – von Kinkel	Orange 1807–1811 poppy red collar, green cuffs and lapels	Yellow
12, raised 1803 Disbanded 1806 Re-raised 1814	von Lowenstein-Wertheim	Orange	White
13, raised 1805 Re-numbered 11 in 1811		Red collar, cuffs and lapels black piped red	White
14, raised 1806 Re-numbered 13 in 1811 Re-raised 1814	1814 – Wrede	Red collar, cuffs and lapels black piped red	Yellow

In 1814 all line infantry facings became red with yellow buttons; the 1st and 2nd Regiments lost their distinctive button hole lace. The buttons showed the unit number.

LIGHT INFANTRY

The Light Infantry units wore a light green uniform coat, changed to dark green in 1809.

The headgear was the raupenhelm worn by the line units.

The distinctive colours were:

REGIMENTAL NO.	REGIMENTAL TITLES	FACINGS	BUTTONS
1	Metzen 1807 – Haberman 1809 – Gedoni 1811 – Hertling 1811 – Fick 1815 – Fortis	Red 1806 – Black cuffs and lapels	White 1804 – Yellow
2	Clossmann 1804 – Vincenti 1805 – Ditfurth 1808 – Wreden 1811 – Treuberg 1811 – Merz 1815 – Sebus	Red 1806 – Black cuffs and lapels	White
3	Salern 1804 – Preysing 1808 – Bernclau 1811 – Scherer Used to reform the 12th Line	Black, edged red	White
4	Salern 1804 – Stengel 1806 – Zoller 1807 – Wreden 1809 – Donnersberg 1810 – Theobald 1813 – Cronegg	Black, edged red	Yellow
5 1806 – to Nürnberg Re-raised 1807	De la Motte 1807 – Dalwigk 1808 – Buttler 1812 – Herrmann 1814 – Treuberg	Crimson 1807 – black cuffs and lapels, yellow collar piped red	White

REGIMENTAL NO.	REGIMENTAL TITLES	FACINGS	BUTTONS
6	Lessel 1804 – Weinbach 1806 – Taxis 1809 – La Roche 1812 – Palm 1814 – Flad	Crimson 1807 – black cuffs and lapels, yellow collar piped red	Yellow
7 raised 1808 from Tyrolian Jäger battalion and disbanded in 1811	Gunther	Collar blue edged red	White

CAVALRY

Whilst the cavalry all wore the raupenhelm, the basic uniform coat colour varied according to the arm of service. When they were formed the hussars and uhlan regiments wore the traditional dolman and pelisse and czapka and kurtka respectively. The kuirassier regiments did not wear a cuirass.

REGIMENTAL NO.	REGIMENTAL TITLE	COAT COLOUR	FACINGS	BUTTONS
1st Kuirassiers	Minucci	White	White collar, scarlet lapels, cuffs and turnbacks	White
1804 – 1st Dragoons	Minucci	White	Scarlet collar, lapels, cuffs and turnbacks	White
1811 – 1st Chevau-légers	vacant	Green	Scarlet 1814 – poppy red with green turnbacks	White 1814 – yellow
2nd Dragoons[1]	Taxis	White	Scarlet collar, lapels, cuffs and turnbacks	Yellow

[1] The 1st Dragoon Regiment had been formed in 1790 and disbanded in 1803. Until the 1st Kuirassier was converted to a dragoon regiment in 1804 there were no 1st Dragoons in the Bavarian Army.

REGIMENTAL NO.	REGIMENTAL TITLE	COAT COLOUR	FACINGS	BUTTONS
1811 – 2nd Chevau-légers	Taxis	Green	Scarlet 1814 – poppy red with green turnbacks	Yellow
1st Chevau-légers 1811 – 3rd, Chevau-légers	Fugger 1809 – Kronprinz	Green	Black, red edging to collar 1814 – poppy red with green turnbacks	Yellow
2nd Chevau-légers 1811 – 4th Chevau-légers	Churfurst 1809 – Konig	Green	Poppy red 1814 – poppy red with green turnbacks	White 1814 – yellow
3rd Chevau-légers 1811 – 5th Chevau-légers	Leiningen	Green	Poppy red 1814 – poppy red with green turnbacks	Yellow
4th Chevau-légers 1811 – 6th Chevau-légers	Bubenhofen	Green	Black 1814 – poppy red with green turnbacks	White 1814 – yellow
1813 – 7th Chevau-légers	Prinz Karl	Shako, Green coat	Light blue	White
1813 – Hussars		Shako, light blue dolman and pelisse	Black fur edging, white lace	White
1813 – Uhlans		Czapka – yellow top Kurtka – dark green	Light blue 1814 – red	White
1814 – Garde du Corps		Brass helmet with bearskin crest, cornflower blue coat, steel cuirass	Poppy red with white lace	White

Horse furniture was scarlet for the kuirassier and dragoon regiments, edged in button colour. For the original chevau-léger regiments and the two dragoon regiments after conversion, as well as the uhlan regiment when formed, the shabraque was poppy red, also trimmed in the button colour.

The hussar regiment had light blue shabraques edged white, and the Garde du Corps had poppy red half shabraques with white sheepskins piped red.

ARTILLERY

The headgear for both foot and horse batteries was the standard raupenhelm. The uniform coat was dark blue, infantry style for the foot battery and cavalry kollet for the horse.

The facings were scarlet for the collar, cuffs and turnbacks, with black piped scarlet lapels. Buttons, etc. were brass.

8. BATTLE HISTORY

(Roman numerals indicate original Corps affiliation; these often changed during the campaign.)

1806–07

B Siege of Breslau, 6 December 1806–6 January 1807
Br Blockade of Brieg, 17 January 1807
G Blockade of Glogau, to 25 November 1806

1809

1L Landshut, 16 April 1809
2L Landshut, 21 April 1809
A Arnhofen, 19 April 1809
Ab Abensberg, 20 April 1809
E Eggmuhl, 22 April 1809
I Innsbruck, 11–13 April 1809
N Neumarkt, 24 April 1809
Ty Actions in the Tyrol, May–November 1809
W Wagram, 5–6 July 1809

1812

1P 1st Polotsk, 16–18 August 1812
2P 2nd Polotsk, 18–20 October 1812
Bo Borodino, 7 September 1812

1813–14

Ar Arcis-sur-Aube, 20–21 March 1814 (Seven National Guard battalions not included)

Ba Bautzen, 20–21 May 1813 (as French allies)

Bs Bar-sur-Aube, 26–27 February 1814 (One National Guard battalion not included)

D Dennewitz, 6 September 1813 (as French allies)

H Hanau, 30–31 October 1813 (Seven National Guard battalions not included)

LR La Rothière, 1 February 1814 (Eleven National Guard battalions not included)

Wu Blockade of Wurzburg, 24 October 1813–2 May 1814 (One National Guard battalion not included)

There was no significant Bavarian involvement in the 1815 campaigns.

UNIT	1806–07	1809	1812	1813–14
Infantry				
1	G, B, Br	VII: Ab, E, Ty	VI: 1P, 2P	XII: D LR, Bs, Ar
2	G, B, Br	VII: A, Ab, E, Ty	VI: 1P, 2P	LR, Wu
3	B	VII: A, Ab, N, Ty, W	VI: 1P, 2P	XII: Ba, D LR, Bs, Ar
4	G, B, Br	VII: Ab, E, Ty	VI: 1P, 2P	XII: Ba, D H, LR, Wu
5	G, B, Br	VII: 1L, E, Ty, W	VI: 1P, 2P	XII: Ba, D H, LR
6		VII: A, Ab, N, Ty	VI: 1P, 2P	H, LR, Ar
7	B	VII: Ab, N, Ty, W	VI: 1P, 2P	XII: Ba H, LR
8		VII: Ab, E, Ty	VI: 1P, 2P	XII: Ba, D H, LR
9		VII: E, Ty	VI: 1P, 2P	XII: Ba, D H, LR

UNIT	1806–07	1809	1812	1813–14
10	G, B, Br	VII: 1L, E, Ty	VI: 1P, 2P	XII: Ba, D LR, Bs
11		I:	VI: 1P, 2P	H, LR
12				
13	B, Br	VII: Ab, 2L, N, Ty, W	X:	XII: Ba, D
14		VII: E, Ty		
Light Infantry				
1		VII: Ab, E, Ty	VI: 1P, 2P	H, LR
2		I:		LR
3	B, Br	I, VII: E	VI: 1P, 2P	XII: Ba LR, Bs, Ar
4	B	I:	VI: 1P, 2P	XII: Ba H, LR
5		VII: 1L, E, Ty	VI: 1P, 2P	XII: Ba
6	G, B	VII: Ab, N, Ty, W	VI: 1P, 2P	XII: Ba
7		VII: 1L, Ty		
Cavalry: listed as at 1811 re-organization				
1 Chevau-légers	G, B, Br	I, VII: A, Ab, E	III Cav: Bo	H, LR, Bs, Ar
2 Chevau-légers	B	VII: 1L, E, Ty	III Cav: Bo	XII: D H, LR, Bs, Ar
3 Chevau-légers	G, B, Br	VII: A, Ab. 2L, E, Ty	IV: Bo	H, LR, Ar
4 Chevau-légers	B, Br	VII: 2L, Ty, W	IV: Bo	H, LR
5 Chevau-légers	B	VII: 2L, N, Ty, W	IV: Bo	H, LR
6 Chevau-légers		VII: E, Ty	IV: Bo	XII: D H, LR, Ar
7 Chevau-légers				H, LR, Bs, Ar

9. TACTICS

Up until the turn of the century, the Bavarian Army fought in the traditional linear formations inherited from Frederick the Great's Prussia. Since it had proven to be a successful way of making war, this is not too surprising.

Having been on the receiving end of French revolutionary tactics, the Bavarian staff decided to update their manuals and in 1804 began to issue new instructions. These stressed integrated, combined arms tactics, with the use of infantry columns for movement, skirmish tactics and firepower. One aspect that received substantial effort was to increase the artillery available to Bavarian commanders.

The Bavarian Army that mainly formed the VI Corps in Russia was well trained and gave a good account of itself at the two battles of Polotsk. However, the huge losses suffered meant that the 1813 army had to be rebuilt from cadres, new levies and discharged old sweats. It took time for this organization to bed down, although it was bad generalship that caused the loss of the Battle of Hanau in October 1813, not the failure of the army itself. There can be little doubt that it formed an important element of the 1814 army that invaded France.

CHAPTER 4

The Army of the Grand Duchy of Berg, 1806–13

1. INTRODUCTION

So far, the armies we have described came from established states, even though they had all gained land and population at the expense of smaller or less successful ones. The Grand Duchy of Berg is very different, being set up as a means to strengthen the French hold on Germany and, ultimately, failing to outlive its creator. In its short life, however, it was to provide some hard fighting units for the various French armies.

2. BACKGROUND

Berg was an artificial creation set up by Napoleon as part of the glacis between France and Prussia. It was built on the foundation of the Prussian territories of Cleve and Wesel, but it also included the ex-Bavarian Ansbach and Berg, given up as Bavaria gained areas closer to its own heartland.

The Grand Duchy was originally given to Joachim Murat, Napoleon's brother-in-law and one of the original marechals. After he gained the throne of Naples in succession to Joseph (himself translated to Spain), the Grand Duchy was given to Napoleon-Louis, the son of Louis Bonaparte, the King of Holland, and Napoleon's nephew. As Napoleon-Louis was under age, it was ruled on his behalf by a commissioner appointed direct by the Emperor.

3. COMMAND STRUCTURE

As Berg became part of the Confederation of the Rhine the army was subject to French command. Indeed, with Murat and then Napoleon as the executive, it would have been unlikely to have been anything else.

The army was too small to be self-sufficient, but formed part of larger formations in Spain and in Russia.

4. OFFICER CORPS

Without a strong military tradition, the original officer corps came from a variety of sources, ex-Prussians and adventurers predominating. The failure to generate sufficient native officers was to bedevil the army throughout its short life. Not having a stake in either their country or with the men they commanded, there was little inclination to enforce discipline.

5. OTHER RANKS

Although recruits had been found for both the Bavarian and the Prussian Army, the idea that there was now a new army in which to serve failed to generate much enthusiasm.

The idea in setting up a new state was to set an example for the rest of Germany, and this included widening the pool of eligible soldiers through conscription. This was a new experience for the population and was widely hated. As a result, many of those called to serve evaded their obligation or, if they reported for service, quickly deserted.

To a great extent, therefore, the Berg infantry arm was felt to be a liability. That it turned in such a good battlefield performance may, perhaps, be put down to the Germans' natural affinity for soldiering.

6. THE MILITARY ESTABLISHMENT

Organization

INFANTRY		
1806: One regiment, formed from 12th Bavarian Regt and a Nassau-Oranien battalion	4 battalions	Each of 8 companies of 100 men
August 1808: Two regiments	Each of 3 battalions, plus composite depot battalion	Each of 4 fusilier, 1 grenadier and 1 voltigeur companies of 140 men each. The depot had no flank companies
October 1808: Three regiments	As above	As above
1811: Four regiments	Each of 2 battalions; one depot company per regiment	As above
1813: Two regiments	As above	As above
CAVALRY		
1806: 1 chasseur à cheval regiment formed from Nassau-Oranien Hussars	4 Squadrons	Each of 2 companies of 125 men.
1809: Converted into a Uhlan (Lancer) regiment and considered to be part of the Imperial Guard	As above	As above
1812: 2 lancer regiments (only the 1st was of guard status)	As above	As above
1813: 1 lancer regiment	As above	As above
ARTILLERY		
One company of foot artillery One company of horse artillery	Eight pieces Six pieces	6 x 8 pdrs, 2 x 6 inch howitzers 6 x 4 pdrs

7. UNIFORMS

INFANTRY

The original regiment first wore Bavarian uniform, but soon changed to a French-style one. They wore a white Spencer coat, closed to the waist with sky blue collar, cuffs and lapels, piped white and sky blue turnbacks for all regiments. The breeches (overalls after 1810) were white.

The shakos were also French style with red plumes for the grenadiers (red epaulettes), although the bearskin was also issued, either with or without the front plate. The '*anse du singe*' was red with a white cross. Voltigeurs had a green tipped white plume and green epaulettes. Fusilier companies had a white piped sky blue shoulder strap in the 1st and 3rd regiments and sky blue piped white shoulder strap in the 2nd and 4th regiments.

The other regimental distinctives were Brandenburg cuffs for the 1st, 3rd and 4th Regiments and Polish cuffs for the 2nd with the following cuff flap patterns:

REGIMENT	CUFFS	BUTTONS
1st	White cuff flaps with sky blue piping	Brass
2nd	No cuff flaps, but the Polish cuffs were piped white	Brass
3rd (October 1808)	Sky blue cuff flaps piped white	Brass
4th (August 1811)	No cuff flaps, but the cuff was split with white piping on each edge	White metal

CAVALRY

When it was first formed the cavalry wore a czapka with an amarante (or, more prosaically, pink) 'box' over a black lower. The plume, cord and flounders (when worn) were white.

The coat was a white kurtka with amarante collar, cuffs, turnbacks and lapels. There was amarante piping on the rear seam of the sleeve which extended down the back to the tail of the coat. The breeches were amarante.

From 1809 this uniform changed radically. The headgear remained the czapka, although an amarante shako was issued for campaign. The elite company wore a colpack. The regiment was now issued with a dark green chasseur, a cheval coatee with amarante collar cuffs and turnbacks, with the lapels dark green piped amarante. Breeches were dark green piped amarante.

When the unit received the lance, it adopted a dark green kurtka with the amarante facings as previously. The lance pennon was pink over white.

The 2nd Regiment wore the czapka and colpacks, but the kurtka had the facings piped dark green.

8. BATTLE HISTORY

(Roman numerals indicate original Corps affiliation; these often changed during the campaign.)

The 1st Infantry Regiment served at the blockade and siege of Graudenz in 22 January–12 December 1807. The service for the rest of the Napoleonic Wars was:

1809

O	Oelper, 1 August

Spain

C	Carpio, 25 September 1811
FD	Fuentes de Oñoro, 3–5 May 1811
G	Siege of Gerona, 6 June–10 December 1809
VdP	Venta del Pozo, 23 October 1812

1812

Be	Berezina, 24–28 November

1813

Ba	Bautzen, 2 May
Le	Leipzig, 16–18 October
R	Reichenbach, 22 May

UNIT	1809	SPAIN	1812	1813
1st Infantry		G	Be	
2nd Infantry		G	Be	
3rd Infantry	O		Be	
4th Infantry			Be	
1st Chasseur à Cheval		FD, C, VdP		Ba, R, Le
2nd Chasseur à Cheval			Be	

9. TACTICS

As far as Napoleon was concerned, the Berg units were an integral part of the French, so much so that any instructions were sent through the Minister of War rather than the Foreign Ministry!

This level of integration and the need to ensure that they could serve and contribute to the mainly French forces with which they served meant that they were trained in French drill and minor tactics.

The 1st and 2nd Regiments that served at Gerona numbered 2,700 officers and men in four battalions in April 1809. It lost 261 men alone when it attempted to storm the walls in September, and by the time the city fell in December had been reduced to the strength of a single battalion.

Post Script

The Congress of Vienna, which started soon after Napoleon's first abdication in April 1814 undid the arrangements underlying the Confederation of the Rhine. Prussia regained her lost provinces and the two infantry regiments were used to form the 28th and 29th Prussian Regiments. The cavalry was used as a cadre for the 11th Hussars and the 5th Uhlans.

CHAPTER 5

The Army of the Kingdom of Denmark, 1804–13

1. INTRODUCTION

DENMARK, WHICH AT the time of the Napoleonic Wars also included Norway, Schleswig and Holstein, tried to maintain a strict neutrality. This brought them up against the British who wanted to maintain an effective blockade of the European coast, and the French who wanted to use the country to launch an attack on Sweden.

After Tsar Alexander and Napoleon had made peace at Tilsit, rumours grew that the Danes would be 'encouraged' to use their fleet to redress the losses suffered at Trafalgar. To stop this, a British fleet and army was sent to Copenhagen to offer to take the Danish ships into safe keeping. Naturally enough, this offer was turned down and negotiations turned to threats, including the bombardment of the city.

Whilst this resulted in the Danes giving up their fleet, it was at the expense of creating an enemy. From then on, any British ships using the Baltic were at risk and it required a Royal Navy squadron to protect them.

Although Denmark made an alliance with France, it was essentially a defensive one, and she supplied no troops to the various expeditions. Even in 1812, her support was limited to protection of the rear areas and, in 1813, protection of her borders.

In the meantime, Crown Prince Karl of Sweden (the ex-Marechal Bernadotte) had got agreement from the Allies that the price for joining them was Norway, to recompense for the loss of Finland to Russia in 1809. In 1814, after Napoleon's first abdication, this was achieved with little or no bloodshed.

2. BACKGROUND

Denmark had been a great regional power from the middle of the seventeenth to the middle of the eighteenth centuries. She had fought with distinction in the Great Northern War, as well as providing hard-fighting regiments to the Maritime Powers fighting against Louis XIV in the Low Countries and along the Rhine. Indeed, as late as the 1740s a Danish army was considered to be one of the best that money could buy!

This martial reputation waned as the Prussian Army became the benchmark and Denmark became more and more a military backwater, concentrating on the fleet to protect her growing overseas trade. The militia battalions supplied a significant part of the army.

3. COMMAND STRUCTURE

King Christian VII had come to the throne in 1766, but his mental state was suspect and his son Frederick had been acting as regent since 1784. Frederick acceded to the throne in 1808 as Frederick VI.

Frederick and his ministers had been accused of Jacobinism in the 1790s, and there can be little doubt that there was some support for France and French ideas.

4. THE MILITARY ESTABLISHMENT

Organization

INFANTRY		
Guard Regiment (Livgarden til Fods)	1 'Regiment'	4 companies. Each company numbered about 130 men
Leib Regiments (Livregimenter)	2 Regiments, each of 2 battalions	1st battalion of 1 grenadier and 4 musketeer companies 2nd battalion of 1 jäger and 4 musketeer companies. Each company numbered about 130 men
Infantry Regiments (1807)	12 Regiments, each of 2 battalions	As above

INFANTRY (Cont.)		
Infantry Regiments (1808)	12 Regiments, each of 4 battalions (I & II regular, III & IV militia)	As above, the 3rd and 4th battalions as the 2nd
Jägers (1808)	1 Regiment, of 2 battalions	Each battalion consisted of 4 jäger companies, plus a grenadier company
Rifles (Skarpskyttekorps)	2 Regiments, each of 2 battalions	As above
Kings Rifle Corps	1 battalion of militia	2 companies of 100 men
CAVALRY		
Lifeguard (Kongelige Livgarde til Hest)		2 squadrons of 74 officers and men each
Dragoons (Ryttere)	4 Regiments	4 squadrons of 177 officers and men each
Light Dragoons (Lette Dragoner)	3 Regiments	As above
Hussars	1 Regiment	6 squadrons of 177 officers and men each
Bosniaks (converted to Uhlans in 1808)	1 Regiment	4 squadrons of 177 officers and men each

5. UNIFORMS

INFANTRY

The Danish Army had adopted a red base for its uniforms earlier in the eighteenth century. The uniform was based on that of the Russian Army's 1792 pattern, which featured small triangular turnbacks at the waist; these were white, as were the skirt turnbacks. The lapels were closed. Collar, cuffs and lapel facings as below distinguished the units themselves.

Musketeers and jägers wore a straight-sided shako (jäger plumes were green, musketeer officer plumes were white), grenadiers and all ranks of the Guard regiment had an Austrian-style bearskin with a light blue over white plume and a red bag, but adopted a shako in 1813.

Breeches were grey, with black gaiters. Belting was white, except for the jäger companies which had black leather.

Information on the jäger battalions is somewhat sparse and conflicting, but essentially the uniform colour was dark green with black facings, piped white. The Grenadier-jäger company wore a bearskin with a red over green plume. Belting was black leather.

There is some evidence that officers of line jäger companies and (by extension) the jäger regiments adopted a dark green pelisse. The fur edging and the braid was silver grey.

UNIT	FACINGS	BUTTONS
Livgarden til Fods	Light blue, no piping	White
Danske Livregiment	Light yellow, no piping	White
Norske Livregiment	Light yellow, piped white	White
Kongens	Light blue, no piping	White
Dronningens	Light blue, no piping	Yellow
Kronprinsens	Light blue, piped white	White
Prince Frederick	Green, no piping	White
Fynske	White, no piping	White
Sjaelland	Green, white piping	White
1st Jyske	Black, white piping	Yellow
2nd Jyske	White, no piping	Yellow
3rd Jyske	Black, white piping	White
Oldensborgske	Green, no piping	White
Slesvigske	Light blue, piped white	Yellow
Holstenske	Green, piped white	Yellow
Slesvigske Jaegerkorps	Black, piped white	?
Sjaellanske Skarpskyttekorps	Black, piped white	White
Holstenske Skarpskyttekorps	Black, piped white	Yellow

CAVALRY

The Livgarde til Hest wore a helmet that looked very similar to a British Tarleton of the period, but with the addition of black falling mane at the rear. The uniform was pale straw-yellow faced red (including the small triangular turnbacks), with pale straw-yellow breeches. Belting was black. The horse furniture was red, edged white.

The four ryttere regiments wore a bicorne which had a white plume. The uniform was red with regimental facings at collar, cuffs and lapels (which were closed). The turnbacks were yellow. For campaign, units wore dark blue overalls. The horse furniture was red, edged white.

Liv-ryttereregiment:	yellow
Sjaellanske	dark blue
Slesvigske	light blue
Holstenske	light green, piped yellow

The Lette Dragoner wore the Tarleton helmet with a facing colour turban, although that of the Livregiment was red. Like the ryttere regiments, the uniform itself was red with facings at the collar, cuffs and closed lapels:

Livregiment	black, piped yellow
Jydske	green, piped white
Fynske	light-blue, piped yellow

Overalls were blue but grey ones were slowly being introduced in 1813; these had leather cuffs and rubbing surfaces. Shabraques were red, edged white, and there is no evidence of sabretaches being used.

The hussar regiment wore a black mirliton (perhaps with a visor by 1812) with a white plume, and may even have adopted a black fur busby. The dolman was light blue, faced crimson, whilst the pelisse was crimson with black fur edging. Lacing to the dolman and the pelisse was white. The breeches were buff leather with crimson Schwaraden, although by 1812 they may have adopted light blue overalls.

The horse furniture was red, with white wolfs-tooth edging. The sabretache was crimson edged white.

The bosniaks originally wore a largely oriental-style costume (much like the original bosniak regiment in the Prussian Army) The fez was red with a white turban, and the long coat was light blue, faced red. On conversion to a Uhlan regiment they adopted the traditional czapka of red top over light blue, a light blue, faced red kurtka and overall trousers. The horse furniture was red edged white and the lances bore a red over white pennon.

ARTILLERY

Both branches wore essentially the same uniform of black shako with blue pom-pons, red-faced blue infantry-style jacket and dark blue breeches, although the Ridende Artilleri wore cavalry overalls.

Danish artillery was painted red with yellow metalwork.

NORWEGIAN REGIMENTS

Most of the regiments were volunteer units, only the Sondenfjaeldske and Nordenfjaeldske being considered regular. It is assumed in addition that the four ryttere regiments were regular: Akerhusske, Smaalenske, Oplandske and Trondhjemske. We have no uniform information on any of these.

Interestingly, the Norwegian forces included ski-troops, who wore a black leather cap and jäger-style uniform.

6. BATTLE HISTORY

The Danish Army did not take part in any long-term campaigns. Apart from the assistance given to putting down von Schill's revolt in 1809,[1] its most lengthy deployment was in 1813 when it supported Marechal Davout in Hamburg.

That being so, the following order of battle for the Danish Auxiliary Corps under General of Infantry Prince Frederick von Hesse at the end of the summer armistice in August 1813 is provided as an example:

Advanced Guard – Colonel S. Waldeck
2nd Battalion, Slesvigske Jägerkorps

[1] I (less the grenadier company) & II Oldensborgske Infanteriregiment; III Holstenske Infanteriregiment; 2 Cos Holstenske Skarpskyttekorps; 1 troop Holstenske Regiment Ryttere; 2 Sqns Hussars.

1st and 2nd Battalions, Holstenske Skarskyttekorps
2nd and 6th squadrons, Hussar Regiment
One battery of Ridende Artilleri with 3 pounders

1st Brigade – Major General G. L. Graf von der Schulenberg
1st, 2nd & 4th (Militia) Battalions, Oldensborgske Infanteriregiment
Jäger company from 3rd Battalion Oldenborgske Infanteriregiment
4th (Militia) Battalion, Holstenske Infanteriregiment
1st Battalion, Dronningens Infanteriregiment
Jäger company of 2nd Battalion, Dronningens Infanteriregiment
Holstenske Regiment Ryttere
One battery of artillery with 6 pounders

2nd Brigade – Major General J. C. Lasson
1st and 2nd Battalions, Fynske Infanteriregiment
1st and 2nd Battalions, Slesvigske Infanteriregiment
3rd (Militia) Battalion, Holstenske Infanteriregiment
Jysdke Regiment Lette Dragoner
1 battery of Ridende Artilleri with 3 pounders
1 battery of artillery with 6 pounders

7. NAVY

In 1807 the fleet consisted of twenty ships of the line (1st to 4th rates) and seventeen smaller vessels. The British captured or destroyed nineteen of the major vessels, sixteen ships 5th rate or lower, ten unrated ships and twenty-five gunboats; the last ship of the line was destroyed in 1808.

This almost total destruction of the fleet meant that the navy had to fall back on using galleys and gunboats, a potent threat to British merchantmen in light breezes or in calms, especially since they were armed with heavy guns.

CHAPTER 6

The Army of the Duchy of Hesse-Darmstadt, 1805–15

1. INTRODUCTION

HESSE DARMSTADT WAS located on the east bank of the Rhine. Part of the Holy Roman Empire (even though it was Protestant), it formed part of the Upper Rhine Kreis.

The Landgravate provided troops to the Reichsarmee but they had fought in the Low Countries during the Wars of the Spanish and Austrian Successions, and the Darmstadt regiment had formed the rearguard at Rossbach in 1757. The regiment continued to serve with the Reichsexsecutionsarmee until the close of the Seven Years War. Indeed, so much was Hesse-Darmstadt seen as a supporter of the Habsburg monarchy that the Landgrave was hereditary inhaber[1] of a regiment of Austrian Dragoons from 1746 to their disbandment at the end of the century.

This martial tradition was to stand her army in good stead during the Napoleonic period. One unit was to serve with distinction in Spain from 1808 to 1812, whilst the rest of the army was to fight at Wagram and in Russia.

[1] This refers to a regiment's colonel-proprietor. This was usually a senior general or member of the ruling house whose name the unit often bore. It could be a form of pension, as the inhaber was responsible for supplying the regiment with clothing and other supplies (and thus took a percentage of the funds), as well as appointing junior officers to vacancies (sometimes for a consideration). In some armies, the proprietor was responsible for the drill being used, although this power was decreasing as armies became more structured.

2. BACKGROUND

Unlike Hesse-Kassel which dropped out of the war against revolutionary France in 1795 (at the same time as her protector, Prussia), Hesse Darmstadt remained loyal to Austria until the Treaty of Luneville in 1801, but the knowledge that a victorious France was only across the Rhine tended to concentrate the Landgrave's mind.

With Austria now largely expelled from German affairs, although the formal ending of the Holy Roman Empire was not to take place until 1806, France was able to 'modernize' some of the more feudal structures of the political scene. One aspect of this was to give the lands of the Imperial Knights or the ecclesiastical holdings to the larger secular states as compensation for losses elsewhere.

Often this was for the cynical reason of tying states to France, for the fear would be that a resurgent Austria would force the disgorgement of these new possessions. Certainly, when the Confederation of the Rhine was set up in 1806, Ludwig X was quick to show his willingness to join. His additional reward was to be elevated to Grossherzog (Grand Duke).

Although the army was to prove a solid support to Napoleon's forces, by the summer of 1813 Grossherzog Ludwig realized that the Allies were likely to prove too strong for them. As a result he started negotiations with the Emperor Franz of Austria. The intention behind this was that by changing sides voluntarily instead of being forced to do so by an occupation force, he would keep all his gains. This proved a wise move, although he had to provide a force to serve with the allies – the blood tax continued as before.

3. COMMAND STRUCTURE

In common with nearly every other state that joined the Confederation of the Rhine, changes had to be made in the method of governance. In order to maintain the strength of the army, to supply it and to provide a supporting infrastructure, changes had to be made to the political and social relationships within the state.

The most obvious of these was to increase the level of bureaucracy, for only through this could the tax rolls be maintained, or the list of potential soldiers kept up to date. Reducing the power of the guilds meant that not only was a loop-hole (by allowing apprentices to escape service) closed, but old soldiers were able to take up employment as a form of pension.

In essence, therefore, whilst there was some degree of absolutism in Hesse-Darmstadt beforehand, now it was put on a systematized basis, with the right of the state to become more deeply involved in the social framework of the population.

4. OFFICER CORPS

When it joined the Confederation of the Rhine, Hesse-Darmstadt's army still reflected the outlook of the late eighteenth century, even down to the basic uniform. However, the officer corps itself was capable and homogenous, having few non-native-born within their ranks, and the early campaigns showed that there was little that needed to be taught either in terms of efficiency or knowledge.

The integration of the fusilier battalions as part and parcel of the brigades allowed them to fully understand and appreciate the full repertoire of modern tactics.

5. OTHER RANKS

French officers had already had an opportunity to see Hessian units in action during the 1806 and 1807 campaigns, and had warranted large amounts of praise. Like the officer corps, the rank and file of the army appear to have been raised from native-born residents, which helped to engender *esprit de corps*.

Like a number of the armies of the German states, a large number of the ordinary soldiers were placed on extended leave unless required for the annual manoeuvres or on mobilization for war. This meant that the government saved their wages but also that the men themselves contributed to the economic life of the state. In addition, by carrying on a trade they were training themselves for a career after retiring from the army (assuming that any wounds were not too debilitating!).

Grand Duke Ludwig's ministers also tried to ameliorate the soldier's conditions through increased pay and other benefits, as well as some pension rights for old servicemen and their dependents.

The fighting value of the Hessian army was recognized by no less a person than Napoleon, who complained when the unit in Spain failed to live up to his expectations (although any problems were short-term), but tried to get Ludwig to field additional units when his generals expressed their entire satisfaction.

6. THE MILITARY ESTABLISHMENT

Organization

INFANTRY		
1803: Line Infantry Regiments	3 regiments of 2 battalions each of 428 all ranks	Each battalion of 4 companies, totalling 103 all ranks
Fusilier Battalions	3 battalions, each of 428 all ranks	As above
1809: Line Infantry Regiments (Central Europe)	2 regiments of 2 battalions, each of 680 all ranks	Each battalion of 4 companies, totalling 170 all ranks
Fusilier Battalions (Central Europe)	2 battalions, each of 680 all ranks	As above
1809: Line Infantry Regiment (Spain). This unit was lost in the fall of Badajoz and not reformed until May 1814	1 regiment of 2 battalions, each of 850 all ranks	Each battalion consisted of 4 centre, 1 grenadier and 1 voltigeur companies, each 140 all ranks.
1812: Line Infantry Regiments (Russia)	2 regiments of 2 battalions, each of 680 all ranks	Each battalion of 4 companies, totalling 170 all ranks
Fusilier Regiment (Russia)	1 regiment of 2 battalions, each of 680 all ranks	As above
1813–15: Line Infantry Regiments	2, later 3, then 4 regiments, each of 680 all ranks	Each battalion of 4 companies, totalling 170 all ranks
Fusilier Regiment	1 regiment of 2 battalions, each of 680 all ranks	As above

CAVALRY		
1803: Chevau-légers	1 Regiment of 3 squadrons	Each squadron, each of 120 men.
1812: Chevau-légers	1 Regiment of 4 squadrons	Each squadrons, each of 120 men
ARTILLERY		
Foot artillery	3 companies	Each 5 x 6 pdr and 1 howitzer

The Hesse-Darmstadt Army was uniquely organized. Each of the three line regiments was provided with a fusilier battalion in order to form a three-battalion brigade as follows:

1803
The Leib-Brigade was formed from the Leib-Regiment and the 2nd Fusilier Bataillon.
The Regiment Landgraf, along with the Fusilier Bataillon Landgraf, formed the Landgraf-Brigade.
The Regiment Erbprinz and the 1st Fusilier Bataillon formed the Erbprinz-Brigade.

In 1806, with the formal dissolution of the Holy Roman Empire, the formation of the Confederation of the Rhine and the resulting promotion of the Landgraf to Grossherzog, the units were renamed as follows:

The Leib-Brigade became the Leib-Garde-Brigade, with the Leib-Garde-Regiment and the Garde Fusilier-Bataillon.
The Brigade-Landgraf became the Leib-Brigade, with the Leib-Regiment and the 1st Leib-Fusilier Bataillon.
The Erbprinz-Brigade became the Brigade Gross- und Erbprinz, with the Regiment Gross- und Erbprinz and 2nd Leib-Fusilier Bataillon.

In 1809, prior to leaving Hesse for service in Spain, Brigade Gross- und Erbprinz was reformed into a two-battalion regiment on the French organization. Essentially, the 2nd Leib-Fusilier Bataillon was disbanded and used to form the two elite companies for the centre companies of the Regiment Gross- und Erbprinz.

In 1812, the Garde-Fusilier Bataillon and the 1st Leib-Fusilier Bataillon were stripped out of their Brigades and used to form the Provisorisches Leichtes Infanterie-Regiment (re-named Garde-Fusilier Regiment in 1813.)

7. UNIFORMS

INFANTRY

Up until 1809 the head gear for all ranks and battalions (irrespective of designation) was the bicorne with white tape edging. There were company pom-pons on the front upper edge.

The coat was of Prussian style in dark blue for the musketeer regiments and in dark green for the fusiliers. The turnbacks were scarlet and brigade facing colours were carried at the collar, cuffs, lapels and shoulder straps:

The Leib-Brigade, then the Leib-Garde Brigade: Red
Landgraf-Brigade, then Leib-Brigade: Light blue
Erbprinz Brigade, then Brigade Gross- und Erbprinz: Yellow
Breeches were white, with black gaiters for campaign wear.

When the Gross- und Erbprinz Regiment was formed for service with the French Army it presented a variegated appearance with the green-clad fusiliers intermingled with the blue-clad musketeers. They were at least given a French-style shako, with the grenadiers having a red plume, the voltigeurs a green plume and the centre companies having the usual company pom-pons.

Eventually all ranks were given a blue jacket with the regimental facings of yellow. The grenadiers had red fringed epaulettes whilst the voltigeurs had green, edged with yellow crescents. Breeches were originally white but shortage of cloth meant that overalls were of various colours, and the regiment came to depend more and more on the French for equipment.

The regiments remaining in Central Europe began to adopt the French shako during the Austrian campaign of 1809, although the Leib-Regiment may not have received them until almost the end of the fighting. All units were issued with white overall trousers, but seem to have worn blue ones for everyday and campaign wear.

When the fusilier battalions were taken out of their brigades they were re-uniformed in blue with scarlet facings.

The Prinz Emil regiment, formed in 1814, was given the facing colour of pink.

CAVALRY

The original headgear was a black leather, kasket-style cap with a black caterpillar crest. This was replaced by a raupenhelm in 1806 with a black over red plume.

The tunic was dark green with red collar and turnbacks and black lapels, cuffs and cuff flaps. The breeches were originally buff, but changed to green overall with a red stripe by 1812.

Horse furniture was a green shabraque, edged white and a green, edged red valise.

ARTILLERY

The artillery companies wore infantry-style uniforms of blue faced black. The lapels, cuffs and turnbacks were piped red. The plumes were black, tipped red. Legwear followed the infantry pattern.

8. BATTLE HISTORY

(Roman numerals indicate original Corps affiliation; these often changed during the campaign.)

1806–07
G Blockade and siege of Graudenz, 22 January–12 December 1807
J Jena, 14 October 1806

Spain
Al Almonacíd, 11 August 1809
B Siege of Badajoz, 17 March–6 April 1812
Me Medellín, 29 March 1809
MI Mesa de Ibor, 17 March 1809
O Ocaña, 18–19 November 1809
T Talavera, 27–28 July 1809
Z Zornoza, 30 October 1808

1809
A Aspern-Essling, 21–22 May 1809
E Ebelsberg, 3 May 1809
P Pressburg, 1–4 June 1809
R Siege of Raab, 15–22 June 1809
W Wagram, 5–6 July 1809
Zn Znaim, 10–11 July 1809

1812
Be Beresina, 26–28 November 1812
Bo Borodino, 7 September 1812

1813–14
Ba Bautzen, 20–21 May 1813
Le Leipzig, 16–19 October 1813
Lu Lutzen, 2 May 1813

1815
Hu Siege and capitulation of Huningen, 15–26 August 1815
R Rheinzabern, 23 June 1815
St Blockade of Strasbourg, 28 June–30 July 1815
Su Suffelweyersheim, 28 June 1815

UNIT	1806–07	SPAIN	1809	1812	1813–14	1815
INFANTRY						
Leib-Garde-Regiment	G		IV: A, W, Zn	I:	III: Lu, Ba, Le	Su, St, Hu
Leib-Regiment	G		IV: A, W, Zn	I: Bo	III: Lu, Ba, Le	Hu
Regiment Gross- und Erbprinz		Z, MI, Me, T, Al, O, B				R, St, Hu
Prinz Emil						Hu
Garde Fusilier-Bataillon	VII: J, G		IV: P, R, W, Zn			

UNIT	1806–07	SPAIN	1809	1812	1813–14	1815
INFANTRY (Cont.)						
1st Leib-Fusilier Bataillon	VII: J, G		IV: P, R, W, Zn			
2nd Leib-Fusilier Bataillon						
Garde Fusilier-Regiment				XI:	III: Lu, Ba, Le	R, Su, St
CAVALRY						
Chevau-légers	G		IV: E, A, W, Zn	IX: Be	IV: Lu, Ba, Le	St

9. TACTICS

In the 1806/07 campaign the Hesse-Darmstadt Army had impressed the French generals under whom they served. It would appear that in preparation for the 1809 campaign those forces remaining in central Europe had undergone training in French drill, but probably fought it using their earlier, Austrian-style repertoire of tactics. The fusilier units were often detached from the main body of the brigade and attached to cavalry brigades as advance guards and for special operations.

By contrast, the Regiment Gross- und Erbprinz received nothing but complaints about its conduct. Marechal Lefebvre, who was the original commander of IV Corps in Spain, felt that they were wholly incapable of mastering the French drill. This should not have been wholly unexpected, since the whole regiment had had to absorb a new organization, new personnel and a new environment.

This led Napoleon to complain to Ludwig that the regiment needed a new cadre of officers. Once this was done the regiment rapidly improved; yet another example of how German soldiers react to positive example.

At Medellín, the battalions of the German Division were interspersed among the regiments of French cavalry, but at Talavera were caught by the British attack. It appears, however, that the blame for the fall of

Badajoz in 1812 was put on the Hessians even though it was one of the last units to surrender.

All told, the Hessian regiments provided the French Empire with a valuable fighting resource that fought with efficiency and valour.

CHAPTER 7

The Army of the Kingdom of Holland, 1804–10

1. INTRODUCTION

TO BE ACCURATE, THE Kingdom of Holland only existed between 1806 and 1810. Prior to this date, what is now the Netherlands was the Batavian Republic. This had been formed in 1794 when the French Revolutionary armies first overran the Austrian Netherlands (modern Belgium) and then crossed into the Netherlands where they were helped by the tacit assistance of a small group of supporters dissatisfied with the oligarchical government of the republic. In one of the most famous episodes of the invasion light cavalry captured the fleet, then ice-bound in the Texel!

The re-born Batavian Republic threw in its lot with the revolution, only for its fleet to be captured by Admiral Duncan's British fleet at the battle of Camperdown, and for most of the Caribbean possessions to be taken by other British forces. Even Cape Colony was lost, and only the logistical difficulties precluded an attack in the East Indies. It was all a far cry from when the news that 'The Dutch are in the Thames!' caused panic in London.

2. BACKGROUND

The long struggle for independence from first Habsburg Spain and then Bourbon France had first raised the Dutch Republic to a leading military role in Europe as well as being a financial centre. Dutch forces had formed the backbone of Marlborough's army in the Low Countries during the Spanish Succession, whilst money had meant that German and Danish 'auxiliaries' could supplement these.

Unfortunately, the Republic's resources were insufficient to compete with Britain, which had learnt the need for a highly efficient financial system from the Dutch. By the middle of the eighteenth century this was almost complete and Holland had been firmly relegated to the 'second-division' of European powers.

The victory of Austerlitz in December 1805 gave the new Emperor Napoleon the opportunity to start restructuring Europe, and one of the first places to be looked at was the Batavian Republic. To energize the country, and to try to ensure that it was able to fulfil his requirements, he arranged for the government to request that he nominate a new head of state. In response he selected his younger brother Louis (who was married to Napoleon's stepdaughter Hortense) to take the throne as King Louis.

Ultimately, this choice proved to be an ill one; Louis had unfortunately misunderstood the reasons for being made king and tried to rule benevolently and with his kingdom's needs uppermost in his mind rather than those of his imperial brother. Where Napoleon tried to stop Dutch ships trading with British ports, and to enforce favourable trading arrangements with France, Louis was prepared to issue trading warrants. Where Napoleon wanted the Dutch fleet rebuilt to replace the ships lost at Trafalgar, and for the Dutch Army to be strengthened to supplement the Imperial forces, Louis tried to evade these demands with prevarications and stonewalling.

Eventually, although Dutch forces had indeed fought well in Spain and Germany, Louis was forced to abdicate in 1810. Holland was absorbed into France and the Dutch Army became part of the French Army. By 1813 this had become too much and the country was ripe to revolt in favour of its hereditary stadtholder Louis. The link with France was broken at the first abdication in 1814, and the Dutch forces went on to form a significant part of Wellington's army at Waterloo in 1815.

3. COMMAND STRUCTURE

If Napoleon expected Louis to act as a loyal brother first and the King of Holland second, he was to be sharply disappointed. Holland may have welcomed the replacement of the old republic in the 1790s, but that did not automatically mean that it subscribed to the ideals of first the revolution and then the Empire. The newly created King Louis saw his duty as lying with his people, not his brother.

Whilst Louis was prepared to make troops available for use in imperial campaigns, there was no movement to introduce the wide-ranging conscription of either France or some of the German states. With its primary economic activity – trade – lost through blockade, there was no money available to fund a large army; besides, historically Holland had used large numbers of mercenaries in previous wars. With Germany now an armed camp, the only way to keep numbers up would be to use native-born soldiers, something that the population would not countenance.

That is not to say that there were no changes made. Louis continued to centralize the government, doing away with the powers of the individual provinces that had so be-devilled political stability in the previous century. Allied to this was an attempt (not completely successful) to curb the influence of the guilds.

In many ways, Louis' brief reign saw some necessary improvements made to Dutch public life, and there was genuine concern when he was forced to abdicate rather than accept the harsh treatment by his imperial brother.

4. OFFICER CORPS

If there was a tradition of service in the Netherlands it was probably directed more towards the Navy and the Merchant Marine. Just as the Dutch Government was willing to hire mercenaries to eke out its military obligations, so most of its officers came from a variety of sources. The Napoleonic period meant that it was forced to rely on its own resources

Senior officers were appointed from the French Army, but there was some traffic the other way, with Merlen and Chasse just two examples.

Hermann Wilhelm Daendels was born on 21 October 1763 at Hatten. The son of a burgermaster, Daendels first served as a major in an insurgent unit during the revolution of 1787. Forced to leave Holland once it collapsed, he moved to France in time for their revolution and in 1792 was the lieutenant-colonel of the 4th battalion of the 'Foreign Legion'.

When Dumouriez led the invasion of Holland in 1794 Daendels was first a general of brigade and later was promoted to general of division. He remained in Holland and fought against the Duke of York's invasion of 1799 at Bergen and Castricum.

In 1806 he was made the colonel-general of the Dutch cavalry, and then sent to defend the Netherlands East Indies in the following year, until replaced by Governor Jansen in 1811.

Surprisingly, he managed to evade British patrols and reached Europe again in time to command the Baden and Hessian units in IX Corps during the Russian campaign of 1812, serving at the Berezina. Retreating to Modlin in Poland, he was given the position of governor and was besieged until December.

Discharged from French service after Napoleon's first abdication in 1814, he joined the new Kingdom of the Netherlands, serving on the army staff during the Waterloo campaign.

5. OTHER RANKS

Unlike other states within Napoleon's empire, the Dutch Government did not institute any form of conscription. Only when Louis abdicated and the Netherlands were incorporated into metropolitan France did this happen, and the 'blood tax' was only one reason for the revolt in favour of the House of Orange in 1813.

In order to keep units up to some standard of establishment, it was decided that fit and healthy male orphans and others being raised by the state were to receive military training when they reached fourteen with the intention of joining an active unit at eighteen.

One advantage that the Dutch did have, of course, was that they had some immunity to the fevers then prevalent in their coastal provinces. This secret weapon was to be decisive in the Walcheren campaign of 1809.

6. THE MILITARY ESTABLISHMENT

Organization

1803 INFANTRY		
7 line demi-brigades of 2,347 officers and men	Each of 3 battalions of 780 officers and men	Each battalion had one grenadier (65 officers and men) and eight fusilier companies (89 officers and men)
4 Jäger battalions		Each battalion had one carabinier and eight jäger companies, as above.
3 Foreign units	2 battalions each	As line infantry
CAVALRY		
2 Light Dragoon regiments (ex-Heavy Cavalry); 650 officers and men		Each of 4 squadrons of 160 officers and men
1 Dragoon regiment		As above
1 Hussar regiment		As above
ARTILLERY		
Horse and foot batteries		8 pieces in foot units and 6 in horse companies
Later 1803		
The 7 line demi-brigades became 21 independent battalions		Each battalion had one grenadier and eight fusilier companies
1805 INFANTRY		
Guard grenadiers	1 battalion	Formed from the grenadier company of the third battalion of each line regiment

1805 **INFANTRY (Cont.)**		
8 Line regiments	Each of 3 battalions	1st and 2nd battalions had 1 grenadier company and 6 fusilier companies. The 3rd battalion only had 6 fusilier companies
2 Chasseur regiments	Each of 2 battalions	Each battalion had 1 carabinier and 6 chasseur companies
2 Foreign regiments	Each of 2 battalions	As line regiments
CAVALRY		
Dragoons of the Guard (became Horse Grenadiers in 1806 and disbanded 1807)		1 regiment of 2 squadrons
Hussars of the Guard		1 regiment of 4 squadrons
2 Dragoon regiments (2nd Light Dragoons disbanded and 1st re-named)		Each of 4 squadrons
1 Hussar regiment		1 regiment of 3 squadrons
ARTILLERY		
4 Foot artillery 'battalions' and 1 Horse artillery company		Each battalion appears to have consisted of only one company. Companies seemed only to have had 4 guns
1809 **INFANTRY**		
Grenadiers of the Guard (ranked as 1st Regiment)	2 battalions	Each of 4 companies
Jägers of the Guard (ex 1st Chasseurs, but still ranked as 1st) Disbanded 1808	2 battalions	Each of 4 companies

1809 **INFANTRY (Cont.)**		
8 Line regiments (numbered 2 to 9)	Each of 3 battalions	Assumed 1 grenadier, 1 voltigeur and 4 fusilier companies
1 Chasseur regiment (numbered 2nd Chasseurs until the Guard Jägers were disbanded then 1st)	2 battalions	Assumed 1 carabinier, 1 voltigeur and 4 chasseur companies
CAVALRY		
Guard Horse Regiment	Comprised both hussars and kuirassiers!	Number of squadrons unknown
2nd Kuirassiers (formed from 2nd Dragoons		3 squadrons
2 Hussar regiments (3rd formed from 1st Dragoons)		3 squadrons each
ARTILLERY		
4 Foot artillery 'battalions' and 1 Horse artillery company		As above

When the Dutch Army was absorbed into the French Army, the Guard Grenadiers were used to form the 3rd Grenadiers à Pied, and the 3rd Hussars and Guard Horse Regiment became the 2nd Chevau-léger Lanciers of the Guard.

The 4th Infantry formed the Régiment Isle de Walcheren, later the 131 Ligne, whilst the other seven regiments were reformed into the 123 to 126 Ligne. The Chasseur regiment became the 33 Léger.

The 2nd Kuirassier was used to form the 14 Cuirassier, and the 2nd Hussars formed the 11th (French) Hussars.

The foot artillery became the 9th Artillery Regiment. It had been thought to use the horse artillery to form a new 7th Regiment, but in the event the two companies were assigned to the 1st instead.

6. UNIFORMS

i) to 1806

INFANTRY

There was strong French influence in the Dutch uniform. In 1803 the line units wore a bicorne, dark blue tunic with demi-brigade facings at the collar, lapels, cuffs and cuff flaps, white breeches and black gaiters. Turnbacks to the skirts were red for the 1st, 4th and Sachsen-Gotha, white for the 2nd, 3rd and 6th, and yellow for the 5th, 7th and Waldeck.

The chasseurs also wore a bicorne, and their tunic colour was dark green (including the turnbacks and lapels) with individual unit facings for the collar, cuffs, cuff flaps and turnback piping.

Facing Colours

1st: Red
2nd: Crimson
3rd: White
4th: White; collar red piped white
5th: Yellow
6th: Light blue
7th: Yellow
Waldeck: Yellow
Sachsen-Gotha: Red
1st Chasseur Bn: Red
2nd Chasseur Bn: Black; lapels black
3rd Chasseur Bn: Black
4th Chasseur Bn: Crimson

When the demi-brigades were re-organized, the individual battalion distinctions became:

UNIT	COLLAR	CUFFS & LAPELS	CUFF FLAPS	TURNBACKS
1	Red, white piping	Red	Red	Red
2	Dark blue, white piping	Red	Dark blue	Red
3	White, red piping 1804: light blue, piped red	Red 1804: Light blue	White 1804: Light blue	Red
4	Crimson, white piping	Crimson	Crimson	White
5	White, crimson piping 1804: crimson, piped white	Crimson	White 1804: crimson	White

UNIT	COLLAR	CUFFS & LAPELS	CUFF FLAPS	TURNBACKS
6	Dark blue, white piping 1804: buff	Crimson 1804: pink	Dark blue 1804: buff	White
7	White, white piping	White	White	White
8	Dark blue, white piping 1804: red, piped red	White 1804: red	Dark blue	White
9	Red, white piping	White	Red	White
10	Red, white piping 1804: yellow, piped white	White 1804: yellow	Red	Red 1804: white
11	Dark blue, piped white 1804: yellow, no piping	White 1804: yellow	Dark blue	Red
12	White, piped red 1804: orange, no piping	White 1804: orange	White	Red 1804: orange
13	Light blue, piped white	Light blue	Light blue	Light blue
14	Dark blue, piped white 1804: light blue, piped light blue	Light blue	Dark blue 1804: light blue	Light blue
15	White, piped light blue	Light blue	White 1804: light blue	Light blue
16	Light blue, piped white	Light blue	Light blue	White
17	Dark blue, piped white 1804: light blue, piped white	Light blue	Dark blue 1804: light blue	White
18	Red, piped white	Light blue	Red 1804: light blue	White
19	Yellow, piped white 1804: yellow, piped yellow	Yellow	Yellow	Yellow
20	Red, piped white	Yellow	Red	Yellow
21	Dark blue, piped white	Yellow	Dark blue	Yellow

When the two chasseur regiments were formed in 1805, the 1st Regiment took yellow facings and the 2nd light blue.

CAVALRY

The Light Dragoon regiments wore a Tarleton-style helmet with black fur crest, red turban and white plume. The tunic was white with black facing for the 1st Regiment and light blue for the 2nd. Facings were carried at the collar, lapels, cuffs and turnbacks. Overalls were grey, and the saddle furniture was crimson edged white for the 1st and yellow edged white for the 2nd Regiment.

The dragoon regiment wore a black bicorne. Their coat was dark blue with pink cuffs, collar, lapels, epaulettes and turnbacks. Breeches were white with high boots, and the saddle furniture was dark blue edged white.

The Tarleton helmets of the light dragoons and the bicornes of the dragoons were replaced by brass dragoon helmets about 1805.

The hussar regiment had shakos, a blue dolman with red collar and cuffs, red breeches and a crimson and white sash. If they wore a pelisse it was possibly white with black fur edging and yellow lace.

ARTILLERY

Both horse and foot units wore a bicorne. The foot units had an infantry tunic of dark blue faced red, whilst the horse had a long-tailed, dragoon-style coat with red facings at the collar cuffs and turnbacks only. Breeches were buff leather.

ii) from 1806

INFANTRY

With the formation of the Kingdom of Holland, the army underwent substantial uniform changes.

The Guard: Both the grenadiers and the jägers wore a black bearskin bonnet without a front plate. The cords were white, and the red top patch had a white grenade for both units. The plume was red for the grenadiers and red-tipped green for the jägers.

The long-tailed coat was white with crimson facings for the collar, cuffs, lapels and turnbacks. The epaulettes were red for the grenadier battalion and yellow-fringed green for the jägers. Epaulettes, etc. were gold for officers. Breeches were white.

Line Infantry: The basic uniform colour was now white, with different facings for each regiment carried at the collar, cuffs, lapels, turnbacks, and the edging to the fusilier's shoulder straps. Facings were:

2nd light blue
3rd red
4th pink
5th dark green
6th grass-green
7th yellow
8th light violet
9th black

The grenadier companies wore black bearskins with a red plume, cords and top patch, with a white cross. The bearskin had a brass front plate, and the epaulettes were red. Voltigeur companies wore a black shako with green flounders and a green side plume. There was a large regimental number on the front. Epaulettes were yellow with green fringes.

The fusiliers also wore a shako with the regimental number on the front. The side pom-pon was in the regimental facing colour.

The breeches white, with short black gaiters

Light Infantry: The uniform coats were dark green with regimental facings at the collar, cuffs and lapel and shoulder-strap piping. The facing colours were light blue for the 2nd Jägers and yellow for the 3rd. Breeches were green.

The carabinier companies wore a bearskin with red plume, flounders and epaulettes, the voltigeurs a shako with a green side plume and yellow epaulettes with green fringes. The jäger companies also wore a shako with a facing colour pom-pon at the side.

CAVALRY

The Guard: The Dragoons of the Guard were almost a mounted version of the Grenadiers. Their headgear was the bearskin with red plumes and cords, white coat with crimson facings, and high boots. When it merged with the Hussars it adopted a French cuirassier helmet, but not the cuirass itself. The shabraque was crimson.

The Hussars of the Guard wore a black busby with red bag and white plume, a scarlet dolman with yellow braid, and a white pelisse with black fur trim and yellow braid. The shabraque was dark blue with yellow edging. When it merged to form the Guard Cavalry, it adopted a crimson shabraque.

Line Cavalry: The 2nd Kuirassiers wore a French cuirassier helmet with a red plume. The coat was white with light blue facings and red epaulettes. The breeches were white. The shabraque was sky blue with yellow edging.

The 2nd Hussars wore a black shako with the regimental number in brass on the front. The plume was black. The dolman and breeches were dark blue and the pelisse was white with black fur edging. Braid was yellow. The 3rd Hussars also wore the shako, but the dolman was now light blue, although the pelisse and braiding were the same as the 2nd. The shabraque was dark blue edged yellow for the 2nd and light blue edged yellow for the 3rd.

ARTILLERY

The foot companies wore infantry style uniforms, including the side plumed shako. The coat and breeches were dark blue, as were the lapels. The collar, cuffs turnbacks and epaulettes were red.

Each company had a different coloured shako pom-pon. The 1st (Guards) was red, the 2nd was white, the 3rd light blue and the 4th yellow.

The horse companies wore a hussar-style uniform. The shako had a red top band, cords and plume. The dolman, pelisse and breeches were dark blue, and the braid was red.

7. BATTLE HISTORY

(Roman numerals indicate original Corps affiliation; these often changed during the campaign.)

1805
Not present at any significant actions

1806–1807
F Friedland, 14 June 1807

H Capitulation of Hameln, 7–22 November 1806
S Blockade of Stralsund, 15 January–20 August 1807

Spain
Al Almonacíd, 11 August 1809
Cu Cuidad Real, 27 March 1809
MI Mesa de Ibor, 17 March 1809
O Ocaña, 18–19 November 1809
T Talavera, 27–28 July 1809
Z Zornoza, 30 October 1808

1809
Sh Schill's Revolt – storm of Stralsund, 31 May 1809

UNIT	1805	1806–07	SPAIN	1809
Dragoons of the Guard				
Hussars of the Guard/ 1st Kuirassiers				
2nd Dragoons/2nd Cavalry/2nd Kuirassiers		VIII: F		X: Sh
2nd Hussars		VIII: F		
3rd Hussars	VIII (as 1st Dragoons)	VIII: H, S	Cu, T, Al, O	
Grenadiers/Jägers of the Guard				
2nd Line	VIII (as 1st)	VIII: H, S	1st Bn only: Z, MI, T, Al, O	
3rd Line	VIII (as 2nd)	VIII: H, S		
4th Line		VIII: H, S	2nd Bn only: Z, MI, T, Al, O	
5th Line		VIII: S		
6th Line		VIII: S		X: Sh
7th Line	VIII (as 6th)	VIII: H, S		X:

UNIT	1805	1806–07	SPAIN	1809
8th Line		VIII: H		X:
9th Line	VIII (as 8th)	VIII: S		X: Sh
1st Waldeck	VIII			
2nd Waldeck	VIII			
Sachsen-Gotha				
2nd Jägers	VIII (as 1st)	VIII: H		
3rd Jägers		VIII: H, S		

7. TACTICS

Napoleon expected to use the Dutch forces to operate as part of the Grand Armée. The fact that they were organized as French units helped. However, except for the 1805 campaign, when Dumonceau's division formed part of one of the main corps, they tended to be used in supplementary roles. Even the units deployed to Spain were only a tithe of the army. One assumes that they were put into the German Division to avoid brigading them with French units, rather than to provide some stiffening for inexperienced German ones.

Those regiments that formed part of X Corps in Saxony and Westphalia in 1809 did not distinguish themselves. Whether it was because of food shortages or slack discipline, the local population hated the Dutch division for their looting and pillaging.

There is, in fact, little to show that the Dutch Army was anything other than a good stolid fighting force. If there was little enthusiasm for Imperial adventuring, that can hardly be blamed on the men in the ranks.

CHAPTER 8

The Army of the Kingdom of Italy, 1804–14

1. BACKGROUND

THE KINGDOM, FORMED in 1805, from Lombardy and the old Cisalpine and Cispadane Republics, was expanded at the end of the year, as a result of the Treaty of Pressburg, by the addition of the Venetian Republic, together with the southern-most part of the Tyrol. Napleon established Eugène de Beauharnais, Josephine's son, as Viceroy and Eugène's first priority was the reorganization of the army. Following the Viceroy's appointment, the structure of the army was, on 1 March 1805:[1]

Guardia del Presidente (President's Guard) – Infantry, Cavalry and Artillery
Fanteria di Linea (Line Infantry) – five regiments
Fanteria Leggera (Light Infantry) – two regiments
Legione Italiano (an Infantry formation which would become an auxiliary regiment)
Cacciatori a Cavallo (Chasseurs à cheval) – one regiment
Hussars – two regiments (later converted to Dragoons)
An artillery corps
A corps of engineers
Gendarmeria nazionale – two regiments

[1] Memoranda of Army States in the *Archives Nationales* in Paris.

Invalidi e veterani – one battalion
A battalion of naval gunners.
There were also some Polish troops in the Italian service: one infantry and one cavalry regiment, these passed into Neapolitan service in 1806.

The Presidential Guard, which was taken into the army (see below) and French regiments stationed in the area who were busily recruiting, came to contain substantial numbers of Italian recruits, however they were still part of the French Army.

Before 1805 was out, the following units had been added:

Royal Guard:
- Corps of Royal Guard of Honour (*Guardia Reale d'Onore*) cavalry – 4 companies
- Corps of Royal Guard Vélites (*Veliti reale*) 3 battalions – 12 companies
- Corps of *Guardia di linea*, comprising:
  - Infantry regiment of 'Line Guard' with a Guard Grenadier (*Granatieri a Piedi)* battalion and a Guard Chasseur (*Cacciatori a Piedi)* battalion.
  - one mounted Dragoon regiment (*Dragoni della Guardia Reale*)
  - one company of Guard horse artillery
  - one battalion of *Cacciatori de Brescia* (October 1805).

NOTE: The guard units (except the *Guardia Reale d'Onore* and the *Veliti reale*) were all formed from the Presidential Guard.

2. ORGANIZATION

i) The Guard

In 1806, the Royal Guard added a 5th company of *Guardia Reale d'Onore* the (*Compagnia de Venezia*), a company of marines (*marini*) and a company of Artillery Train. Then, in 1808, a sub-division of the *Gendarmeria Scelta* was re-attached to the Guard Dragoon regiment.

At the end of 1808, the Italian Royal Guard was organized as follows:

THE GUARD

INF. REGT	BNS	CO./BN	MEN/CO.	CAVALRY	SQNS/COS	MEN/SQN
Guardia de linea	1 (Granatieri)	5	105	Dragoni	2 Sq. (each 2 Cos)	104/Co.
	1 (Cacciatori)	5	105	G.R. d'On.	5 Cos	108/Co.
Veliti	3	5	120	Gend. Scelta	1 Co.	43
Marini		1	60			
ARTILLERY	**SQNS**	**COS**	**GUNS PER CO.**			
HORSE	–	1	No certain data but probably 8 x 6pdr (Austrian) pieces			
FOOT	–	1	No certain data but probably 8 x 6pdr (Austrian) pieces			

The three Veliti were effectively junior units to the two main guard infantry regiments, one being grenadiers and the two others cacciatori (later, in 1810, called *carabinieri*).

In 1810, there was a reduction in the veliti to two battalions (one of granatieri and one of carabinieri). In the Guardia de linea regiment, the Cacciatori became known, as in the French Army, as Carabinieri. A regiment of two battalions of Conscripts of the Guard (*Conscriti*) were raised in 1810.

Also in 1810, regimental artillery companies, with train, (having the same composition as in the line infantry) were organized for the Vélites, the *Guardia di linea* and the Conscriti.

In 1811, there was a reorganization of the marini of the Guard so that it then formed a crew (of 152 men) and organization of a company of foot artillery (100 men).

After the Russian campaign, in January 1813, the Guard Infantry Regiment took the name *Granatieri della Guardia*, and comprised two battalions, and the Conscriti became the *Cacciatori della Guardia* (also with two battalions). In March of the same year, the Cacciatori was increased to four battalions. Also at the beginning of 1813, the *Guardia d'Onore* was reduced to a single company.

ii) The Line & Light Infantry:

The line and light infantry were organized as in the following table:

ITALIAN INFANTRY 1805

APPROXIMATE PAPER STRENGTHS	LINEA	LEGGERA
NO. OF REGTS	5	2
BNS/REGT	2	2
COS/BN	Fusilier (*Fuciliere*) – 8 Grenadier (*Granatiere*) – 1 Voltigeur (*Volteggiatore*) – 1	Chasseur (*Cacciatore*) – 8 Carabinier (*Carabiniere*) – 1 Voltigeur (*Volteggiatore*) – 1
MEN/CO.	Grenadier 83 Fusilier/ Voltigeur 123	Carabinier 83 Chasseurs/ Voltigeur 123

The following infantry units were created in 1806 :

Royal Istrian Battalion (*Battaglione Reale del 'Istria*) (738 men)
1st Dalmation Battalion (738 men)
2nd Dalmation Battalion – attached to the *Marini* (738 men)
The Royal Dalmation Legion (*Legione Reale di Dalmata)*

In the same year:

A second battalion was added to the *Cacciatori di Brescia* Regiment, which then took the title *Cacciatori Reale di Brescia.*
The Italian Legion (organized in 1803) became the 'Auxilliary Regiment' (Reggimento Ausiliario of two battalions) and was then re-titled 6th regiment of the line (July 1806).
All line and light regiments added a third battalion.

APPROXIMATE PAPER STRENGTHS 1806	LINEA	LEGGERA
NO OF REGTS	5	2
BNS/REGT	3	3
COS/BN	Fusilier (*Fuciliere*) – 7 Grenadier (*Granatiere*) – 1 Voltigeur (*Volteggiatore*) – 1	Chasseur (*Cacciatore*) – 7 Carabinier (*Carabiniere*) – 1 Voltigeur (*Volteggiatore*) – 1
MEN/CO.	Fusiliers 83 Grenadiers/ Voltigeurs 104	Chasseurs 83 Carabiniers/ Voltigeurs 104

In July 1807, the *Cacciatori Reale di Brescia* became the 3rd Light Infantry Regiment.

The next major events were in 1808, with the addition of a seventh line regiment (from ex-Papal troops) and the change to the French establishment of five battalions (four field and one depot). The field battalions were composed of six companies, including two '*élite*' companies (*granatieri* and *volteggiatori* for the line, *carabinieri* and *volteggiatori* for the light infantry). The Royal Dalmatian Regiment was formed out of the 1st and 2nd battalions of the Dalmatian Legion, whilst the City of Venice Guard Regiment (eight companies and one of gunners) was raised to perform a militia-style defence for its locality.

APPROXIMATE PAPER STRENGTHS 1808	LINEA	LEGGERA
NO OF REGTS	7	3
BNS/REGT	4 +1 depot	4 +1 depot
COS/BN	Fusilier (*Fuciliere*) – 4 Grenadier (*Granatiere*) – 1 Voltigeur (*Volteggiatore*) – 1	Chasseur (*Cacciatore*) – 4 Carabinier (*Carabiniere*) – 1 Voltigeur (*Volteggiatore*) – 1
MEN/CO.	140	140

1809 saw the Istrian Battalion disbanded and its men distributed among the 1st and 2nd light regiments.

In 1810 the *Battaglione Coloniale*, of 600 men, was formed around some malcontents of the 6th line regiment and it was installed as garrison of Elba; regimental artillery was added to all line and light units. There were now seven line and three light regiments, plus the Royal Dalmatian Regiment. The Venice Guard battalion was split and became a two-battalion regiment with a regimental artillery company.

During 1811 the following new formations were raised:

1) A fourth light infantry regiment of five battalions and one artillery company was formed.
2) The Milan National Guard (*Battaglione Guardia alla Città di Milano)* of six companies, of which two were élite, plus one independent company of 'sappers and firefighters of Milan'.
3) A regiment of veterans and invalids (*Reggimento Veterani e Invalidi*) bringing the army and navy veteran units together. This unit comprised one battalion of veterans and one of invalids. These had grown to two battalions of veterans (six companies each) and one of invalids of four companies.
4) Finally that year, each 'departement' raised a company of reserve or militia troops for local defence. These varied in

strength from 120 to 240 men; they were not officially part of the army.

In 1813, the *Battaglione Coloniale* became a regiment of two battalions and, at the end of 1813, a rifle-armed Volunteer Jäger Battalion (*Battaglione Bersaglieri Volontari*) was formed from forest rangers who were already skilled in the use of the weapon. Its strength was of four 120-man companies.

Some volunteer battalions were raised in Milan and Bologna to be formed, in 1814 into the Volunteer Regiments Nos 1 and 2.

iii) The Line Cavalry

The original hussars were converted to dragoons (1st Hussars became *Dragoni della Regina* on 3 July 1805 and 2nd Hussars became *Dragoni Napoleone* on 5 February), and the *Cacciatori a Cavallo* became *Cacciatori Reale Italiano*. The cavalry organization was thus constituted as under:

ITALIAN CAVALRY 1805

APPROXIMATE PAPER STRENGTHS	DRAGONI	CACCIATORI A CAVALLO
NO. OF REGTS	2: 'Regina' & 'Napoleone'	1: 'Reale Italiano'
SQNS/REGT	4	4
COS/SQN	2	2
MEN/CO.	116	116

A depot squadron of two companies, each containing 27 men was formed in 1806 for each regiment.

In 1808, a second regiment of *Cacciatori* was formed ('*Reale Principe*'). In 1808, a second regiment of *Cacciatori* was formed ('*Principe Reale*'), then, in September 1810, *Reale Italiano* became 1st *Cacciatori* and the *Principe Reale* became 2nd *Cacciatori* ; a third regiment being raised later the same year, apparently not being named.

ITALIAN CAVALRY SEPTEMBER 1810

APPROXIMATE PAPER STRENGTHS	DRAGONI	CACCIATORI A CAVALLO
NO. OF REGTS	2: 'Regina' & 'Napoleone'	3 Rgts Nos. 1, 2 & 3
SQNS/REGT	4 (+depot Co.)	4 (+depot Co.)
COS/SQN	2	2
MEN/CO.	132 (depot 21)	132 (depot 21)

1811 saw the formation of the 4th *Cacciatori a Cavallo* then, in 1812, of the 'General Depot' of *Cacciatori a Cavallo* which comprised the depot companies.

There was one other body which has not been dealt with, that of the '*Gendarmeria Legione*', which was initially composed of two regiments (two squadrons of three companies apiece). It had increased to three legions by 1808, each of which comprised two squadrons of four companies.

iv) The Line Artillery and Engineers

ITALIAN ARTILLERY END 1805

APPROXIMATE PAPER STRENGTHS	ARTIGLIERIA A PIEDI	ARTIGLIERIA A CAVALLO
NO. OF REGTS	1	1
BNS/REGT	2	2
COS (BATTERIES) /BN	10	10
GUNS/CO.	6 x 8pdr + 2 x 6" howitzers (or 6 x 12pdr + 2 x 8" howitzers)	6 x 4pdr (sometimes + 2 howitzers)

There were two companies of gunners and four of train included in the above organization, together with mechanics and pontonniers. In addition, there was a company of miners and a battalion of sappers.

In 1806, the regiment of artillery, mechanics and pontonniers formed a single regiment composed of two battalions of ten companies, each of 100 men. In each battalion there were two companies of specialists (mechanics, armourers, pontonniers, etc.).

In November 1806, the miners and sappers formed the Battalion of Sappers (six companies of 100 men, of which the 1st was an élite company of miners).

The depot company of the *Artiglieria a Piedi* was formed in 1807 as was a detachment of the engineer train which was placed in the service of the battalion of sappers.

In 1808, the *Artiglieria a Piedi* comprised twenty-three companies, including the depot company, thus now totalling two battalions each of eleven companies, plus the depot.

July 1810 saw the formation of seven companies of coast guard gunners (with an eighth added in 1813). The battalion of sappers increased to nine companies each of 100 men.

ITALIAN ARTILLERY 1811

APPROXIMATE PAPER STRENGTHS	ARTIGLERIA A PIEDI	ARTIGLERIA A CAVALLO
NO OF REGTS	1	1
BNS/REGT	3	1
COS (BATTERIES) /BN	11	6
GUNS/CO.	Various	Various

In addition, there was a single train battalion of eight companies.

In 1812, the train was organized as two battalions, each of six companies, and a depot company. The engineer train was now a company of 128 men.

3. UNIFORMS

THE GUARD

Guard uniforms were basically similar to the line (see below), except that the infantry grenadiers and carabiniers had bearskins. Grenadier and carabinier collars, cuffs and turnbacks were scarlet, lapels and grenadier cuff-flaps were white; pockets were piped scarlet. The epaulettes of the grenadiers were scarlet, whilst those of the carabiniers were green straps with scarlet fringes. Breeches and waistcoats for both were white.

Vélites wore bearskins and their coats were white with grass-green facings, piped white (except turnbacks) and worn on lapels, collar, turnbacks, cuffs and cuff flaps. The only differences between the grenadier and carabinier battalions were the epaulettes which followed the parent regiments, en-pointe pockets, lapels and cuffs for the carabiniers, and the turnback insignia (a grenade and hunting horn respectively).

Conscripts had line-type shakos. Coats were light infantry style, dark green with white-piped lapels, cuffs and turnbacks. Collars, and cuff flaps were scarlet, piped white.

From 1811, marines sported a black 'top hat' with curled brim and a square white-metal lozenge plate to the front. Breeches and coats were dark green with scarlet collars and cuffs. The turnbacks were green, piped scarlet. Prior to 1811, the same uniform as the French Sailors of the Guard was worn but with green in place of blue and white in place of yellow.

Guard dragoons although organized first, were attired very similarly to those of the French (and Italian) line dragoons except that the helmet 'turban' was of leopard skin. The dark green coat collar, white lapels and green cuffs and turnbacks were not piped and breeches were white.

Before 1810 the distinctive colours of the four (later five) Guards of Honour companies were:

Milan – red coat and blue facings

Brescia – white coat and blue facings

Bologna – blue coat and red facings

Romagna – green coat and red facings

Venice (1806) – green coat and orange facings

From 1810, they took French-style carabinier helmets with black crests. Coats were dark green and waistcoats and breeches were white. Each company wore its new facings on collar, cuffs, turnbacks and cuff-flap piping, as follows:

Milan – Pink

Brescia – Buff

Bologna – Yellow

Romagna – Scarlet

Venice – Orange

Gendarmes were almost indistinguishable from their French equivalents. Even the coat was dark blue and the breeches were buff. Facings (lapels, collar, cuffs, turnbacks and cuff-flap piping) were crimson. The headgear was a black bearskin. In 1813, the uniform became green.

Guard Horse Artillery was uniformed like the French Garde Impériale, with hussar-type clothing. The foot artillery wore the bearskin of the grenadiers but without the plate, the coat was green, with black distinctives, lapels, epaulettes and turnbacks were red.

The train was like that of the line but with grass green aiguillettes on the right epaulette.

LINE INFANTRY

Until 1807, Line Infantry uniforms were similar to the French but were dark green where the French were blue, and regimental facing colours were worn. In 1807, the main colour changed to white. Bicornes were worn until 1808 when the regiments were equipped with shakos (bearskins for the grenadiers, which disappeared in 1812).

The facings and locations were as shown on p. 214 (the colour after the oblique stroke is the piping colour).

LINE INFANTRY

UNIT	1812 COAT PIPING	FACING COLOURS					
		COLLAR	CUFFS	CUFF FLAPS	TURNBACKS	POCKETS	LAPELS
1st Regt	Green	Green	White/Green	Scarlet	White/Green	White/Green	White/Green
2nd Regt	Scarlet	White/Scarlet	White/Scarlet	Green	White/Scarlet	White/Scarlet	Scarlet
3rd Regt	Green	Scarlet/Green	Green	Scarlet	White/Green	White/Green	Green
4th Regt	Scarlet	Scarlet	White/Scarlet	Green	White/Scarlet	White/Scarlet	White/Scarlet
5th Regt	Green	Green	Scarlet/Green	Green	White/Green	White/Green	Scarlet/Green
6th Regt	Scarlet	White/Scarlet	White/Scarlet	Scarlet	White/Scarlet	White/Scarlet	Green/Scarlet
7th Regt	Green	Scarlet	Green	Green	White/Green	White/Green	Scarlet

Volteggiatore shako plumes were green, yellow, green tipped yellow or yellow tipped green. On campaign, a carrot-shaped tuft was worn in either green or yellow.

LIGHT INFANTRY

Light regiments wore the dark green uniform throughout their existence and had dark green breeches and waistcoats (except for 1st Regiment, which were yellow, piped green) – again, matching the French but with green instead of blue. The facing colours were used on collar and cuffs, and as piping to the waistcoats, lapels, turnbacks and pockets.

The Bersaglieri and Dalmatian (4th) regiments wore the 'Corsican' hat (left side of brim turned up).

Facing colours were as follows:

1st Regiment	Dark Yellow
2nd Regiment	Scarlet
3rd Regiment	Orange
4th Regiment	Light Claret
Bersaglieri	Dark green breeches & 'Spencer' coat with mid-green facings on collar, cuffs, lapels & turnbacks; lapels & cuffs piped dark Green; pockets & shoulder straps piped mid-green.

LINE DRAGONI

French-style dragoon helmets with black horsehair tail and turban, except for the first company of the first squadron, which had bearskin bonnets. Coats were similar to the French Dragoon style, with facing colours on lapels, collar, cuffs and turnbacks: pink for the Regina Regiment and deep crimson for the Napoleone Regiment. Breeches were white. Whilst on campaign in the Peninsular War, the 2nd Regiment wore dark brown coats with claret facings. This was by force of necessity, since the Spanish *guerrilla* attacks on French supply lines prevented the arrival of replacement uniforms. The ersatz replacements were produced locally.

LINE CACCIATORI A CAVALLO

The 1st Regiment wore the czapka until 1806, when it was replaced with a shako. The 2nd and 4th regiments wore the shako, with elite companies wearing hussar colpacks, bagged in the facing colour and piped white (1st Regt) or green (2nd & 4th Regts). All of the 3rd regiment's squadrons wore the colpack but without bags.

Coats for 1st & 2nd regiments were of the '*surtout*' style in dark green, with facing colour on the collar, cuffs, turnbacks and pocket piping. The 3rd and 4th regiments had a 'kinski' jacket which was like the surtout but with shorter tails. The other regiments adopted this style in 1812. The 3rd Regiment's élite company had a full hussar-style uniform, which practice extended to the other regiments in 1814. Dark green was always the breeches, waistcoat and coat colour and facing colours were as follows:

1st Regiment	Deep yellow
2nd Regiment	Scarlet
3rd Regiment	Bright orange
4th Regiment	Claret

GENDARMERIA LEGIONE

Bicorne hat with white lace and tassels, dark green habit-veste coat faced crimson, buff breeches.

FOOT ARTILLERY

Black bicorne until 1808, when it was replaced by a shako without a peak and bearing a scarlet carrot tuft. A standard shako was supposed to replace the peakless version in 1812 but there are drawings of the peakless version still being worn after that year. Breeches and coats were the national dark green with black lapels, scarlet piped collar, scarlet cuffs, cuff flaps and turnbacks. Black over-knee gaiters were worn.

HORSE ARTILLERY

Until 1811, the czapka (black) was worn, with a scarlet plume (later black, tipped with green) for dress or carrot tuft. The peakless shako replaced the czapka in 1811 and, later the standard shako was adopted.

A dark green hussar-style dolman was worn until 1806, with scarlet collar, cuffs and breast lace. In 1806, this gave way to a cavalry-style habit-veste jacket with black collar and cuffs, the latter piped scarlet, scarlet turnbacks and breast lace. Breeches and waistcoats were dark green.

ARTILLERY TRAIN

Headgear as for the Horse artillery. Jackets were mid-grey with light green collar, cuffs and turnbacks which colour was also used on the breast lace. Waistcoats were mid-grey and breeches buff.

4. ENGAGEMENTS

Italian Guard Regiments

Unit	Raised	Engagements* (with at least 1 Bn present) in approx. date order
Grenadieri	1805	Soave,[1] Castelcerino, R. Piave, Raab, Wagram, Malojaroslavetz, San Marco e Volano, St Marein, Weichselburg
Carabinieri	1805	Soave, Castelcerino, R. Piave, Raab, Wagram, Malojaroslavetz, San Marco e Volano, Feistritz/ Rosenthal, St Marein, Weichselburg, Tchernütz, San Marco e Volano
Veliti	1805	El Bruch, **Mataro, Gerona,** (Soave?, Castelcerino?), R. Piave, Raab, Wagram, Malojaroslavetz, San Marco e Volano
Marini	1805	(Soave?, Castelcerino?)
Cacc. di Brescia	1805	Became 3rd Leggera in 1807 – q.v.
Conscriti	1810	Malojaroslavetz
Dragoni	1805	R. Piave, Raab, Wagram, Moskowa, Malojaroslavetz
Gend. Scelta	1808	R. Piave, Raab, Wagram, Malojaroslavetz

* Bold type indicates a city defence or siege (in which the unit either defended or laid siege).

[1] Smith, D., (*The Greenhill Napoleonic Wars Data Book* Greenhill, 1998, p. 295) simply says that 3 Bns of the Italian Guard were present; we have arbitrarily assumed the three shown, but it could have included a vélite battalion plus any two of the three we indicate. This applies equally to Castelcerino. It should be borne in mind that elements (probably 1 Bn each) of all three regiments were also in Spain.

Italian Line Infantry Regiments

Regiment	Raised	Engagements* (with at least 1 Bn present) in approx. date order
1st	1805	**Colberg, Stralsund**, Sacile,[1] Soave, Castelcerino, Tarvis, Raab, Königswartha, Dennewitz, Wartenburg, Leipzig, Lippa, Tchernütz, Reggio, R. Taro
2nd	1805	**Mataro, Gerona**, Soave, Castelcerino, Tarvis, Raab, **Sta. Maura**, Pla,[2] Malojaroslavetz, Bautzen, Katzbach, Jelsane, Tchernütz, Peschiera
3rd	1805	Tarvis, Raab, Malojaroslavetz, Jelsane, Tchernütz, Peschiera
4th	1805	**Colberg, Stralsund, Mataro, Gerona, Rosas**, Cardadeu, Molins de Rey, Igualada, Valls, Klagenfurt, Raab, **Hostalrich, Tortosa**, Pla, **Tarragona, Saguntum,**[3] **Valencia**, San Pelayo, **Castro Urdiales**, Tolosa, R. Nivelle, Lützen,[4] Königswartha, Gross-Beeren, Dennewitz, Wartenburg, Leipzig, R. Mincio, Parma
5th	1805	**Mataro, Gerona, Rosas**, Cardadeu, Molins de Rey, Granollers, Mollet, Sta. Parpetua, **Hostalrich, Tortosa,** Pla, **Tarragona, Saguntum, Valencia,** Bautzen, Katzbach, Dohna, Leipzig, Hanau, R. Mincio, Parma
6th	1805	**Rosas**, Cardadeu, Molins de Rey, Igualada, Valls, **Hostalrich, Tortosa, Tarragona, Saguntum, Valencia,** San Pelayo, **Castro Urdiales**, Tolosa, R. Nivelle, Lützen, Königswartha, Dennewitz, Wartenburg, Leipzig, Parma, Peschiera
7th	1808	**Rosas**, Cardadeu, Molins de Rey, Igualada, Valls, Sacile, Malghera, Raab, Pla,[5] Roda, **Tarragona**, Lützen, Königswartha, Dennewitz, Wartenburg, Leipzig, Reggio
B. G. Cittá di Milano	1811	Königswartha, Dennewitz, Wartenburg, Leipzig, Peschiera

* Bold type indicates a city defence or siege (in which the unit either defended or laid siege).

[1] Smith, D. op. cit., p. 287 says 8 Bns of 1st and 7th Line Regts were present. However, at this time, each regiment had only 3 Bns and one of the 7th Rgt was in Spain.

[2] This is Oman's name for the action which Smith, D. op. cit., p. 353 calls L'Illa.

[3] There was a simultaneous battle and siege. We can not ascertain which infantry battalions were at which.

[4] The line infantry regiments were represented by a combined battalion of their élite companies.

[5] Smith, D. op. cit., p. 353 says 8th Regt, but there were only seven. It was the 7th that was with Pino at this time.

Italian Light Infantry Regiments

Regiment	Raised	Engagements* (with at least 1 Bn present) in approx. date order
1st	1805	**Colberg, Stralsund, Rosas**, Cardadeu, Molins de Rey, Igualada, Valls, Klagenfurt, Raab, **Hostalrich, Tortosa**, Pla, Malojaroslavetz, Königswartha, Dennewitz, Wartenburg, Leipzig, Jelsane, R. Mincio
2nd	1805	**Colberg, Stralsund, Rosas**, Cardadeu, Molins de Rey, Igualada, Valls, Klagenfurt, **Hostalrich, Tortosa**, Pla, **Tarragona, Saguntum, Valencia**, San Pelayo, **Castro Urdiales**, Tolosa, R. Nivelle, Königswartha, Bautzen, Dohna, Leipzig, Lippa, Jelsane, Tchernütz, R. Mincio, Parma, Reggio
3rd	1807	Raab, Malojaroslavetz, Tersain, San Marco e Volano, Peschiera
4th	1811	Lützen, Novacco, Tersain, San Marco e Volano
Dalmatian	1806	Tarvis, **Raab**, Malojaroslavetz, Lippa, Jelsane, Tchernütz
Istrian	1808	R. Piave, Klagenfurt, Raab
Bersaglieri	1813	

* Bold type indicates a city defence or siege (in which the unit either defended or laid siege).

Italian Dragoon Regiments

Regiment	Raised	Engagements* in approx. date order
1st (Regina)	1805	**Colberg, Stralsund**, Montebello, Tavernelle, Olmo, R. Piave, Raab, Wagram, Moskowa, Malojaroslavetz, St Marein, Weichselburg
2nd (Napoleone)	1805	**Colberg, Stralsund**, Sacile,[1] Cardadeu,[2] Molins de Rey, Valls, Raab, Vich, **Tortosa, Tarragona**, Saguntum, **Valencia**, Las Rozas, San Pelayo, Lützen, Bautzen, Leipzig, Hanau, Peschiera

Italian Cacciatiori a Cavallo Regiments

Regiment	Raised	Engagements* in approx. date order
1st (Reale Italiano)	1805	**Colberg, Mataro, Gerona**, Cardadeu, Molins de Rey, Valls, Malghera, Raab, Wagram, **Tortosa**, Parma, R. Taro
2nd (Reale Principe)	1808	R. Piave, Klagenfurt, Raab, Moskowa, Malojaroslavetz
3rd	1810	Moskowa, Malojaroslavetz, Wiasma, R. Mincio, R. Taro
4th	1811	Bautzen, Jelsane, Caldiero, R. Mincio, Parma

* Bold type indicates a city defence or siege (in which the unit either defended or laid siege).

[1] Smith, D. op. cit., p. 272 shows four squadrons of Drag. Napoleone as present. At least one squadron was in Spain, so it would appear the depot squadron must have been in the field, or else that it was not the 1st Dragoons which were involved.

[2] Smith, D. op. cit., p. 272 indicates the presence of '7th Drag. Regt' under Gen. Fontana (commanding 2nd brigade, which comprised the 2nd Light & 7th Line Infantry Regts, and 2nd Dragoons, in Pino's division). There were only two Italian Dragoon Regts. and it was the 2nd that fought at Cardadeu. We believe the error could have come from Oman, Sir C. op. cit., Vol II p. 84 [footnote for Molins de Rey], where he talks about the '7th' Italian Dragoons. Oman indicates that the cavalry charged against disordered Spanish troops and captured some guns later in the battle.

5. FIGHTING METHODS

As part of the French Army, Italian regiments were expected to adopt French tactical and grand-tactical formations. Their structure was virtually identical and they can, to all intents and purposes, be considered to replicate the fighting methods of their French comrades.

6. GENERAL OFFICERS

Italian general officers do not seem to have excited the same interest with historians as do their French, British, Prussian, Austrian or even Russian counterparts. Since they fought as part of the French Army, this is probably not surprising. Notwithstanding this comparative anonymity, they fought with personal bravery and not a little success. Italian regiments were in the thick of the fiercest fighting in many of the most difficult theatres and were found in the hell hole of Zaragoza, the bitter conflicts against Spanish regiments and patriots in Catalonia and Valencia and the ice and snow of the doomed Russian campaign of 1812. As a result of this neglect, it is very difficult to locate any personal biographies.

Consequently we will limit ourselves to listing the complement for two years in the history of the Italian Army under French service, with a little data on specific officers. It should be borne in mind that the Italian generals held command ranks in the French Army. Where known, we show first names as well as surnames.

i) 1808

GÉNÉRAUX DE DIVISION

Pasquale Fiorella*	
Dabrowski*	
Giuseppe Lecchi*	
Domenico Pino*	Primero Capitane della Guardia Reale
Fillipo Severoli	

GÉNÉRAUX DE BRIGADE

Giorgio B. Bertolosy*

Antonio Bonfanti*	
G. B. Bianchi d'Adda	Spettore generale del Inghinieri
Calori	Spettore generale del Artiglieria
Luigi Campagnola	
Giuseppe Danna	
Giacomo Fontane*	
Achille Fontanelli*	Commandante di Veliti Reale
G. Francesco Julhien	
Teodoro Lechi*	Comm. di Fanteria di Linea della Guardia Reale
Luigi Mazzucchelli*	
Andrea Milosevitz	
Ottavy	
Luigi Peyri	
Pietro Polfrancheschi	Spettore generale della Gendarmeria Reale
Luigi Viani*	Commandante di Dragoni della Guardia Reale

ii) 1810

GÉNÉRAUX DE DIVISION

Antonio Bonfanti*
Pasquale Fiorella†
Achille Fontanelli§
Giuseppe Lecchi†
Domenico Pino†
Fillipo Severoli

GÉNÉRAUX DE BRIGADE

Antonio Bertoletti
Giorgio B. Bertolosy*
G. B. Bianchi d'Adda
Luigi Campagnola
Giuseppe Danna
Giacomo Fontane*
Frederico Guillaume
G. Francesco Julhien
Lafond
Teodoro Lechi*
Luigi Mazzucchelli*

Andrea Milosevitz
Giuseppe Palombini
Luigi Peyri*
Pietro Polfrancheschi
Luigi Viani*
Carlo Zucchi*

* Membre de la Légion d'Honneur
† Aigle de la Légion d'Honneur
§ Grand Officier de la Légion d'Honneur

CHAPTER 9

The Army of the Kingdom of Naples, 1804–15

1. INTRODUCTION

THE ITALY OF the eighteenth and early nineteenth century was almost as fragmented politically as Germany, but without the, sometimes, nebulous authority of the Holy Roman Empire. Whilst Austria had a substantial presence in the north, and the Papal States anchored the centre, the rest of Italy consisted of often oligarchic republics, dukedoms and kingdoms. One of the largest, that of Naples, extended from the 'heel' of Italy up to approximately Terracina on the Tyrrhenian Sea and the River Tronto on the Adriatic. The kingdom also included the island of Sicily.

In the cabinet wars of the eighteenth century, Naples had been only a pawn, exchanged as part of the general rearrangements usually made as part of the peace at the conclusion of hostilities. At one time ruled by the House of Habsburg, the kingdom passed to the Spanish Bourbons in 1735. In 1805, the reigning monarch was Ferdinand IV, the brother of Charles IV of Spain, and the husband of Maria Carolina, sister of Marie-Antoinette, the late Queen of France. With these connections it was, perhaps, not to be wondered that the Neapolitan courts had such hatred of France, even if there was an inability to do much about it.

2. BACKGROUND

Naples was a somewhat quiescent coalition partner during the 1st

Coalition (1792–97), but the arrival of Rear Admiral Horatio Nelson after his victory at the Nile in 1798 caused the country to take a more active role during the 2nd (1799–1801).

Under the command of the Austrian Karl Mack von Leiberich, the Neapolitan Army had advanced north and taken Rome in November 1798, but had then fallen back in disorder on the approach of a French army. Ferdinand and Maria Carolina fled Naples to the city of Palermo in Sicily, leaving their capital in turmoil as the mob turned their anger on those suspected of collusion with the invaders. The invaders were therefore welcomed with open arms by the middle and upper classes.

The new French administration set up the Parthenopean Republic in January 1799, but defeats in Northern Italy meant that it was cut off from support. The presence of Nelson's fleet gave control of the sea to the Allies. Eventually, Ferdinand developed a counter-revolution, which regained control of the mainland part of his kingdom but used the opportunity to wreak vengeance and wholesale retribution on all who had supported the republic.

When the war with newly Imperial France broke out afresh in 1804, Ferdinand attempted to maintain a wary friendship whilst at the same time keep in contact with the allied states. Unfortunately, the 3rd Coalition went down to disaster at Austerlitz in December 1805. With this triumph, Napoleon was able to begin the dismantling of Austrian power in Germany and North Italy, but it also gave him the opportunity to deal with the Neapolitan Bourbons whom he saw as potential troublemakers.

The Bourbons were forced to leave the mainland again for Sicily where they were protected by a British garrison and a British fleet. Napoleon then gave Naples to his eldest brother, Joseph, who was crowned King of Naples on 30 March 1806; Ferdinand took the title of King of Sicily. In 1808, however, an opportunity arose in Spain, and Joseph abdicated and the throne was then taken by Napoleon's brother-in-law, Joachim Murat. Murat was the Grande Armée's cavalry commander and one of the original Marshals of the Empire.

As might be expected, Napoleon expected King Gioacchino Napoleone to support the empire both with money and with men for the army. This Murat did, expanding the army several times over the next nine years, with units seeing service in Spain, Russia and Germany. Unlike most of the other monarchs or rulers in other parts of Napoleonic Europe, he was enthusiastic about offering troops for the various armies, as this meant that payment became a matter for the French exchequer, not the Neapolitan one.

So used was Murat to the role of king (or so ambitious was his wife Caroline, Napoleon's sister), that from 1812 onward he began intriguing with the Austrians to enter the war on the Allied side in return for keeping the throne. By the beginning of 1814, matters had reached a head, and Murat led an army north to support the Austrians against the Viceroy Eugene's Italian one, although in the event Napoleon's first abdication meant that he avoided fighting his old comrades in arms.

The Allies refused to confirm any of these arrangements and in 1815 Murat then set himself up as a guarantor of Italian independence. He hoped that this rallying call would cause Napoleon's old Italian veterans to flock to his standard whilst the Allies themselves were involved in putting down Napoleon's restoration, but even before Waterloo was fought, the Austrians had defeated Murat's invasion and he was forced to flee. Attempting to emulate the Emperor, in October 1815 Murat landed in Calabria to get back his throne, but was captured, tried and executed, the second marshal to die this way.

The Congress of Vienna re-instated the Bourbons who now took the title of rulers of the Two Sicilies. Ferdinand tried to roll back some of the liberal policies brought in by both Murat on the mainland and the British in Sicily, but his reactionary rule led to a rising in 1820.

3. COMMAND STRUCTURE

Joseph did not reign long enough to make a substantial input into modernizing or liberalizing the laws of his new kingdom, but French administrators were brought in to use their experience and to train native-born bureaucrats. Some of these often proved to be more radical and 'nationalistic' than their ministers. Even before the introduction of the Code Napoléon in 1810, Ministers were working to wrest judicial powers away from the aristocracy and to deal with other areas of feudalism still found in Neapolitan society, including such things as land reform to give the rural peasants access to agriculture, etc.

One area that did require special measures was the Neapolitan custom of banditry. The local bands often sheltered behind the nobility, but an assault on the powers of one affected the other. The use of the army to put down some of the bands showed that the state would protect itself, and it had largely been successful up to 1809.

In that year, Murat introduced conscription to keep the army up to strength. This meant that draft evaders reinforced the bandits. By 1811, much of the previous successes had been lost, especially since the British and the Sicilians saw an opportunity to destabilize Murat's regime by arming and supporting some of the larger and more effective bandit gangs. By 1811, there were areas that were no longer under the control of the Neapolitan Government; in Michael Broer's phrase, 'if Spain was Napoleon's Vietnam, then Calabria was his Cambodia.'

4. OFFICER CORPS

A large part of the Neapolitan Army had left for Sicily with the Royal family, and Joseph and Murat were forced to reform their armed forces. Many of the senior officers were either native or at least Italian, and few Frenchmen served in the Neapolitan Army.

Officers were obtained from the nobility, from the middle classes who supported the liberalization of the government and the law and, with experience, from the educated ranks.

Throughout the period, however, the army was renowned for its indiscipline and propensity to desert given an opportunity, and there must therefore be a question mark on the level of professionalism in the officer corps.

5. OTHER RANKS

Joseph tried to form his army by incorporating the local prison population within its ranks, a failure that was never quite eradicated. Voluntary enlistment was difficult to maintain, but conscription was never the success it was in France, Germany or elsewhere in the Empire.

The problem seems to be that there was no real local tradition of service, and it was easy for someone to evade the draft if they really wanted to do so. Joseph poached troops from the Polish regiments which participated in the invasion of Naples, whilst Murat tried to recruit from units in the French garrison, and even retained the services of the escort from his previous principality, the Grand Duchy of Berg. One unit, the 7th Royal African, was raised from the ex-French regiment of pionniers noirs, the remnants of the Haitian prisoners of war!

6. THE MILITARY ESTABLISHMENT

Organization

1806 GUARD			
Granatieri a Piedi della Guardia Reale	1 Regiment of 2 battalions. Regimental strength about 1,150 officers and men	Each battalion had 4 companies. Battalion strength was approx. 570 officers and men	Each company had 140 officers and men
Volteggiatorre a Piedi della Guardia Reale (2nd Vélites in 1809)	As above	As above	As above
Veliti a Cavallo della Guardia Reale	1 Regiment; regimental strength approx. 390 officers and men	2 Squadrons; squadron strength about 190 officers and men	Each squadron had2 companies, each of 95 officers and men
LINE			
Reggimenti d' Infanteria di Linea	2 Regiments. The field strength was approx. 2,160 officers and men	Each 2 field battalions, plus a depot battalion. The field battalions were approx. 1,080 officers and men	Each field battalion had 1 granatiere, 1 volteggiatore and 7 fuciliere companies, each of approx. 120 officers and men. The depot consisted of 4 fuciliere companies
Reggimento d'Infanteria Leggera	1 Regiment. Field strength was approx. 2,160 officers and men	2 field battalions, plus a depot battalion. Strength as above	Each field battalion had 1 carabinieri, 1 volteggiatore and 7 cacciatori companies, each of approx. 120 officers and men. The depot consisted of 4 cacciatori companies

LINE (Cont.)			
Real Corso (Royal Corsicans)	Organized as the Reggimento d'Infanteria Leggera		
Cacciatori a Cavallo	2 Regiments, plus a depot company. Field strength was approx. 580 officers and men	3 field squadrons, each of 190 officers and men; it was probable that only 2 squadrons were mounted	Each field squadron consisted of two companies. The first company of the first squadron was an elite company. Company strength was approx. 95 officers and men
Foot artillery	1 Company		6 Austrian 6lb guns and 2 howitzers
1809 **GUARD**			
Granatieri a Piedi della Guardia Reale	1 Regiment of 2 battalions. Regimental strength about 1,150 officers and men	Each battalion had 4 companies. Battalion strength was approx. 570 officers and men	Each company had 140 officers and men
Veliti della Guardia Reale	2 Regiments, each of 2 battalions. Regimental strength about 1,150 officers and men	Each battalion had 4 companies. Battalion strength was approx. 570 officers and men	Each company had 140 officers and men
Marino della Guardia Reale	1 Battalion	2 Companies	Each company approx. 140 officers and men
Guardia d'Onore	1 Squadron, approx. 190 officers and men	2 Companies	Each company had approx. 95 officers and men
Veliti a Cavallo della Guardia Reale	1 Regiment; regimental strength approx. 390 officers and men	2 Squadrons; squadron strength about 190 officers and men	Each squadron had 2 companies, each of 95 officers and men

1809 **GUARD** (Cont.)			
Guard Artillery	1 Company each of horse and foot artillery		The horse company had 4 x 4lb guns and 2 howitzers; the foot company had 6 x 8lb guns and 2 howitzers
LINE			
Reggimenti d' Infanteria di Linea	7 Regiments. The field strength was approx. 3,120 officers and men.	Each 3 field battalions, plus a depot battalion. The field battalions were approx. 850 officers and men	Each field battalion had 1 granatiere, 1 volteggiatore and 4 fuciliere companies, each of approx. 140 officers and men. The depot consisted of 4 fuciliere companies
Reggimento d'Infanteria Leggera	3 Regiments. Strength as above	Each 3 field battalions, plus a depot battalion. Strength as above	Each field battalion had 1 carabinieri, 1 volteggiatore and 4 cacciatori companies, each of approx. 140 officers and men. The depot consisted of 4 cacciatori companies
Real Corso	Organized as the Reggimenti d'Infanteria Leggera		
Cacciatori a Cavallo	2 Regiments, plus a depot company Field strength was approx. 580 officers and men	3 field squadrons, each of 190 officers and men; it was probable that only 2 squadrons were mounted	Each field squadron consisted of two companies. The first company of the first squadron was an elite company. Company strength was approx. 95 officers and men
Foot Artillery	4 (?) companies		Each 6 guns and 2 howitzers

1812 GUARD			
Granatieri a Piedi della Guardia Reale	1 Regiment of 2 battalions. Regimental strength about 1,150 officers and men	Each battalion had 4 companies. Battalion strength was approx. 570 officers and men	Each company had 140 officers and men
Veliti della Guardia Reale	2 Regiments, each of 2 battalions. Regimental strength about 1,150 officers and men	Each battalion had 4 companies. Battalion strength was approx. 570 officers and men	Each company had 140 officers and men
Marino della Guardia Reale	1 Battalion	2 Companies	Each company approx. 140 officers and men
Guardia d'Onore	1 Squadron, approx. 190 officers and men	2 Companies	Each company had approx. 95 officers and men
Veliti a Cavallo della Guardia Reale	1 Regiment; regimental strength approx. 390 officers and men	2 Squadrons; squadron strength about 190 officers and men	Each squadron had 2 companies, each of 95 officers and men
Guard Artillery	2 companies each of horse and foot artillery		The horse companies had 4 x 4lb guns and 2 howitzers; the foot companies had 6 x 8lb guns and 2 howitzers
LINE			
Reggimenti d' Infanteria di Linea	8 Regiments. The field strength was approx. 3,120 officers and men.	Each 3 field battalions, plus a depot battalion. The field battalions were approx. 850 officers and men	Each field battalion had 1 granatiere, 1 volteggiatore and 4 fuciliere companies, each of approx. 140 officers and men. The depot consisted of 4 fuciliere companies

LINE (Cont.)			
Reggimento d'Infanteria Leggera	4 Regiments. Strength as above. The Real Corso was re-numbered as the 1st, and the original three moved down in seniority	Each 3 field battalions, plus a depot battalion. Strength as above	Each field battalion had 1 carabinieri, 1 volteggiatore and 4 cacciatori companies, each of approx. 140 officers and men. The depot consisted of 4 cacciatori companies
Cacciatori a Cavallo	2 Regiments, plus a depot company. Field strength was approx. 580 officers and men	3 field squadrons, each of 190 officers and men; it was probable that only 2 squadrons were mounted	Each field squadron consisted of 2 companies. The first company of the first squadron was an elite company. Company strength was approx. 95 officers and men
Foot Artillery	12 (?) companies		Each 6 guns and 2 howitzers
Horse artillery	2 (?) companies		Each 4 guns and 2 howitzers
1815 GUARD			
Granatieri a Piedi della Guardia Reale	1 Regiment of 2 battalions. Regimental strength about 1,150 officers and men	Each battalion had 4 companies. Battalion strength was approx. 570 officers and men	Each company had 140 officers and men
Veliti della Guardia Reale	2 Regiments, each of 2 battalions. Regimental strength about 1,150 officers and men	Each battalion had 4 companies. Battalion strength was approx. 570 officers and men	Each company had 140 officers and men

1815 **GUARD (Cont.)**			
Marino della Guardia Reale	1 Battalion	2 Companies	Each company approx. 140 officers and men
Volteggiatorre a Piedi della Guardia Reale	1 Regiment of 2 battalions. Regimental strength about 1,150 officers and men	Each battalion had 4 companies. Battalion strength was approx. 570 officers and men	Each company had 140 officers and men
Guardia d'Onore	1 Squadron, approx. 190 officers and men	2 Companies	Each company had approx. 95 officers and men
Ussaro della Guardia Reale	1 Regiment; regimental strength approx. 770 officers and men	4 Squadrons; squadron strength about 190 officers and men	Each squadron had 2 companies, each of 95 officers and men
Guard Chevau-légers	As above	As above	As above
Guard Chevau-léger Lancier	As above	As above	As above
Guard Cuirassiers	As above	As above	As above
Guard Artillery	1 Company each of horse and foot artillery		The horse company had 4 x 4lb guns and 2 howitzers; the foot company had 6 x 8lb guns and 2 howitzers

LINE			
Reggimenti d' Infanteria di Linea	12 Regiments. The field strength was approx. 3,120 officers and men	Each 3 field battalions, plus a depot battalion. The field battalions were approx. 850 officers and men	Each field battalion had 1 granatiere, 1 volteggiatore and 4 fuciliere companies, each of approx. 140 officers and men. The depot consisted of 4 fuciliere companies
Reggimento d'Infanteria Leggera	4 Regiments. Strength as above	Each 3 field battalions, plus a depot battalion. Strength as above	Each field battalion had 1 carabinieri, 1 volteggiatore and 4 cacciatori companies, each of approx. 140 officers and men. The depot consisted of 4 cacciatori companies
'Chevau-léger Lanciers'	4 Regiments, plus a depot company. Field strength was approx. 770 officers and men.	4 field squadrons, each of 190 officers and men; it was probable that only 2 squadrons were mounted	Each field squadron consisted of 2 companies. The first company of the first squadron was an elite company. Company strength was approx. 95 officers and men
Foot Artillery	12 (?) companies		Each 6 guns and 2 howitzers
Horse Artillery	2 (?) companies		Each 4 guns and 2 howitzers

7. UNIFORMS

THE GUARD

Granatieri a Piedi della Guardia Reale: The senior foot regiment of the guard was modelled on the Grenadier regiments of the Imperial Guard. They wore a black bearskin bonnet without a front plate, and the red rear patch had a white grenade; the plume and flounders were red. Murat changed these fittings to carmine in 1809 and to amarante (a pink shade) in 1812.

King Joseph issued the regiment with a scarlet long-tailed coat, faced black, but this changed to dark blue in 1809 (amarante in 1812). The collar, cuffs, lapels, turnbacks and epaulettes were carmine. White breeches and gaiters were issued for parade, black gaiters for campaign, although it is likely that overalls were also issued.

Volteggiatorre a Piedi della Guardia Reale: The original regiment wore the same uniform as the Granatieri, except that the collar was yellow and the lapels white. Epaulettes were (probably) green with a red fringe. A shako with a yellow plume replaced the bearskin bonnet.

The new regiment formed in 1814 also wore a shako with a green plume, but the habit-veste was white with yellow collar and amarante lapels, cuffs and turnbacks. The breeches were white with black gaiters.

Veliti della Guardia Reale: The original bearskin bonnet was black but changed to brown by 1812. The rear patch was carmine, with a yellow grenade; the flounders were green. Plumes were green tipped carmine for the 1st Regiment and plain green for the 2nd. Shakos were worn in the field.

The habit-veste was white for both regiments, but the collar, cuffs, lapels and turnbacks were rose (scarlet from 1812) for the 1st and amaranth for the 2nd. Epaulettes were yellow with green fringes. Breeches were white, but grey trousers were worn in the field.

Marino della Guardia Reale: This small unit was issued with a shako, with a red plume and flounders. The jacket was blue, with red collar, cuffs, lapels and turnbacks; epaulettes were red, with green crescents. Breeches were blue.

Guardia d'Onore: Based on a cadre from Berg, it wore a czapka with a carmine box, piped white, and with a white plume. The kurtka was white, faced carmine at the collar, cuffs, lapels and turnbacks. The shoulder straps were piped carmine, as were the rear coat seams. For campaign, grey overall trousers were worn. From 1812 until the regiment became the Garde du Corps, the front rank carried a lance with a carmine over white pennon.

The shabraque was carmine edged white.

Garde du Corps: When converted in 1813, the unit adopted a bicorne, edged white with a white plume. The coat was red, with yellow cuffs, collar and turnbacks. The front of the coat had horizontal white lacing. The shoulder straps were red, piped yellow.

The shabraque was blue, edged white.

Veliti a Cavallo della Guardia Reale: Originally, the unit wore a czapka with a yellow box, piped blue; the plume was white. The kurtka was blue with yellow collar, cuffs, plastron and turnbacks. The epaulettes were yellow, fringed red. The overalls were blue piped yellow and the shabraque was blue edged yellow.

In 1810, the regiment adopted a shako with a yellow top edging, and the tunic lost the plastron for yellow horizontal lacing.

Ussaro della Guardia Reale: The shako was carmine with a white top band, yellow flounders and white plume; officers had black colpacks for full dress, but may have worn them for everyday wear as well. The bags were carmine, edged and piped yellow.

The dolman was white, laced yellow, and the pelisse was carmine, with black fur edging and yellow braid. Breeches were carmine, piped yellow. Shabraques were white.

Guard Chevau-légers: The regiment wore the czapka with a carmine box, piped white and with a white plume. The green coat had carmine collar, cuffs and turnbacks, with white horizontal lacing across the front. Grey overalls were worn for campaign.

Shabraques were carmine, edged yellow.

Guard Chevau-léger Lancier: The unit wore a light blue 'shako rouleau' with a black falling plume. The jacket was light blue with yellow collar, cuffs and turnbacks. The front of the coat had white horizontal lacing. The breeches were light blue, piped yellow. The front rank were issued with lances, the lance pennons were white with either a yellow or amaranth triangle.

The shabraques were red, edged white.

Guard Cuirassiers: The regiment wore a French-style uniform of a steel helmet with a brass comb, black horse hair mane and white plume. The blue coat had carmine facings and white fringed epaulettes. The steel cuirass had carmine edging. Breeches were white, worn with knee-high boots.

The shabraque was blue with white edging.

Guard Artillery: The foot artillery wore a shako with a carmine plume and cords. The coat was blue with carmine collar, cuffs, lapels, epaulettes and turnbacks. Breeches were blue with black gaiters.

The horse companies wore a black colpack with carmine ornaments. The tunic was dark blue with a carmine collar and piping to the lapels and cuffs, and the dark blue breeches were worn with hussar boots.

THE LINE

Reggimenti d' Infanteria di Linea: Under King Joseph, the line units wore a bicorne with a red plume for the granatieri, green for the volteggiatore and company pom-pons for the fuciliere companies. The granatieri wore a bearskin bonnet with a scarlet rear patch for parades.

Under Murat's reorganization, the units adopted the shako for all companies (granatieri for service wear). Plumes were red for the granatieri (amarante by 1811), volteggiatorri yellow, and the fusilieri had company pom-pons.

The habit-veste was white, with the following facing colours which were worn on the collar, cuffs, lapels, turnbacks and the piping to the shoulder straps; volteggiatorri had yellow collars. Epaulettes were red/amaranth for the granatieri and green or yellow, fringed green, for the volteggiatorri. Buttons were white metal, except for the 11th and 12th which were brass:

1st	Re	Sky Blue
2nd	Regina	Scarlet
3rd	Real Principe	Black
4th	Real Samnite	Amaranth
5th	Calabria	Dark Green

6th	Napoli	Orange
7th	Real Africa	Golden Yellow
8th		Rose Pink
9th		Royal Blue
10th		Mid-blue
11th		Amarante
12th		Dark Green

Breeches were white, with black gaiters

Reggimenti d'Infanteria Leggera: It is likely that the regiment adopted a shako on formation, with a bearskin for the carabinieri company. This had a red plume and cords, whilst the volteggiatorri had yellow and the cacciatore had green.

The habit-veste and waistcoat were blue, and regimental facings were worn at the collar (volteggiatorri yellow, piped facing colour), cuffs, lapels, turnbacks and shoulder strap piping. Carabinieri had red epaulettes, volteggiatorri yellow, fringed green. The facing colours were:

1st (later 2nd)	red
2nd (later 3rd)	yellow
3rd (later 4th)	orange

Breeches were blue.

In 1814, the dark blue coats, waistcoats and breeches were changed to sky blue, but the distinctives remained the same.

Real Corso: The uniform was essentially similar to that worn by French Legere regiments. The shako was worn by the cacciatore and volteggiatorri companies, and a bearskin cap by the carabinieri, with the usual company distinctions. The regimental distinctive of green (black from 1807) was worn at the collar and cuff flaps, but all piping was white. The volteggiatorri had yellow collars.

Cacciatori a Cavallo: The two cacciatore a cavallo regiments were uniformed like the French chasseurs à cheval, with green-plumed shakos (colpacks with a green bag and a red plume for the elite company). Up to 1808 the regiments wore a green dolman, braided with yellow, and with red collar and cuffs for the 1st Regiment and yellow for the 2nd.

In 1808 the units were issued with green tunics and red breeches, with grey overall trousers for campaign wear. The facings were red for the 1st Cacciatori and yellow for the 2nd. The facings were worn as piping to the collar, cuffs, lapels and shoulder straps, and on the turnbacks. The elite companies had red epaulettes. When converted to chevau-légers in 1813, the 2nd Regiment may have retained this uniform.

The white sheepskin had dog-tooth edging in the facing colour.

Chevau-léger Lanciers: When the first Chevau-léger regiment was formed in 1806 it wore a French shako and was issued with a light blue jacket (piped rose, then amaranth) and breeches.

In 1813, when the Cacciatori were re-designated as Chevau-légers, the 1st Chevau-légers became the 3rd and the 4th newly formed. All regiments were to adopt the light blue uniform of the original regiment of this arm, although the 2nd does not seem to have done so. Piping was red for the 1st, yellow for the 2nd, yellow for the 3rd and orange for the 4th.

When the lance was issued, the pennon was crimson over white; the sheepskin had facing colour dogs-tooth edging.

Artillery: The foot companies wore a shako with an amaranth plume, blue piped amaranth coat and blue breeches with black gaiters.

The horse companies also wore a shako; the blue hussar dolman was braided amaranth and the blue overalls had amaranth piping.

8. BATTLE HISTORY

The Neapolitan Army was kept largely concentrated to act as a garrison for the vulnerable Italian peninsula. The only significant deployments outside were:

Spain: 1st Reggimento d' Infanteria di Linea
Storm of Mataro, 17 June 1808
Failed Storm of Girona, 20 June 1808
Failed siege of Girona, 24 July–16 August 1808
Capture of Girona, 6 June–10 December 1809
Siege and capture of Tortosa, 16 December 1810–2 January 1811

2nd Reggimento d' Infanteria di Linea
Molins del Rey, 21 December 1808
Capture of Girona, 6 June–10 December 1809
Siege and capture of Tortosa, 16 December 1810–2 January 1811

1st Reggimento d'Infanteria Leggera
Siege and capture of Tortosa, 16 December 1810–2 January 1811

2nd Cacciatori a Cavallo
Failed siege of Girona, 24 July–16 August 1808
Siege and capture of Tortosa, 16 December 1810–2 January 1811

In 1811, the survivors of the two infantry regiments were recalled to Naples and used to form a new 8th Reggimento d' Infanteria di Linea; the two depots, with additional conscripts, then re-formed the two old regiments.

Russia, 1812: The 33rd Division formed part of the XI Corps under Marshal Augereau. The units were the Guardia d'Onore, Veliti a Cavallo della Guardia Reale, Veliti della Guardia Reale, Marino della Guardia Reale, and the 5th, 6th and 7th Reggimenti d' Infanteria di Linea, plus a company of horse artillery. The division served on lines of communication duties.

Germany, 1813: A composite regiment formed of the elite companies of the 5th, 6th and 7th Reggimenti d' Infanteria di Linea (presumably one battalion of six companies of granatieri and another of volteggiatorri) served at Lutzen, 2 May 1813, and Leipzig, 16–19 October 1813 as part of XI Corps.

The 4th Reggimento d'Infanteria Leggera were also in XI Corps at Leipzig.

The 2nd Cacciatori a Cavallo recorded officer casualties whilst serving in II Cavalry Corps at Dresden, 26–27 August 1813.

Parts of the fucilieri companies of the 5th, 6th and 7th Reggimenti were in garrison at Dresden and Danzig during the sieges of these cities.

In 1815, Murat's army at Tolentino (3 May) consisted of:

The Guard Infantry Division of the two Veliti regiments, the Volteggiatorri and artillery and engineers serving as infantry, and twelve guns;

The Guard Cavalry Division and eight guns;

Three divisions, each consisting of one Leggera and three Linea units and twelve guns;

One cavalry brigade, consisting of two Chevau-léger Lancier regiments.

9. TACTICS

It is extremely difficult to be objective about the Neapolitan Army, as much is coloured by what we think we know about the Italians in 1940. Matters are not helped by Napoleon's remark not to send any more Neapolitan troops to Spain as they only deserted and formed bandit groups, or that of a regimental colonel who suggested withdrawing his mens' firearms so that when they did desert at least they left their guns behind!

Both Joseph and Murat had to use large numbers of impressed men to keep their regiments up to strength. It is, perhaps, more charitable to say that the average Neapolitan was a cast-iron realist. Unlike his German counterpart, there was no tradition of service, no incentive to make him want to put on a uniform and march off to the wars, no urge to seek glory.

When it was necessary, he could and would fight, but the wars in which he fought were not his wars, and Napoleon was not his emperor; all in all, perhaps this was not a bad philosophy.

CHAPTER 10

The Army of the Kingdom of Saxony, 1806–15

1. INTRODUCTION

IT IS DIFFICULT to read the history of the Saxon Army during the eighteenth and the first two decades of the nineteenth centuries and not come the conclusion that it was one of the unluckiest ever.

Forced into supporting Prussia's threat to Napoleon's Empire in 1806, Saxon units fought at Saalfeld and Jena, finally covering the defeated army as it withdrew. Elevated to a kingdom after joining the Confederation of the Rhine, the army was mobilized for the 1809 Austrian campaign. Commanded by Marechal Bernadotte, a man distrusted by his Emperor, they fought well at Wagram but suffered through association when their commander was sacked.

In 1812, in Russia, the Saxons formed a complete corps – the VII – and fought alongside the Austrian Hilfskorps on the southern front. Whilst they might not have suffered the agonies of the main army, one complete brigade was lost to an avoidable surprise attack by an energetic Russian commander. To counterbalance this, the Saxon heavy cavalry brigade took the Great Redoubt at Borodino in a brilliant, almost unique, charge, only for Napoleon to give the credit to his own, unsuccessful cuirassier units.

The army was rebuilt for the 1813 campaign and was again involved in the desperate fighting in Central Germany. King Friedrich August would have been more than willing to throw in his lot with the Allies, but his capital, Dresden, was the main French garrison in Saxony and the King was a virtual prisoner. Captured after Leipzig, Friedrich August was kept incommunicado and the kingdom placed under a Russian governor until Napoleon's first abdication in the spring of 1814.

Leipzig, too, provided the leitmotif to the whole story of the Saxon Army; a complete division – 5,000 men – marched out of the French ranks and joined the Allies in broad daylight and in full sight of both armies. This 'treachery' if so it was, seemed typical of the Saxon Army throughout the Napoleonic period

Saxony's fate now fell into the hands of the diplomats meeting at Vienna. Whereas those states whose leaders had declared independence from Napoleon were usually allowed to continue to exist, Friedrich August's inability to do so was compounded by Prussia's desire for expansion. Saxony was forced to cede almost half of the kingdom, whilst the army was also divided.

Faced with uncompromising Prussian demands that they be fully integrated into Blücher's army in time for the final, Waterloo, campaign in 1815, some 15,000 Saxons refused to serve, and were sent home. Understandable perhaps, but it is somewhat difficult to escape the conclusion that the Saxon Army would have been far happier for the whole Napoleonic experience to have passed them by.

2. BACKGROUND

Once a regional power, but situated with borders resting on both Austria and the nascent state of Prussia, it was natural that the electorate, then the kingdom, of Saxony, would be forced to make hard choices, be fought over and, eventually, ruined.

As part of the Holy Roman Empire, Saxony threw in her lot with Austria during the 2nd Silesian War only to taste defeat at Hohenfriedberg and Kesselsdorf. In the first campaign of the Seven Years War (1756–63), Frederick the Great's Prussians invaded without warning and forced the Saxon Army to capitulate. In scenes that shocked even a cynical Europe, entire regiments were impressed into the Prussian Army and marched off to fight their erstwhile Austrian allies.

In the event, most of the men quickly deserted, forming a new Saxon Army in exile that fought with the French in Western Germany, but Frederick was able to use the electorate's resources for several years. When peace was eventually restored, agriculture and industry alike had been ruined. Frederick's policy was to look for the eventual absorption of Saxony into Prussia, something that was to be partly achieved by his heirs in 1815.

In the War of the Bavarian Succession (1778–79), Saxony supported Prussia against Austria, and then supported Austria and Prussia during the initial campaigns against the French Revolution. The electorate followed the Prussian lead in leaving the coalition in July 1796. When Prussia determined on war against France in 1806 to resolve what she saw as insults, Saxony was forced to become a reluctant ally.

Unlike the defeated and dismembered Prussia, however, Napoleon saw Saxony as an opportunity for building a counterweight. Elevated to a kingdom through the Treaty of Posen, re-establishing the previous links with Poland through the Grand Duchy of Warsaw, Saxony was now ready to fight as a loyal French ally.

3. COMMAND STRUCTURE

Strangely, Friedrich August had a great deal of sympathy for the ideals of the French Revolution, but was slow to bring any modernization to his own state. The higher direction continued to be through cabinet functions rather than by the appointment of ministers, and there was no representative assembly, even one as neutered as the French.

4. OFFICER CORPS

Up until 1809 the Saxon Army suffered from having an ageing officer corps, with generals barely able to mount their horses or lead troops into action. They were just not up to the strain and pace of modern warfare.

After the close of the Austrian campaign, the army had to undergo a reappraisal of its fitness, and this allowed retirements and the bringing forward of younger men, although at no time would a Saxon actually command anything higher than a division. An example was Thielmann, who would command the Saxon Division in X Corps in 1809, but would have to join the Prussian Army to command Blücher's III Corps in Belgium in 1815.

5. OTHER RANKS

The 1806 army was composed of volunteers or, more accurately, those members of society incapable of earning a crust in any other way. Because commanders owned the companies, any saving that could be made (for instance, pocketing the pay of fictitious soldiers, allowing excess furloughs, etc.) represented profits. For the soldiers themselves, smartness in drill and appearance were all that were expected of them, whilst promotions to NCO rank came through long service and obedience.

In 1811, this changed. Conscription necessarily lead to a better class of soldier coming forward, even if it meant that some of the previous restrictions on apprenticeships and guilds were removed. Rewarding soldiers with promotions based on ability and leadership potential meant that joining the army could be seen as honourable and offering professional advancement.

This 'social contract' meant that solders who retired on account of age or wounds had earned the state's gratitude. Arrangements were made either for worthwhile employment or to pay a decent pension.

6. THE MILITARY ESTABLISHMENT

Organization

1806 INFANTRY		
Leib-Grenadier-Garde	1 regiment of 2 battalions, each 4 grenadier and 1 'flugelkompagnie'. Total (with staff) 1,754 officers and men	Each company consisted of 174 officers and men
12 infantry regiments	Each of 2 battalions of 4 musketeer and 1 grenadier companies. Total (with staff) 1,754 officers and men	Each company consisted of 174 officers and men. Each musketeer company had 11 sharpshooters to act as skirmishers
7 grenadier battalions	1 combined battalion made up of the grenadier companies of 2 regiments. Total 696 officers and men. The two flugelkompagnien from the Leib-Grenadier-Garde formed a separate unit by themselves.	Each company consisted of 174 officers and men

CAVALRY		
Garde du Corps	4 Squadrons, totalling 429 men	Each squadron consisted of 104 officers and men
3 heavy regiments	Each of 4 squadrons, totalling 734 officers and men	Each squadron consisted of 180 officers and men
4 chevau-léger regiments	As above	As above
1 hussar regiment	8 squadrons totalling 1,065 officers and men	Each squadron consisted of 131 officers and men
ARTILLERY		
Regimental artillery	4 guns per infantry regiment	Either 6 or 3 pdr
1 regiment of 2 battalions	Each battalion had 6 companies	Each company had 4 guns and 2 howitzers. The Saxon artillery used 4, 8, and 12 pdr guns and 8 pdr howitzers.
1809 **INFANTRY**		
Leib-Grenadier-Garde	1 regiment of 2 battalions, organized as above, totalling 2,073 officers and men	Each company consisted of 203 officers and men
12 infantry regiments	Each of 2 battalions of 4 musketeer and 1 grenadier companies. Total (with staff) 2,081 officers and men	Each company consisted of 203 officers and men. Each musketeer company had 11 sharpshooters to act as skirmishers which were stripped out to form a separate unit
7 grenadier battalions	As 1806	Each company consisted of 203 officers and men
2 schutzen battalions	Each battalion consisted of 4 companies formed from the battalion sharpshooters. Total battalion strength was 700.	Each company totalled 174 officers and men
Jäger company	–	126 officers and men

CAVALRY		
As 1806		
ARTILLERY		
Regimental artillery	4 guns per infantry regiment	Either 6 or 3 pdr
1 artillery regiment	2 battalions, each of 6 companies	Each company had 4 x 8 pdr guns and 2 x 4 pdr howitzers
1810 **INFANTRY**		
Leib-Grenadier-Garde	As 1809	As 1809
8 infantry regiments	As 1809	As 1809. 4 x 4 pdr guns, manned by the regiment were attached for the Russian campaign
2 schutzen regiments	Each of 2 battalions of 4 companies. Total strength 1,653 officers and men.	Each company totalled 204 officers and men
Jäger company	–	As 1809
CAVALRY		
Garde du Corps	4 squadrons, totalling 786 officers and men	Each squadron totalled 192 officers and men
2 heavy regiments	As above	As above
4 chevau-léger regiments. In 1811 one regiment was converted to Uhlans	As above	As above
Hussar regiment	8 squadrons, totalling 1,074 officers and men	Each squadron totalled 132 officers and men
ARTILLERY		
1 artillery regiment of 2 battalions	Each battalion had 8 companies	Each company 4 guns and 2 howitzers. The guns were 6 and 12 pdr.
1 'Brigade' of horse artillery	2 companies	Each company 4 x 6 pdr and 2 howitzers

In 1813, the losses of the Russian campaign could not be made good and some infantry regiments consisted of only one battalion. The cavalry could only form one kuirassier, one uhlan and one hussar regiment, at reduced strength.

When Saxony passed into the Allied camp after Leipzig, the state of the army meant that four units (Niesemeuschel, Rechten, Low and Steindel) had to be disbanded and the remaining line regiments used to form three provisional regiments:

Provisional Garde-Regiment from the Leib-Grenadier-Garde, Konig, and the remnants of the two grenadier battalions (see below for details).

Provisional 1st Line Regiment, consisting mainly of the two battalions of Prinz Anton.

Provisional 2nd Line Regiment, from Prinz Maximilian, von Rechten and von Steindel.

Provisional 3rd Line Regiment, from Prinz Friedrich August.

1st Light Infantry Regiment from von Lecoq, returned convalescents and ex-prisoners of war.

2nd Light Infantry Regiment also used ex-prisoners of war as a source, but also included men from von Sahr.

The Allies also insisted that additional Landwehr forces be provided. These numbered four, three-battalion regiments, two light infantry battalions and an additional unit of hussars.

The allocation of forces to Prussia falls outside the scope of this book.

Grenadier Battalions

The composition of the Grenadier battalions changed between campaigns.

COMMANDING OFFICER	CONSISTING OF THE GRENADIER COMPANIES OF	AND
1806		
Leib-Grenadier	Leib-Grenadier-Garde	
Von Winkel	Prinz Maximilian	Von Rechten
Von Thiollaz	Prinz Xavier	Prinz Clemens
Von Hundt	Prinz Anton	Von Niesemeuschel
Von Metsch	Prinz Friedrich August	Von Thummel
Von Lecoq	Von Sanger	Von Low
Von Leichtenstein	Kurfurst	Bevilqua
1809		
Leib-Grenadier	Leib-Grenadier-Garde	
Von Bose	Prinz Friedrich August	Von Burgsdorf
Von Hake	Prinz Clemens	Von Oebschelwitz
Von Radellof	Prinz Anton	Von Niesemeuschel
Von Winklemann	Von Cerrini	Von Low
Von Einsiedl	König	Von Dyherrn
Von Wolan/Von Stutterheim	Von Rechten	Originally two (perhaps four) depot companies, then the grenadier companies of Prinz Maximilian
1812		
Leib-Grenadier	Leib-Grenadier-Garde	
Von Brause/Eychelburg	König	Von Niesemeuschel
Von Anger	Prinz Anton	Von Low
Von Stutterheim/von Speigel	Prinz Maximilian	Von Rechten

COMMANDING OFFICER	CONSISTING OF THE GRENADIER COMPANIES OF	AND
1812		
Von Liebenau	Prinz Friedrich August	Prinz Clemens
1813		
Von Speigel	Prinz Maximilian	Von Rechten, Prinz Friedrich and von Steindel
Von Sperl	König	Von Niesemeuschel, Prinz Anton and von Low

The two 1813 grenadier battalions were used to form the 3rd Battalion of the Provisional-Garde-Régiment. Eventually, three new battalions were formed, but not until 1815.

7. UNIFORMS

i) 1806–1809

INFANTRY

The Leib-Grenadier-Garde wore an Austrian-style bearskin with a brass front plate; the bag was yellow. The coat was red with yellow collar, cuffs, and lapels; the turnbacks were in the coat colour. The waistcoat was yellow and the breeches white.

The musketeers in the line regiments wore bicornes and the grenadiers wore the bearskin, with the cloth bag in the regimental facing colour. The schutzen detachments had a green plume.

The coats were white, with regimental distinctives at lapels, collar and cuffs. The turnbacks were in coat colour, and the breeches and waistcoat were white with the long gaiters black.

1806 REGIMENT	CHANGES TO 1809	FACING	BUTTONS
Kurfurst	1806 – König	Red	Yellow
Von Sanger	1808 – von Cerrini	Red	White
Prinz Anton		Dark blue	Yellow
Prinz Clemens		Dark blue	White
Prinz Maximilian		Yellow	Yellow
Von Thummel	1808 – von Burgsdorff	Yellow	White
Prinz Friedrich August		Light green	Yellow
Von Low		Light green	White
Prinz Xavier	1806 – Von Oebschelwitz	Light blue	Yellow
Von Bevilaqua	1808 – von Dyherrn	Light blue	White
Von Niesmeuschel		Crimson	Yellow
Von Rechten		Crimson	White

CAVALRY

The heavy cavalry wore a black bicorne with a white plume. The tunic was buff with regimental distinctives at cuffs, turnbacks and collar and the waistcoat. The breeches were buff. Whether all units wore the cuirass is an open question, but if they did it was only the breast plate. The cuirass was iron, laquered black.

The cheveauleger regiments also wore a bicorne with plume. The coat was red, with collar, cuffs, lapels, turnbacks and waistcoats of the facing colours. The breeches were grey for campaign.

1806 REGIMENT	CHANGES TO 1809	FACING COLOUR	BUTTONS
Heavy Cavalry			
Garde du Corps		Royal blue	–

1806 REGIMENT	CHANGES TO 1809	FACING COLOUR	BUTTONS
Karabiniers	–	Scarlet	–
Kurfurst Kuirassier	1806 – König 1807 – Leib	Scarlet	–
Kochtitsky Kuirassier	1808 – von Zastrow	Yellow	–
Chevau-léger	–	–	–
Prinz Clemens	–	Light green	Yellow
Prinz Albrecht	–	Dark green	Yellow
Prinz Johann	–	Black	Yellow
Von Polenz	–	Light blue	

The shabraque for all regiments was in the facing colour with yellow edging. All horse furniture was black leather. The chevau-légers had a black sheepskin saddle cover.

The Hussar regiment wore a black mirliton with a light blue wing. The dolman was white with light blue collar and cuffs, and the pelisse was light blue with black fur edging and white braiding. The breeches were white.

The shabraque was light blue with white edging.

ARTILLERY

The headgear was the infantry bicorne with yellow lace trim. The coat was dark green with scarlet collar, cuffs, lapels and turnbacks. Breeches were buff (possibly leather for campaign) with black gaiters. Artillery equipments were dark grey with brass metalwork.

ii) 1810 onwards

INFANTRY

In 1810 the Saxon Army took on a more modern appearance by adopting the shako and a habit-veste that had closed lapels.

The Leib-Grenadier-Garde retained the bearskin for parade, but for campaign the shako was adopted. It had a white plume (rather than the more usual red for grenadiers) with white cords and flounders. The habit-veste was red, with lemon yellow collar, cuffs, lapels and turnbacks. The epaulettes were white with fringes. Breeches were white, with white overalls for campaign wear.

The musketeer shakos of the line regiments had a white plume tipped with the facing colour for parade, and a pom-pon for campaign. The grenadiers had a scarlet plume or pom-pon and cords.

The habit-veste was white, with facing colours showing at the collar, cuffs, lapels and turnbacks, and the shoulder straps were piped in the facing colour. There is no indication that the grenadiers wore epaulettes.

Breeches were white, but overalls were issued from 1811 in a variety of colours including white, light grey and brown.

1809 REGIMENT	CHANGES TO 1814	FACING	BUTTONS
König		Scarlet 1813 – Poppy red	Yellow
Von Cerrini	Disbanded 1810		
Prinz Anton		Dark blue	Yellow
Prinz Clemens	1813 – von Steindel	Grass green	White
Prinz Maximilian		Yellow	Yellow
Von Burgdorff	Disbanded 1810		
Prinz Friedrich August		Grass green 1813 – Light blue	Yellow
Von Low		Dark blue	White
Von Oebschelwitz	Disbanded 1810		
Von Dyherrn	Disbanded 1810		
Von Niesemueschel	1810–13 – Vacant	Scarlet 1813 – Poppy red	White
Von Rechten		Yellow	White

The two Light Infantry regiments formed after 1809 also wore the shako with dark green plumes and pom-pons for parade and campaign respectively, and dark green cords.

The habit-veste was dark green with black collar, cuffs and lapels, all piped scarlet. The turnbacks were dark green, and the shoulder straps were also dark green, piped scarlet. The breeches and, later, overalls, were grey.

The jäger company wore almost exactly the same uniform, except that the lapels and collar were dark green, piped scarlet.

CAVALRY

The three remaining heavy cavalry regiments (the Karabiniers having been disbanded in 1810) had now adopted a brass, French-style, crested helmet, similar to that worn by the later carabinier regiments. The crest and turban was black fur and the plume was white.

The tunic for the Garde du Corps was buff, whilst that for the Leib and the Zastrow Kurassiere was white. Facings remained as for the 1806 uniform. Opinion is split on whether the cuirass was actually worn. If so, it was only a black lacquered breastplate. Breeches were buff.

The provisional regiment formed in 1813 wore the uniform of the Leib-Kurassier-Garde.

The chevau-léger regiments had also taken on a more modern appearance, taking into wear a black shako, with white plume and cords. The tunic continued to be red, and the facings were the same as with the 1806 uniform. Grey overalls were worn on campaign.

The Prinz Clemens adopted the lance in time for the Russian campaign in 1812 (and were renamed the Prinz Clemens Uhlans). The lance pennon was red over white to reflect the association with Poland, but other sources give green and red. There are references to the re-formed 1813 Uhlan Regiment wearing a czapka with a light blue box, and the tunic being light blue with black facings.

The Hussar Regiment also adopted the shako, with white plume and cords. The dolman, pelisse and breeches were light blue, with the collar and cuffs on the dolman black. Fur edging to the pelisse was black.

The shabraques of the heavy cavalry were in facing colour, those for the chevau-légers were red with facing colour edging , whilst the hussars had light blue with black edging.

ARTILLERY

The foot artillery companies wore a uniform similar to the infantry, but the shako had a red plume. The tunic was green faced red, and the turnbacks were green piped red. Breeches were grey.

The horse artillery companies also wore a green tunic, but modelled on that of the cheveauxleger regiments. Facings, including the turnbacks, were red, breeches were grey, and all ranks had adopted black knee boots.

8. BATTLE HISTORY

(Roman numerals indicate original Corps affiliation; these often changed during the campaign.)

1806–07

D	Blockade and siege of Danzig, 10 March–24 May 1807 (as French allies)
F	Friedland, 14 June 1807 (as French allies)
J	Jena, 14 October 1806 (as Prussian allies)
S	Saalfeld, 10 October 1806 (as Prussian allies)

1809

R	Raszyn, 19 April 1809
Sx	Defence of Saxony, April–July 1809
U-L	Urfahr-Linz, 17 May 1809
W	Wagram, 5–6 July 1809

1812

Be	Beresina, 26–28 November 1812
Bo	Borodino, 7 September 1812
G	Gorodeczna, 11–12 August 1812
K	Kobryn, 27 July 1812
Wo	Wolkowysk, 14–16 November 1812

1813

Ba	Bautzen, 20–21 May 1813
D	Dennewitz, 6 September 1813
Dr	Dresden, 26–27 August 1813
GB	Gross-Beeren, 23 August 1813
Le	Leipzig, 16–19 October 1813

REGIMENT	1806–07	1809	1812	1813
Leib-Grenadier-Garde		IX:U-L (1 Bn only), W,		VII: Ba (1 Bn), GB (1 Bn)
Kurfurst – König	S, J	IX: U-L, W	VII: K	VII: GB (I Bn)
Von Sanger – von Cerrini		IX: W		
Prinz Anton	X: D	IX: W	VII: G, Wo	VII: GB, Le (1 Bn)
Prinz Clemens – von Steindel	S, J	IX: W	VII: G, Wo	VII: GB, D (1 Bn), Le (1 Bn)
Prinz Maximilian	J, X: D	IX: U-L, W	XI:	VII: GB (I Bn)
Von Thummel – von Burgsdorff	J			
Prinz Friedrich August	J	IX: U-L, W	VII: G, Wo	VII: GB, D (1 Bn), Le (1 Bn)
Von Low	J	IX: W	IX:	VII: GB
Prinz Xavier – Von Oebschelwitz	S, J	R, Sx (I Bn), IX: (II Bn), W		
Von Bevilaqua – von Dyherrn	J, X: F	IX: (I Bn only) U-L, W		
Von Niesmeuschel – Vacant	J	IX: W	VII: K	VII: GB (II Bn), Le (II Bn)
Von Rechten	J		IX:	VII: GB (II Bn), D (II Bn), Le (II Bn)
1st Schutzen Regt		IX (as 1st Sch. Bn): W	VII: G, Wo	VII: Ba (1 Bn), GB, D, Le (1 Bn)
2nd Schutzen Regt		IX (as 2nd Sch. Bn): W	VII: G, Wo	VII: GB, Le (1 Bn)
Garde du Corps		IX (2 Sqns): W	IV Cav: Bo	

REGIMENT	1806/07	1809	1812	1813
Karabiniers	J,	IX (2 Sqns): W		
Kurfurst Kurassier – König – Leib	X: D, F	IX: W		I Cav: Dr, Le
Kochtitsky Kurassier – von Zastrow	J	Sx,	IV Cav: Bo	I Cav: Dr, Le
Prinz Clemens	J, X: F	IX: W	VII: K (3 Sqns), G (4 Sqns), Wo	VII: GB, Le
Prinz Albrecht	J	IX: (1 Sqn) U-L, W	III Cav: Bo	
Prinz Johann	J, X: F	IX: W	IX: Be	
Von Polenz	J	Sx (3 Sqns),	VII: G	
Hussars	S (5 Sqns), J	R (2 Sqns), Sx (3 Sqns) IX: (3 Sqns) U-L, W	VII: Wo	VII: GB, Le

GRENADIER BATTALIONS	ACTIONS PRESENT
1806	
Leib-Grenadier	
Von Winkel	J
Von Thiollaz	J, X: D, F
Von Hundt	J
Von Metsch	J
Von Lecoq	J, X: F
Von Leichtenstein	J
1809	
Leib-Grenadier	

GRENADIER BATTALIONS	ACTIONS PRESENT
1809 (Cont.)	
Von Bose	IX: U-L, W
Von Hake	IX: U-L
Von Radellof	IX: W
Von Winklemann	IX:
Von Einsiedl	R, Sx
Von Wolan/Von Stutterheim	R, Sx
1812	
Leib-Grenadier	
Von Brause/Eychelburg	VII: G, Wo
Von Anger	VII: G, Wo
Von Stutterheim/von Spiegel	VII: G, Wo
Von Liebenau	VII: G, Wo
1813	
Von Speigel	VII: GB, D, Le
Von Anger/von Sperl	VII: Ba, GB, Le

9. TACTICS

The Saxon infantry did not change its organization in any significant form, keeping the same four-company battalion structure after they joined the Confederation of the Rhine. The company retained the manoeuvre element, so that columns were formed on a company frontage.

Without a designated voltigeur or jäger company, battalions were unable to generate a large number of skirmishers and these duties fell on the (1809 onwards) shutzen battalions and regiments.

It was generally acknowledged that the best arm in the Saxon Army was its cavalry, and the taking of the Great Redoubt at Borodino is surely evidence of this. None the less, the lapse in reconnaissance before Kobryn led directly to the loss of an entire infantry brigade, which seriously compromised the strength of VII Corps for the rest of the campaign.

There can be little doubt that, overall, the Saxon Army did all that was required of it, fighting and dying at the behest of a French emperor who cared nothing for it (*what are the deaths of a million men to a man such as I*?). Little wonder that, in 1813, once it had been ground down once and unfairly blamed for the loss of a battle more the fault of yet another French marshal, it should choose to opt out of a war not of its own making.

CHAPTER 11

The Armies of the Smaller German States, 1806–15

1. INTRODUCTION

The Holy Roman Empire had been such an enduring entity in middle Europe that few people could begin to think of its demise. When it came in 1806, it was because it had failed to adapt to the new pressures of modern politics.

The role of emperor was subject to election. Up until the seventeenth century this meant that it could change between rulers, but latterly it had become almost totally vested in the House of Habsburg, although even this was not a foregone conclusion; in 1742 the House of Wittelsbach had been elected. Religious differences, dating from the Reformation, had tainted the unity of the Empire, but were containable, even though Frederick the Great might play on these fears for his own ends.

Not all states had the role of electing the Emperor. Those that did, such as Hanover, were known as electorates, but the smaller ones were grouped together in order to provide a voice at the Imperial Diet. All were grouped in geographical Kreis, which gave a structure to the Empire as a whole.

Because the role of the Diet was to act as a forum for mediating disputes between states, the only likely threat came from outside. Few states kept anything like a large standing army and, if one were required, it had to be voted on, with states being assessed on their ability to provide money and men. The onset of the French Revolution, therefore, came as a profound shock to the states, for not only did the invading armies pose a threat to the rulers, but their states were unprepared for the demands of total war.

By 1800, many German principalities were exhausted, having been marched over many times. Disillusionment with Austria for its failure to provide protection was rife. The larger states, such as Prussia and Bavaria, which had lost provinces along the Rhine, were prepared to make compensating gains at the expense of the free cities and ecclesiastical states within their borders.

After Austria's defeat at Austerlitz in December 1805, and the resulting Peace of Pressburg, Emperor Franz II realized that it was now possible for Napoleon to be elected as the next Holy Roman Emperor using the votes of his German clients. Rather than let this happen, Franz voluntarily gave up the Imperial throne and dissolved the Empire.

2. BACKGROUND

The dissolution of the Empire left a power vacuum in Germany, which Napoleon quickly filled. Although the larger states were allowed to gain territory and their rulers to become kings, there were still a significant number of small states. To replace the Holy Roman Empire, and to provide a focus for these, Napoleon sponsored the formation of the Confederation of the Rhine.

The ex-Archbishop of Mainz, Karl von Dalberg was nominated as Prince Primate and eventually provided with the Grand Duchy of Frankfurt. This turned out to be something of a poisoned chalice, for few of the rulers were prepared to defer to anyone. Whilst Napoleon wanted to see the Confederation as a conduit for reform, it was also a means to provide him with additional forces: it would take a brave ruler to refuse Napoleon's call for men.

Recognizing that some of the states were too small to form effective units, Napoleon insisted that individual companies be formed into composite battalions, and composite battalions into regiments. Even if the units so formed were not efficient, or able to take a place in the battle line, they could be used for garrisons and secondary duties whilst they were brought up to a high standard. The ultimate intention was that the need to produce an efficient army would drive the improvements to the state structure.

3. COMMAND STRUCTURE

The role of the Confederation was political rather than military, and the regiments thus formed were ultimately to be commanded within the Imperial hierarchy. Whilst there were intentions in 1809 to form a German corps, this failed to occur due to the need to get units into the Danube valley as quickly as possible. In addition, units sent to Spain stayed there until they ceased to be effective.

One thing the Confederation did find out was that Napoleon's demand for men was insatiable. Whereas the old Empire may have required troops, once the campaign was over, the troops returned to their homes. After 1806, units were expected to be kept up to strength. This continual drain on manpower soon turned German support to anger and thoughts of vengeance.

4. OFFICER CORPS

Originally, the small armies were officered by a mixture of the local nobility and adventurers from all over Germany. The strain of continuing warfare acted as a winnowing, and those unwilling or unable to serve through age and infirmity were soon replaced by others, including men promoted from the ranks.

5. OTHER RANKS

The incessant demand for troops and the need to keep the units supplied required the states to modernize the processes to achieve this. In order to keep up the pool of potential recruits, it was important that opportunities to evade service – such as apprenticeships – were kept to the minimum. Tax rolls had to be kept up to date, leading to an increased and professional bureaucracy.

6. THE MILITARY ESTABLISHMENT

Organization

The regiments formed by the small states were organized as follows:

UNIT	FROM	UNIFORM
1st Confederation	2nd Nassau Regiment 2 Bns, both from Nassau-Usingen	The 1st Grenadier Co. wore a raupenhelm, all other companies a shako. Green coat with black collar, cuffs and shoulder straps, grey breeches and buff belting. Grenadiers had red plumes and epaulettes, volitigeur yellow over green plumes and green epaulettes. In 1810, the grenadiers adopted a colpack with red plume
2nd Confederation	1st Nassau Regiment[1] 2 Bns, both from Nassau-Weilburg, but including Isenburg-Birstein, Hohenzollern-Sigmaringen & Hohenzollern-Hechingen	As above
3rd Confederation	Wurzburg[2] 2 Bns, both from Wurzburg	Shako; red plume and ornaments for grenadiers, green for voltigeurs. White coat, with red collar, cuffs, lapels and turnback piping. Red epaulettes for grenadiers, yellow with green fringes for voltigeur and white with red piping for centre companies. White trousers
4th Confederation	Saxon Duchies 1st Bn from Sachsen-Gotha & Sachsen-Koburg. 2nd Bn from Sachsen-Gotha, Sachsen Meiningen & Sachsen-Koburg. 3rd Bn[3] from Sachsen-Weimar and Sachsen-Hildburghausen	The grenadier companies in the 1st and 2nd Bns wore bicornes in 1809; red plumes (shakos issued after end of Austrian campaign); dark blue coats with red collar, cuffs, lapels and turnbacks; red epaulettes; white equipment. The voltigeurs in the 1st and 2nd Bns wore shako with green plumes, dark green coats with yellow collar and cuffs and red turnbacks, light blue breeches and white equipment. The centre companies of the 1st and 2nd Bns wore bicornes in 1809, but adopted the shako after. Dark blue coats with red collar, cuffs, lapels and turnbacks; red epaulettes; white equipment. The 3rd Bn wore bicornes (shako after 1809), dark green coat with yellow collar patches and turnbacks, grey breeches and buff leather equipment

Footnotes on p. 265.

UNIT	FROM	UNIFORM
5th Confederation	Anhalt-Lippe 1st Bn from Anhalt-Dessau, Anhalt-Bernburg & Anhalt-Kothen. 2nd Bn from Lippe-Detmold & Schaumburg-Lippe	The 1st Bn wore a shako with red plumes and ornaments for the grenadiers, green for the voltigeurs; dark green coats with rose collar, cuffs and turnbacks, red epaulettes for the grenadiers, green epaulettes for the voltigeurs; grey breeches; black equipment. 2nd Bn wore a shako with the usual company ornaments, white coat, dark green collar, cuffs, lapels and turnbacks; white trousers, white equipment
6th Confederation	Reuss, Schwarzburg and Waldeck (each bn only had four companies) 1st Bn from Sondershausen & Rudolstadt. 2nd Bn from Reuss & Waldeck	1st Bn wore a shako, with a dark green Prussian coat with red collar, cuffs and turnbacks; grey breeches. 2nd Bn also wore a shako, white coat with facings at collar, cuffs and lapels (Reuss – medium blue, Waldeck – dark blue); white trousers, white equipment
7th Confederation	Mecklenburg-Schwerin[4] 1st Bn from Mecklenburg-Schwerin 2nd Bn from Mecklenburg-Schwerin 3rd Bn from Mecklenburg-Strelitz	The Schwerin battalions wore a uniform based on the current Prussian style, with a shako, dark blue coat with yellow (1st) or white (2nd) collar, cuffs and turnbacks; grey breeches, white equipment. The Strelitz battalion wore a similar uniform but with red facings. In 1812, all battalions had red facings
8th Confederation	Frankfurt (one, four-company battalion in 1809; two battalions in 1812, plus the separate unit in Spain)	In 1809, the unit wore a shako (no elite companies). The coat was white, with red collar, cuffs, lapels and turnbacks. The 1812 unit wore a shako, with the usual elite company distinctions. Dark blue coats, with red or green epaulettes; dark blue collar, red lapels, cuffs and turnbacks; white breeches; white equipment

[1] Instead of contributing troops, the Duchy of Aremberg, and the Principalities of Salm-Salm, Salm-Kyburg, Liechtenstein and Hohengeroldseck all contributed subsidies.

[2] Some references reverse the derivation of the troops for the 3rd and 8th Confederation Regiments.

[3] III/4th Confederation was a light battalion, but had no elite companies.

[4] Mecklenburg-Schwerin did form a third battalion itself, but it was used as a depository for those troops in the rest of the regiment unable to take the field.

UNIT	FROM	UNIFORM
OTHER UNITS		
Frankfurt Battalion in Spain	Frankfurt	Originally uniformed as the 8th Regiment they re-equipped themselves at Spanish expense. All companies wore the shako, with red plumes and ornaments for the grenadiers and green plumes and ornaments for the voltigeurs. The coat was blue as was the collar. The lapels, cuffs and turnbacks were red for the grenadiers and fusilier companies, and green piped red lapels, cuffs and turnbacks for the voltigeurs. Grenadiers had red epaulettes and the voltigeurs had yellow with green fringes
Bataillon des Princes	From Schwarzburg-Sondershausen, Schwarzburg-Rudolstadt, Lippe-Detmold, Schaumburg-Lippe, Reuss & Waldeck	As for the corresponding companies in the 5th and 6th Regiments (above)
Nassau Reitende Jäger	Nassau (2 Sqns only)	The original headgear was a raupenhelm, dark green coat and breeches with white piping at the collar, cuffs and seams. This uniform changed to a black fur colpack with green bag, dark green dolman, dark green pelisse with black fur and white braiding, and dark green overalls. Horse furniture was a black sheepskin

7. BATTLE HISTORY

1ST CONFEDERATION

The first service of the Nassau troops was when the old 3rd Battalion (later part of the 1st Confederation Regiment) served with the French VII Corps in the Jena campaign in October 1806, and then in the Polish campaign of 1807, where they served at the sieges of Stralsund and Colberg.

In 1808, the newly re-organized 2nd Nassau was selected to form part of the Division Allemande under General de Division Jean Leval, part of IV Corps for the second invasion of Spain. They participated in the battles of Medellín, Talavera, Almonacíd and Ocãna, until the division was split up to carry out garrison duties.

The Nassauers remained with the Baden and Frankfurt units in the Army of the Centre, and were present at the decisive Battle of Vitoria on 21 June 1813 against Wellington's Allied Army, which effectively ended the Bonaparte Kingdom of Spain. Falling back into France, it defended the southen frontier, but in December 1813 its commander, Colonel August von Kruse, received instructions to defect to the British.

Having done so, the Regiment was shipped home to act as a cadre for the re-built Nassau Army that would perform so well during the Waterloo campaign in 1815.

2ND CONFEDERATION

Like its sister unit, the 1st Nassau's constituent battalions had their baptism of fire during the 1806 campaign in Germany and the 1807 in Poland.

The 1st Nassau remained in garrison until 1809 when it was ordered south to join General de Division Marie-François Rouyer's Division Princière which was forming at Wurzburg. The division was to have been assigned to Marechal Massena's IV Corps, then to Davout's III Corps, but in the event was to serve with neither. They were present as part of the Vienna garrison during the Battle of Wagram on 5–6 July 1809.

The division was next sent to Spain, where it arrived in March 1810, and deployed in Catalonia. After suffering a defeat at Manresa, the Nassauers were sent to garrison Barcelona where they missed the disasters that befell the rest of the division. Unlike the 2nd Nassau, it did not pass over to the Allies in December 1813, and was disarmed, the men becoming prisoners of war, although some officers and men elected to join the French.

3RD CONFEDERATION

Like the first two Confederation regiments, Wurzburg's contingent first saw action at the sieges of Stralsund and Colberg. After this the Wurzburg regiment was sent to Spain, where it arrived in Catalonia in April 1809.

Almost immediately it took part in the siege of Girona, 6 June to 10 December 1809. By the time it fell, death in all its many forms had reduced the regiment from 1,700 to a battalion of 420. By the time that it, too, was disarmed in December 1813, it was reduced to some 200–300 men.

Not content with having condemned one Wurzburg regiment to service in Spain, Napoleon insisted on the principality fulfilling its obligations again in 1812, when it was used to provide some stiffening to the penal regiments in the 32nd Division of XI Corps.

The Wurzburg regiment was again reinforced for service in 1813, when it formed part of VII Corps at Gross-Beeren, Dennewitz and Leipzig. In 1814, Wurzburg was assigned to Bavaria.

4TH CONFEDERATION

In 1806, the 4th Confederation Regiment served at Colberg in 1807, but was again mobilized as part of Rouyer's division in 1809. Like the rest of this formation, it initially served as separate garrisons along the Danube, but in July was sent, with the 5th and 6th Regiments, to support Marechal Lefebvre and the Bavarians in the Tyrol.

Fighting the Tyrolian insurgents would prove to be good training for future service in Spain, but the learning curve was steep; fighting in the Eisack valley would cost them close to 43 per cent of their strength in forcing their way along overhung roads and attacks on small garrisons.

Sent to Spain the following year with the rest of the Division Princière, the 4th Confederation Regiment began to suffer desertion as it marched through France, and losses in Catalonia grew until it was consolidated with the 5th and 6th Regiments and sent home to be recruited up to strength for Russia, where it was again reduced to a cadre.

In 1813, the composite battalion of the 4th, 5th and 6th Regiments was part of the garrison of Danzig. By this time, Napoleon's army had been pushed back out of Germany, and new volunteer units were raised in the Saxon Duchies for service with the Allies.

5TH AND 6TH CONFEDERATION REGIMENTS

Formed in 1809, these units served alongside the 4th in Austria, Spain and Russia.

7TH CONFEDERATION

The two Mecklenburg duchies had historical ties with Prussia, and were occupied by French forces after the defeats at Jena and Auerstadt. Pressure from Tsar Alexander resulted in their restoration, but they were forced to join the Confederation of the Rhine.

In 1809, the 7th Regiment was used to provide garrisons in Pomerania, and was involved in Schill's revolt, the II/7 being badly mauled at Damgarten on 24 May 1809 just before the insurrection was put down and Schill killed on the 31st.

In 1812, the Mecklenburg-Strelitz battalion served in I Corps, and part of it marched to Moscow, being present at Borodino, whilst the Mecklenburg-Schwerin units served in IX and then III Corps.

Mecklenburg did not reform its units in 1813, instead joining the Allies as two of the first principalities to renounce their allegience to Napoleon. The newly formed hussar regiment took a flag from the Matelots de la Garde at Leipzig.

8TH CONFEDERATION

Ignoring the unit then serving in Spain, Frankfurt's new contribution in 1809 was used to garrison Erfurt.

In 1812, the regiment (now recruited up to three battalions) was assigned to XI Corps, and retreated into Danzig where it was part of the garrison during the siege in 1813. Yet another unit was formed in 1813, and was besieged in Glogau.

With the end of the Confederation in late 1813, Frankfurt raised a volunteer force to fight with the Allies.

FRANKFURT BATTALION IN SPAIN

Originally, Napoleon demanded a regiment of two battalions for service in Spain, but reduced it to one when it proved difficult to find recruits.

Part of Leval's German Division, it served at Medellín, Talavera,

Almonacíd and Ocãna before the division was split up and itself sent into garrison as part of the Army of the Centre. Like the 2nd Nassau, with which it was brigaded, it fought at Vitoria and with Soult's refreshed army trying to defend the line of the Pyrenees. Also like the Nassauers, the few remaining Frankfurters defected to the Allies in December 1813.

BATAILLON DES PRINCES

Called to serve as a first tranche from their parent duchies, the Bataillon crossed the Pyrenees in April 1809 for service in Catalonia. Hard work and no reinforcements meant that its strength was soon whittled down from its original 800 in April to 200 in September.

In June 1810 it was combined with the survivors of the 5th and 6th Regiments, themselves a shadow of their former selves, and returned to Germany.

NASSAU REITENDE JÄGER

The 2nd squadron of this small regiment began its service in Spain in November 1808, and often served with Leval's division, although not formally part of it. It served with distinction in battles and escort duties alike.

Having been part of the French Army that retreated to Bayonne after Vitoria in 1813, it was reinforced by the 1st Squadron of the regiment. They were re-deployed to Suchet's army in Eastern Spain, and disarmed along with all the other German units in December 1813.

8. TACTICS

The units that went to form the Confederation regiments all had different traditions and methodology, depending on whether they were in the Prussian or Austrian sphere of influence.

This, together with the need to make effective combined units, could have been a nightmare (and on occasions it was) but these regiments proved to be resilient and adaptable. French commanders vied with each other to pay them compliments on their fighting abilities.

In the end, however, their rulers proved to have little confidence in the political union promised by the Confederation and threw in their lot with the seemingly victorious Allies.

CHAPTER 12

The Army of the United States of America, 1812–15

1. INTRODUCTION

As the late Colonel John Elting was at pains to point out, at no stage was the fledgling United States in any sort of formal alliance with Imperial France; indeed, at one stage she was at war with it. Accepting this, and acknowledging that there was a shooting war with Great Britain, we have had to decide in which volume to put a chapter on the American Army.

It seemed logical, therefore, to put it in the second Handbook, since it includes all those armies with which the United Kingdom was at one time or another opposed. If this offends purists or sophists, please accept our apologies.

We have also decided to treat the American Army in what could be seen as a truncated form. Although on paper the regular forces totalled some 63,000 men in March 1814, the field strength was only 31,000, with units spread from the Canadian border, along the Western frontier and down to New Orleans at the mouth of the Mississippi. Admittedly, a large force of militia supported them, but of the 198,000 called out in 1814, most were used as garrisons, whilst some states did not call out units at all. Indeed, the war itself was not supported wholeheartedly across the country, the western states being the most enthusiastic, whilst New England shipowners, who had traded with belligerents in Europe faced ruin from the British blockade.

2. BACKGROUND

The most effective weapon that the British Government had at its disposal was the Royal Navy, which it used to enforce a blockade of ports in France and those of her allies. Cruiser squadrons swept the seas for French merchantmen, and soon there were few ships flying the tricolor left.

In these circumstances, France turned to the neutral powers to carry the supplies she needed, and none was more dedicated to this than that of the fledgling United States, independent from Great Britain in 1783 and owing a debt of gratitude to France.

Faced with the threat of having the blockade undermined, the Royal Navy boarded every ship that it could to ensure war supplies did not slip through, whilst Napoleon issued decrees that any ships allowing themselves either to be searched or which put in to British ports would make themselves liable to seizure. In addition, the Royal Navy's voracious need for seamen was such that boarding parties also searched for any member of the crew who could not prove his American citizenship; failure to provide a certificate often meant impressment.

On the western frontier, settlers were demanding increased security from raids carried out by Native Americans thought to be either controlled by, or having sanctuary in, Canada. The thought was that, with Great Britain largely involved in Europe, a punitive war would either destroy this threat, or capture Canada itself.

The American Army that was to fight in the War of 1812 was very new. At the end of the Revolutionary War, Washington's victorious forces had been rapidly demobilized until there was effectively only a guard left on the main arsenal. With the need to defend the western frontier, however, Congress ordered the raising of the 1st American Regiment from militia troops. This was, at best, only half a solution, for there was little effort made to bring the unit up to strength. In November 1791, two battalions of the regiment, together with militia, were caught up in the United States' biggest Native American disaster along the Wabash in present-day Ohio.

This was avenged in August 1794, when 'Mad Anthony' Wayne took his reformed American Legion to Fallen Timbers, but shortly afterwards the army was reduced again. From then, Congress authorized increases in the army's establishment, only to reduce it again when the perceived threat disappeared. Some of this was also political; in the developing democracy, a standing army was seen by some as potentially subversive. A citizen's militia, defending the people's rights, was seen as far safer.

In addition, America felt safe through its remoteness. Any European army would need to cross the Atlantic before invading. A strong navy and coastal defences were therefore seen as a potential deterrent. It was only with the growth of the 'War Hawks' that real need for expansion of the standing army became important. Unfortunately, for various reasons this proved to be beyond the army's capabilities.

This is obviously not the right place to rehearse the full story of the land operations along the Canadian border. The small British garrison, the Canadian militia, and those allied Native American tribes, threw back the several invasions, capturing large numbers of Americans in the process. The campaign see-sawed along the Great Lakes as first one side then the other obtained temporary naval supremacy and launched attacks, only to suffer catastrophe and withdraw. By 1814, despite the introduction of large numbers of Wellington's veterans, the effective stalemate could not be broken, even through expanding the war to the Chesapeake, burning the White House in Washington, or attacking Baltimore.

The Treaty of Ghent, signed on 24 December 1814 ended the war on a status quo ante bellum – too late to stop Packenham's disaster at New Orleans, but the American Army that resulted was now highly professional.

3. COMMAND STRUCTURE

Under the Constitution, the role of Commander in Chief was lodged firmly with the President, an elected position. In 1812, the President was James Madison. Madison had been instrumental in drawing up both the Constitution and the Bill of Rights. As Secretary of State, he had finalized the Louisiana Purchase that had opened up the Mississippi Basin. The result of this massive accretion of land was the western expansion into the Great Plains.

Madison had no military experience; indeed, he distrusted the military and thought it capable of subverting the republic. As such, he took only as much interest in it as was required to ensure that it was capable of meeting the country's security needs.

Under him were several executive officers, the most important of whom in this context were James Monroe, the Secretary of State (something like a Foreign Minister) and first William Eustis, then John Armstrong as the Secretary of War. Monroe was to succeed Armstrong in September 1814. Both the President and the executive were responsible to Congress for the decisions they made. At Bladensburg on 24 August 1814, Madison, Armstrong and Monroe all rode out to the battlefield, where they interfered with the arrangements and deployments of the actual commander, William Winder.

In addition, under the Federal system, the individual states were responsible for certain aspects of defence, not least the organization, maintenance and training of their militia. Whilst Congress commissioned regular officers, the states were responsible for providing generals for their militia. This situation was rife with opportunities for patronage.

At the beginning of the War of 1812, the ranking general was Brigadier-General James Wilkinson, one of the strangest men ever to rise to that level of responsibility. He was in the pay of Spain, then the ruling power in Mexico, and passed on information about American plans on westward expansion, in addition to which he speculated in land purchases. His successor was Henry Dearborn, who had previously held the role of Secretary of War in Jefferson's administration.

4. OFFICER CORPS

The need to expand the American Army resulted also in a need to find sufficient officers to command it. The Academy at West Point had been set up by Act of Congress in 1802 to train specialists in artillery and engineering, not staff duties, and there were too few graduates available anyway.

The available pool consisted of ageing veterans from the Revolution, or political appointees within the militia. Like their counterparts found in the armies of the *ancien régime*, they may have been willing, but the pace of modern warfare, and the need to plan campaigns at the end of long lines of communication left many floundering.

By 1814, natural selection and the winnowing of ranks through casualties had brought men like Jacob Brown and Winfield Scott to command positions. Scott, in particular, was an avid reader and collector of contemporary military treatises, and trained his brigade using a translation of the 1791 French manual.

5. OTHER RANKS

Like the British soldier, the American Regular was a volunteer; only the militia was made up from universal service, although the regiments were only called out for a specific period of time.

In a time of full employment, it was very difficult to recruit troops; only the unemployable were likely to want to serve in the ranks. Congress tried to stimulate recruitment by offering limited service periods (sometimes as short as twelve or eighteen months, with a land grant in the west as an added inducement), but most regiments only fielded 50 per cent of their authorized strength. An analysis of recruits indicates that the majority (some 76 per cent) were native-born Americans, as the vast influx of emigrants had not yet started. Only in the 1840s would large numbers of Irish and Germans find their role in the army.

When war did break out there was, as might be expected, the spur of patriotism, but since the war was largely unsupported in New England (most of whose potential recruits probably went into the privateering service anyway) this was not an abundant recruitment pool. Only when the British threatened to invade from 1813 onwards was there a resurgence.

Those men who did join up were expected to receive their training with their units, rather than in regimental depots, although a depot company was authorized per infantry battalion. Only the artillery received anything like a formal education. Those joining the rifle regiments were required to be expert shots.

At the beginning of the War, any training was very haphazard, and the early engagements showed that the Amercian military were at the bottom of a very steep learning curve. By 1815, the best regiments were able to slug out a dog-fight with Wellington's veterans in close range firefights. General Riall's 'Those are Regulars by God!' as he saw Winfield Scott's brigade wheel into line at Chippewa (5 July 1814) may be seen as a compliment to the effort put in by their officers and sergeants.

6. THE MILITARY ESTABLISHMENT

Organization

Organization of the Regular forces available at the beginning of the war was as shown in the tables on pp. 276–8.

ORGANIZATION OF THE MILITARY ESTABLISHMENT

1812 **CAVALRY**			
Light Dragoons	2 regiments, each of approx. 600 officers and men	Each of 4 squadrons, strength approx. 150 officers and men	Each squadron had 2 troops of approx. 75 officers and men
INFANTRY			
Infantry regiments	17 regiments	Each of 1 battalion,[1] totalling 1,000 officers and men	Each of 10 companies, each of 100 officers and men[2]
Rifle Regiment	1 regiment	As above	As above
Rangers	7 companies		Authorized strength probably 100 officers and men
ARTILLERY			
Foot artillery	3 regiments	Each of 20 companies[3]	Each able to man about 3 guns
Light artillery	1 regiment	10 companies[4]	As above
1813 **CAVALRY**			
Light Dragoons	2 regiments, each of approx. 600 officers and men	Each of 4 squadrons, strength approx. 150 officers and men	Each squadron had 2 troops of approx. 75 officers and men

[1] The ten new regiments (8th to 17th) authorized in January 1812 were to have two battalions, each with nine companies, but were quickly adjusted to the original organization.

[2] There are some references to flank companies, but this may have been theoretical rather than actual.

[3] These also manned the guns in coastal forts, and were not necessarily available for field use.

[4] The light artillery were expected to be the mobile artillery, similar to horse companies in European armies, but only one was fully equipped at the outbreak of the war.

INFANTRY			
Infantry regiments	44 regiments	Each of 1 battalion, totalling 1,000 officers and men	Each of 10 companies, each of 100 officers and men
Rifle Regiment	1 regiment	As above	As above
Rangers	17 companies		Authorized strength probably 100 officers and men
ARTILLERY			
Foot artillery	3 regiments	Each of 20 companies	Each able to man about 3 guns
Light artillery	1 regiment	10 companies	As above
1814 **CAVALRY**			
Light Dragoons	1 regiment, of approx. 600 officers and men	4 squadrons, strength approx. 150 officers and men	Each squadron had 2 troops of approx. 75 officers and men
INFANTRY			
Infantry regiments	48 regiments	Each of 1 battalion, totalling 1,000 officers and men	Each of 10 companies, each of 100 officers and men
Rifle Regiment	4 regiments	As above	As above
Rangers	17 companies		Authorized strength probably 100 officers and men

ARTILLERY			
Corps of Artillery	12 battalions	Each of 4 companies	Each able to man about 3 guns
Light artillery	1 regiment	10 companies	As above

It should be noted that no unit ever fielded its full authorized strength (which was why the two cavalry regiments were amalgamated in 1814), and some of the junior infantry regiments existed as 'paper' units only.

7. UNIFORMS

CAVALRY

The original helmet worn by the Light Dragoons was leather, with an upright front, behind which was a white over blue plume. The false turban was intended to look like leopard skin, and the falling horse hair mane was white.

In 1813, this was replaced with a new helmet that looked like that now worn by the British heavy cavalry, with a white over blue plume and a white horse-hair mane.

The coat was based on that of the British light dragoons. It was dark blue, including the cuffs and collar, and had white braiding around both. The braiding across the front and along the seams was blue. Overalls were either blue or white, and knee boots were worn.

The shabraque was dark blue, with white trimming.

INFANTRY

As the war progressed, so the infantry uniform got progressively simpler. The first uniform, worn by the seven pre-war regiments consisted of a cylindrical felt cap with a white front plume and white cords. Officers wore a bicorne. The blue coat had a red collar and cuffs, with white turnbacks. The front of the coat was decorated with a double row of buttons with white braiding across the front. The breeches were blue for winter or white for summer, worn with gaiters.

In 1812, the cap became more like that worn by the French Army, wider at the top than the bottom, and with a white metal front plate, but still with a white front plume. The coat still had a red collar and cuffs with white turnbacks, but now there was only a single row of buttons, with braiding across the front. Blue gaiter trousers were worn in winter, and white in summer.

The final change came in 1813, when a new cap, similar to the British Belgic shako, was taken into wear. It had a false front, white metal front plate, and the white plume was moved to the side.

The jacket was simplified still further, losing the red collar and cuffs in favour of them remaining as the coat colour, and the braiding was removed from the jacket front.

The rapid expansion of the army meant that some expedients had to be carried out, such as replacing the blue uniforms with black cloth, or providing non-regulation uniforms, such as brown coats. Perhaps the most famous example is that of Winfield Scott's brigade in 1814. The blue uniforms having been diverted to another command, all that could be offered for the 9th, 11th, 21st and 25th were grey jackets and pantaloons. The four regiments were dressed in the grey alternative, and wore them proudly as they advanced on Riall's British redcoats at Chippewa.

The Rifles wore a uniform based on the line infantry, but in grass green with black collar and cuffs. Before the war actually broke out, they were ordered to adopt a dark, bottle green. Breeches were also green as was the cap plume.

For service dress, the regiments were issued with a green hunting frock, fringed in yellow or straw.

By 1814, the search for stocks of green cloth resulted in the rifles being issued with a simple all grey uniform.

ARTILLERY

The artillery wore a uniform based on that of the infantry, but with red turnbacks trimmed yellow. The 1st Regiment wore a bicorne for a short time in 1812, but, like the other two regiments, soon adopted the cap. Instead of the infantry's white cords and front plate, the artillery adopted yellow.

The Light Artillery regiment wore a blue coat with blue collar and cuffs, to differentiate the unit from its 'heavy' brethren. Overalls were blue, and hussar boots would be worn for mounted service.

THE MARINE CORPS

Although the Marines fought mainly on board ships, a small detachment served at Bladensburg. The uniform was similar to that of the infantry at the start of the war, but the cap plume was red, and the metal cap plate, cap cords and braiding were yellow.

MILITIA

The uniforms to be worn by the militia or volunteers largely depended on what was available. Some wore uniforms, some hunting frocks.

The Washington militia that fought at Bladensburg wore a round hat (like a top hat), with a bearskin fitted across it, and a blue coat with white pantaloons. The Virginia militia, which also served in the defence of Washington, wore blue hunting shirts trimmed red, and a round hat, turned up on the left with a red and black plume.

The Marylanders at Baltimore wore a regular infantry cap with red over black plumes, and blue coats faced red; pantaloons were white.

The New York units which served along the Canadian border wore either bicornes or round hats, and their coats were blue, faced red. Some of the units that served in the Niagara campaign in the summer of 1814 seemed to have been issued with regular uniforms.

8. BATTLE HISTORY

Despite the large number of units formed, very few actually got to fire a shot in anger, and the war itself was largely one of raids and pinpricks.

The battles that were fought would not have counted as skirmishes in the mass warfare being carried out in Europe. As an example of one of the larger engagements, we have included the American Order of Battle for Lundy's Lane, 25 July 1814.

First Brigade:	
9th Infantry	200
11th Infantry	200
22nd Infantry	300
25th Infantry	380
Second Brigade:	
1st Infantry	150
21st Infantry	432 (includes cos of 17th and 19th)
23rd Infantry	300
Third Brigade:	
New York Militia	250
5th Pennsylvania	246
Canadian Vols	50

Biddle's, Ritchie's and Towson's artillery companies, with a total of 200 gunners, served some 6-pounders, two howitzers and three 12-pounders. The cavalry, consisting of a troop of the US Dragoon Regiment and a company of New York Dragoons, totalled seventy officers and men.

9. TACTICS

In 1812, the manual in use harked back to the days of Steuben, drill master to Washington's army at Valley Forge. This in turn drew on the author's familiarity with the Prussian drill of the 1770s. Arrangements were, however, in hand to adopt a more modern manual, based around the dominant French 1791 Règlement. Training was very much in the hands of the regimental and general officers; if they were ineffective, then so were their men. The early campaigns showed that much work needed to be done.

Because of the small size of the forces engaged, usually the equivalent of a small division, generals were able to concentrate on training individual brigades. Most recruits only started their training when they reached their regiments as there were no depots to do this as in the European armies. In view of this, it is perhaps not too surprising that campaigns tended to be short.

The column was the prime manoeuvring formation. It was usually formed on a division (two companies) front. Since it tended not to be shielded from fire by a skirmish screen, units would deploy into line for combat. Like the British, fire combat was not considered to be an end in itself, but a mechanism to destroy the opponents cohesion. Once an enemy formation started to waver, the (hopefully) still steady victor would attempt to charge home to break their morale.

The United States went into the war badly prepared. Logistical support for the fighting troops was either bad or non-existent. Elderly, or political generals found it difficult to adapt to the needs of modern warfare. By the end of it, however, America found it had a new pride in her army and had learnt some important lessons.

To advise the politicians in Washington, and to avoid overt meddling, the nucleus of a general staff system had been formed. Service schools had begun to be developed to train specialists, and arsenals were set up in strategic locations to assist in the arming of new units.

Winfield Scott was to lead an American Army to Mexico City in 1848, training officers who would go on to lead the Union and Confederate Armies during the Civil War; Scott himself was still the commanding general in 1861, a strange link with what has sometimes been described as the 'last Napoleonic War'.

CHAPTER 13

The Army of the Grand Duchy of Warsaw, 1807–13

1. INTRODUCTION

AT ONE TIME, the Kingdom of Poland was the largest in Europe, extending round the Baltic coast into modern day Lithuania, and deep into the Ukraine and Belarus. A fiercely Catholic country, it was a bulwark against both Slav and Turkish expansionism. Indeed, Jan Sobieski was to lead the relief army that defeated the Turkish siege of Vienna in 1683.

Unfortunately, the state became atrophied and failed to mature. The kings were elected by the nobility rather than being hereditary, with the result that bargaining and agreements became important. The great noble families controlled the country, and were not above calling for outside assistance in the event of disputes.

This process of a weak government spurred on the surrounding jackals as Brandenburg-Prussia, Russia, and Sweden all saw opportunities. With few allies, these threats could only be met with limited means, and usually resulted in loss of territory. By the middle of the eighteenth century Poland was falling into the Russian sphere of influence, so much so that, on at least one occasion, the Russians had ensured the election of their candidate for king.

In 1772, Prussia (now a European power thanks to Frederick the Great) and Austria (still eager for land) agreed with Catherine the Great's Russia that the peace of eastern Europe demanded that, if Poland could not be governed efficiently, they would govern it themselves. In this 'First Partition of Poland', Prussia gained West Prussia, Russia Belarus and Austria part of the Ukraine.

The loss of some 29 per cent of its territory was a spur to limited reform in what was left of Poland, but a strong Poland was not what the Eastern powers wanted. (Tragically, this was not wanted by some of the more reactionary nobles either.) In the Second Partition, in 1793, Prussia gained Danzig and its surrounding area, whilst Russia got what was left of Poland east of the Bug.

Although this further loss spurred on Polish patriots to seek assistance from revolutionary France, this was not forthcoming. A rising liberated some parts of Russian-held Poland, but reinforcements under Alexander Suvorov arrived and stormed Warsaw, sacking much of the city. As a result, in the final, Third Partition of 1795, Prussia took Warsaw, Austria received a bridgehead north of the Carpathians around Cracow and Russia absorbed everything else. Poland had ceased to exist.

2. BACKGROUND

Recognizing that revolutionary France was now their only hope, a large number of patriots sought the aid of the French leaders. As an earnest of their intention, the Poles' military leader-in-exile, General Jan Henryk Dombrowski, began to form a Polish Legion. Because the French Constitution did not allow the enlistment of foreign troops, the Legion was put in the pay of the Cisalpine Republic, newly formed following Napoleon Bonaparte's victories in Italy in 1796.

By May 1797 the strength had increased to allow a second legion to be formed. Both units consisted of infantry and artillery, the first cavalry regiment only being formed after the invasion of the Kingdom of Naples in December 1798. Disaster soon ensued when an Austro-Russian army invaded Northern Italy in 1799. This army, under Suvorov, swept away many of the French backed Italian republics. Both Legions fought at Magnano (5 April), but the 2nd Legion retired into Mantua where they were captured after the city's fall, and the men forcibly returned to the Austrian regiments from which many had deserted.

In the meantime, the 1st Legion went on to fight at the Trebbia (17–19 June 1799), Novi (15 August) and during the recovery of Italy after Suvorov led his Russians north into Switzerland during the autumn. With the closure of the campaign, and Napoleon (newly returned from Egypt) as First Consul, the remnants of the two Legions were reorganized into the Italian Legion, whilst also forming a new Legion of the Danube which served along the Rhine. Whilst the Danube

Legion fought at Hohenlinden in December 1800, the Italian legion was still organizing and missed Marengo (14 June 1800).

The two Legions were now concentrated in Northern Italy, where they were disbanded and converted into the 1st, 2nd (from the Italian Legion) and 3rd Demi Brigades Étrangère. There was already some discontent that the Treaty of Luneville, which had been imposed on Austria on 26 January 1801 did not include any provision for the restitution of Poland, and it might have been with the intention of lancing this boil that two of the Polish units were sent to their deaths in the West Indies in 1803. The remaining 1st Demi Brigade stayed in Italy, serving at Maida in July 1806 before being ordered to Central Europe in early 1807 where more tumultuous events had been unfolding. One wonders if, during their marches, these men saw the great Benedictine abbey at Cassino, where some 140 years later another Polish Army in exile was to bleed and (ultimately) be betrayed by their ostensible allies.

On 14 October 1806, Napoleon had defeated the Prussian Army at Jena and Auerstadt and the pursuit of the remainder had led the French spearheads into Prussia's Polish provinces. Just as he intended to reward his German supporters with lands stripped from the Hohenzollern's western and southern holdings, so would the Brandenburg rump be fenced in from the east by a new French client state – the Grand Duchy of Warsaw. The new Duchy would require an army, and the nucleus would be found from a cadre of veterans of the 1st Demi Brigade Étrangère, as well as a newer unit, the Légion du Nord, formed from Prussian and Austrian prisoners of war.[1]

The new army had, as its Minister of War, Prince Josef Poniatowski (1763–1813) who had served in the Austrian Army against the Turks in 1788, then in the Polish Army against the Russians in 1794 but had spent his time since then on his family estates. Originally, the new army used a legion organization, but this was soon superceded by that of a combined arms divisional structure. On 1 March 1807, Poniatowski's 1st Legion consisted of the 1st to 4th Infantry, the 1st Chasseur à Cheval and the 2nd Uhlans; the 2nd Legion (under Zayonczek) had the 5th to 8th Infantry, the 3rd Uhlans and the 4th Chasseurs, whilst the 3rd Legion (Dombrowski) had the 9th to 12th Infantry, the 5th Chasseurs and the 6th Uhlans. All three Legions also had artillery battalions, originally consisting of only a single company.

[1] Another such unit, the Vistula Legion, was also raised through Poles serving in the Italian theatre, including the remnants of the 1st Demi Brigade Étrangère. In this instance, however, the units remained in French pay, and so are discussed in the French chapter.

These formations seem to have been administrative groupings, as the units that fought during the 1807 campaign were made up from different legions. After the Treaties of Tilsit were signed on 7 and 9 July 1807, when the Duchy of Warsaw formally annexed Prussia's Polish provinces, the army could be concentrated and properly organized. There were, however, significant financial problems as the Duchy had to support a French garrison as well as build its own forces. Some help was given when Napoleon agreed to take three infantry regiments into French pay for service in Spain. This detachment, plus the need to find garrisons for the Polish fortresses, effectively meant that the three divisions could not be maintained, and the field force was therefore reduced to two divisions.

In 1809, the Grand Duchy was invaded by the Austrians, but the successes along the Danube allowed the war to be carried into Austrian Galicia, a move which allowed the recruiting of new regiments. Indeed, under the Peace of Schönbrunn in October 1809, these Austrian provinces were absorbed into the Grand Duchy and the new units became permanent.

By 1812, the Grand Duchy was able to provide a complete corps to the Imperial order of battle, as well as provide significant numbers of light cavalry to act as scouts in the heavy cavalry corps. As the French Army advanced across the border into the once-Polish lands of Lithuania, recruits flocked to their standards, although the regiments they provided were ephemeral, and were destroyed in the retreat.

The advancing Russians crossed back into Poland in February 1813, with the capital itself falling in February. Notwithstanding this disaster, the Poles provided yet another corps for Napoleon's German campaign. Again ground down, and with Poniatowski, now a marshal of France, dead at Leipzig, Polish regiments continued to fight and die for an Emperor who could no longer assist them in their dream for a restored Poland – only honour kept them in the ranks. The cadre of a Polish infantry regiment continued under the Bourbons, but it could not be mobilized in time to take the field in 1815. The squadron of Guard Lancers had, of course, accompanied the exiled Napoleon to Elba, and fought at Waterloo with the 2nd (Dutch) Lancers of the Guard.

3. COMMAND STRUCTURE

When the French forces first entered Poland, the liberated provinces were governed by a Committee. With the creation of the Grand Duchy and the appointment of the King of Saxony as its Grand Duke after Tilsit, this was replaced by a State Council of ministers, although the French Resident was an important influence, helping to prevent any outbreak of radicalism.

The constitution was based on that of the French. Serfdom was abolished, and the Code Napoléon introduced, even down to the departments. However, Poland was never allowed to forget that it was a French client state and was in almost a perpetual financial quagmire with a stagnant economy and difficulties in collecting taxes.

4. OFFICER CORPS

There was little difficulty in finding officers for the developing army. Many came from the various legions formed during the revolutionary period or the early empire, but others came from service in the Prussian or Austrian armies, whilst still others came from the nobility.

Almost alone amongst the Confederation forces, Polish formations were commanded by national officers rather than French appointees. Napoleon himself had Polish aides-de-camp. Polish officers proved to be dedicated and experienced. One additional advantage that they had was the ability to converse with Spanish priests using Latin.

5. OTHER RANKS

Conscription was embraced with enthusiasm, with little of the avoidance found in parts of Germany. Lack of funds meant that units tended to be under strength for this reason, not from lack of willing. Polish units were tough fighters, perhaps because they were fighting for a cause and had to prove themselves. Some observers thought they could be brutal: survivors of Colborne's brigade at Albuera in May 1811 accused Uhlans from the Vistula Legion of spearing the wounded.

Polish soldiers also gained a reputation for pillaging, and were not averse to stealing from other units if the opportunity or the need arose.

As will be seen below, cavalry formed a disproportionate element of the army. This was the traditional arm of the Polish forces, and it re-introduced the lance to western armies.

6. THE MILITARY ESTABLISHMENT

Organization

1807 INFANTRY		
12 regiments, with approx. 1,600 all ranks. This was about 66 per cent of authorized strength	2 battalions, each of 800 officers and men	Each battalion had 1 grenadier, 1 voltigeur and 7 fusilier companies, each of 95 officers and men
CAVALRY		
3 regiments of uhlans, each of 812 all ranks	4 squadrons	Each squadron was approx. 200 all ranks
3 regiments of chasseurs à cheval	As above	As above
ARTILLERY		
3 battalions of foot artillery	Each battalion had only 1 or 2 companies	Each company had 6 x 8lb guns and 2 howitzers
1809 INFANTRY		
2 'Home' regiments (10th & 11th), with approx. 2,500 officers and men at authorized strength	With 2 field and 1 garrison battalion, each of 6 companies, with 850 officers and men	Each battalion had 1 grenadier, 1 voltigeur and 4 fusilier companies, each of 140 officers and men
7 'Home' regiments	With 2 battalions, each of 9 companies, with approx. 1,200 officers and men	Each battalion had 1 grenadier, 1 voltigeur and 7 fusilier companies, each of 140 officers and men
3 'Spanish' regiments (4th, 7th and 9th)	With 2 battalions, each of 9 companies, with approx. 1,200 officers and men	Each battalion had 1 grenadier, 1 voltigeur and 7 fusilier companies, each of 140 officers and men
6 'Franco-Galician' regiments, with approx. 3,950 officers and men	Each with 4 field battalions with approx. 850 officers and men, and 1 depot battalion with approx. 560 officers and men	Each field battalion had 1 grenadier, 1 voltigeur and 4 fusilier companies; the depot battlion had only 4 fusilier companies. Each company had 140 officers and men.

CAVALRY		
3 chasseur à cheval regiments of approx. 600 officers and men	Each of 4 squadrons (3 only in practice)	Each squadron had approx. 200 officers and men (1st company was elite)
5 uhlan regiments, approx. 600 officers and men	As above	As above
1 hussar regiment of approx. 600 officers and men	As above	As above
7 'Franco-Galician' regiments (mainly uhlans)	Each of 4 squadrons	Each squadron had approx. 200 officers and men
ARTILLERY		
3 battalions of foot artillery	Each of 4 companies	Each company had 4 guns and 3 howitzers
Horse artillery	2 companies	As above
1812 **INFANTRY**		
14 infantry regiments, each of approx. 3,000 officers and men	Each of 3 field battalions of approx. 800 officers and men, and 1 depot battalion of approx. 500 officers and men	Each field battalion had 1 grenadier, 1 voltigeur and 4 fusilier companies; the depot battalion had 4 fusilier companies. Each company had 136 officers and men
3 infantry regiments (5th, 10th and 11th), each of approx. 3,500 officers and men	Each of 4 field battalions of 840 officers and men, plus a depot company of 140 officers and men	Each field battalion had 1 grenadier, 1 voltigeur and 4 fusilier companies, each of 140 officers and men
5 Lithuanian regiments	Probably 3 battalions per regiment	None were up to strength
2 Lithuanian light regiments	3 battalions per regiment	None were up to strength
CAVALRY		
3 chasseur à cheval regiments	Each of 4 field squadrons (983 officers and men) and 1 depot squadron	Each squadron consisted of 245 officers and men. There was one elite company

CAVALRY (Cont.)		
10 uhlan regiments	As above	As above
2 hussar regiments	As above	As above
1 cuirassier regiments	2 field squadrons and 1 depot company	The field strength was 499 officers and men
ARTILLERY		
1 foot artillery regiment	3 battalions	4 companies, each with 4 guns and 2 howitzers
1 horse artillery regiment	1 battalion	2 companies, each with 4 x 6 pdr guns and 2 howitzers
1813 **INFANTRY**		
The 4th, 7th & 9th regiments were merged into one regiment	2 battalions, each of 450 officers and men	Each of 1 grenadier, 1 voltigeur and 4 fusilier companies
7 other infantry regiments	As above	As above
CAVALRY		
Krakus Regiment	4 squadrons	Approx. 700 officers and men
2 chasseur à cheval regiments	As above	As above
1 hussar regiment	As above	As above
5 uhlan regiments	As above	As above
1 cuirassier regiment	2 squadrons	Approx. 200 officers and men
ARTILLERY		
6 foot companies		Each 4 guns and 2 howitzers
1 horse company		As above

7. UNIFORMS

i) 1807–1810

INFANTRY

The original uniform adopted by the Duchy's infantry was intended to show the Legion and Divisional assignment. All ranks wore the traditional czapka in black felt, decorated with a large sunburst plate on the front, although it is possible that a French-style shako was worn during the initial raising of the army. The grenadiers had a red plume or pom-pon and cords, the voltigeurs yellow, and the fusiliers light blue. Some grenadier companies were issued with bearskins.

The tunic was a dark blue kurtka with yellow cuffs and lapels with red collar for the 1st Legion/Division (1st–4th Regiments); crimson cuffs, lapels and collar for the 2nd Legion Division (5th–8th Regiments) and white cuffs, lapels and collar for the 3rd Legion/Division. Grenadiers had red epaulettes, voltigeurs light green and the fusiliers had shoulder straps piped in the distinctive.

Breeches were dark blue with the outside seam piped in the distinctive.

The three units that formed the Duchy's contribution to the Iberian war in August 1808 (4th, 7th and 9th Infantry) were re-equipped from French stores. They retained their original distinctives.

CAVALRY

On their formation, the first six regiments of the Duchy's cavalry wore the same style of uniform, irrespective of the arm of service. The headgear was a black shako, although the elite companies may have had bearskin colpacks, and some of the uhlans may have had a black czapka with a black plume. The elite companies had a red plume, colpack bag if applicable and cords.

The kurtka was dark blue, and carried divisional distinctives: those assigned to the 1st Legion or Division (1st Chasseurs and 2nd Uhlans) had poppy red collars with yellow cuffs and lapels, all piped white; those from the 2nd Legion or Division (3rd Uhlans and 4th Chasseurs) had crimson facings, piped white, whilst the units for the 3rd Legion or Division (5th Chasseurs and 6th Uhlans) had white distinctives.

For campaign, the breeches were grey with a side stripe in the divisional colour.

From 1808 the 1st and 4th Chasseur regiments adopted a dark green kurtka, whilst the 5th continued to wear a dark blue one. Collar, cuffs, turnbacks and piping was now red for the 1st, crimson for the 4th and orange for the 5th. The distinctive was also used for the busby bag of the elite companies. Breeches were green.

All units carried the lance, with a red over white pennon.

ARTILLERY

The foot artillery wore a black shako with red pom-pon and cords, and a dark green kurtka with black facings including the turnbacks, all piped red; the epaulettes were red. Breeches were white, black with a green side stripe for full dress.

When the horse artillery was formed, it was issued with a czapka with red pom-pon and cords. The kurtka was cavalry-style with black collar, cuffs and turnbacks piped red; the front of the kurtka was piped red. The breeches were dark green with black side stripes.

FRANCO–GALICIAN UNITS

The state of the Duchy's economy meant that there was little opportunity to provide a formal uniform for these newly raised units. Most wore a white-sleeved waistcoat and trousers, although the 13th Regiment was provided with a white coat faced light blue from captured Austrian stocks. The shako was French.

ii) 1810–1814

INFANTRY

Except for the three units in Spain and the 13th Regiment, all units adopted a common uniform style:

> The grenadiers wore a peaked bearskin bonnet, which had a red patch with a white cross. The plume and cords were red. The voltigeurs were issued with a czapka with a yellow-over-green plume and yellow cords, whilst the fusiliers had white cords and black plumes.

The kurtka remained dark blue with white lapels and turnbacks, with crimson collar, cuffs and piping. Exceptions were the dark blue collar of the grenadiers and the yellow collar of the voltigeurs. In addition, the 1st, 2nd and 3rd Regiments and the voltigeur companies of the 5th had yellow cuffs. Epaulettes were red for grenadiers, green for the voltigeurs and the shoulder straps were piped crimson for the fusiliers. Breeches were dark blue for winter and campaign wear and white for the summer.

The 13th Regiment now wore a czapka for all companies with the usual additions, including red top edging for the grenadiers, white kurtka with light blue collar, cuffs and turnbacks. The breeches were white.

The three units in Spain continued to wear French-style uniform even when they returned to Central Europe for service in Russia. The 4th had yellow cuffs and lapels. Grenadier shakos were edged red, whilst the voltigeur's were edged yellow.

CAVALRY

The Chasseur regiments continued to wear a shako (elite companies had a colpack without the bag), dark green kurtka with regimental facings (1st poppy red, 4th crimson and 5th orange), and green breeches.

The two hussar regiments both had a dark blue dolman with crimson collar and a dark blue pelisse. The 10th Regiment had yellow lace and black fur edging, whilst the 13th had white braiding and fur edging. Shakos were black, (the 13th's changed to light blue) with black plumes. The elite companies had a black or brown colpack with light blue bags, red plumes and cords.

The 14th Cuirassiers looked almost the same as the French regiments, the only difference being the substitution of gold epaulettes for the officers and yellow buttons for the men. The helmet was steel, with a black horse-hair crest and red plume, the dark blue habit-veste had crimson collar and cuffs, and the breeches were white leather. The back and breast plates were steel and were trimmed with red at the arms and waist, although these were not available during the 1813 campaign.

The Uhlans continued to wear a czapka (black lambskin or colpack for the elite companies) with black plumes (red for elite companies). The kurtka was dark blue, with the facing colours shown in the table on p. 296.

CAVALRY

UNIT	COLLAR	TURNBACKS	CUFFS	TROUSER STRIPE
2nd	Poppy red, piped white	Dark blue, piped yellow	Poppy red, piped white	Yellow
3rd	Crimson, piped white	Dark blue, piped white	Crimson, piped white	Yellow
6th	White, piped crimson	Dark blue, piped crimson	Dark blue, piped crimson	Crimson
7th	Yellow, piped poppy red	Dark blue, piped poppy red	Yellow, piped poppy red	Yellow
8th	Poppy red, piped dark blue	Dark blue, piped dark blue	Poppy red, piped dark blue	Poppy red
9th	Poppy red, piped dark blue	Dark blue, piped white	Dark blue, piped poppy red	Poppy red
11th	Crimson, piped dark blue	Crimson, piped white	Dark blue, piped crimson	Crimson
12th	Crimson, piped white	Dark blue, piped white	Dark blue, piped white	Crimson
15th	Crimson, piped white	Crimson, piped white	Crimson, piped white	Crimson
16th	Crimson, piped white	Dark blue, piped crimson	Crimson, piped white	Crimson
17th	Crimson, piped dark blue	Dark blue, piped crimson	Crimson, piped dark blue	Crimson
18th	Crimson, piped dark blue	Crimson, piped white	Crimson, piped dark blue	Crimson
19th	Yellow, piped dark blue	Dark blue, piped yellow	Yellow, piped dark blue	Yellow
20th	Crimson, piped dark blue	Yellow, piped dark blue	Yellow, piped dark blue	Yellow
21st	Orange	Orange (piped dark blue?)	Orange	Crimson

Breeches were dark blue.

Known lance pennons were red over white for the 2nd, 3rd, 15th and 16th Regiments, with a dark blue triangle superimposed for the 7th to 12th, and blue over white for the 17th to 21st. It is likely that the remainder were red over white.

In 1813 the 4th Chasseurs were converted to Uhlans with crimson czapkas, crimson facing colours and crimson breeches.

When originally formed the Krakus regiment wore a red czapka with a black or white lambskin turban, long russet-red coats and pantaloons. As supplies became scarce, they adopted colpacks and blue litewkas, although by 1814 a crimson 'beret' was being worn. The lances did not carry pennons.

ARTILLERY

There was little change from the earlier foot artillery uniform, which continued to be a black shako, with a red plume or pom-pon and cords, a dark green faced black infantry style kurtka and green or white breeches.

The horse artillery now adopted the colpack with a dark green bag instead of the czapka. The cords and plume were red. The chasseur style kurtka was dark green, still with black facings, and the green breeches had a black side stripe.

8. BATTLE HISTORY

(Roman numerals indicate original Corps affiliation; these often changed during the campaign.)

1806–07

D	Siege and capture of Danzig, 10 March–24 May 1807
F	Friedland, 14 June 1807

Spain

Al	Almonacíd, 11 August 1809
Fu	Fuengirola, 13 October 1810
O	Ocaña, 18–19 November 1809
T	Talavera, 27–28 July 1809
Ta	(failed) Siege of Tarifa, 19 December 1811–5 January 1812

1809

K	Krakau, 14 July 1809

R Raszyn, 19 April 1809
S Sandomierz, 26 May 1809

1812
Be Beresina, 26–28 November 1812
Bo Borodino, 7 September 1812
Bv Borisov, 21 November 1812
M Mir 10 July 1812
Ri Blockade of Riga, 24 July–18 December 1812
S Smolensk, 17–18 August 1812
W Winkowo, 18 October 1812

1813–14
Bl Blockades of Zamosc (10 February–22 December 1813) & Modlin (23 February–25 December 1813)
D Siege and Capture of Danzig, 16 January–29 November 1813
De Dennewitz, 6 September 1813
Le Leipzig, 16–19 October 1813

UNIT	1806–07	SPAIN	1809	1812	1813–14
1st Inf			R, K	V: Bv	VIII: Le
2nd Inf			R, K	V: S, Bo, W	Le
3rd Inf			R, S, K	V: S, Bo, W	
4th Inf		IV: T, A, Ol, Fu (4 Cos)		XI: Be	Le
5th Inf			R	X: Ri	D
6th Inf			R, S, K(?)	V: Bv	
7th Inf		IV: Al, O, Ta		XI: Be	
8th Inf			R	V: S, Bo, W	VIII: Le
9th Inf		IV: Al, O, Ta		XI: Be	
10th Inf	X: D, F			X: Ri	D

UNIT	1806–07	SPAIN	1809	1812	1813–14
11th Inf	X: D, F			X: Ri	D
12th Inf	X: D, F		S	V: S, Bo, W	VIII: Le
13th Inf				V: S, W	Bl
14th Inf				V: Bv	VIII: Le
15th Inf				V: S, Bo, W	VIII: Le
16th Inf				V: S, Bo, W	VIII: Le
17th Inf				V: Bv	
18th Inf					Bl
19th Inf					
20th Inf					
21st Inf					
22nd Inf					
1st Chasseur à Cheval			R, S (1 Sqn, K)	V: Bo, W	IV Cav: Le
2nd Uhlans			R, K	IV Cav: M, Bv	De, Le
3rd Uhlans			R	IV Cav: M, Bo	IV Cav: Le
4th Chasseur à Cheval				V: S, Bo, W	De, Le
5th Chasseur à Cheval	X: D (1 Sqn), F (3 Sqns)		R	V: S, Bo, W	
6th Uhlans	X: D (2 Sqns), F (3 Sqns)		R (1Sqn)	I Cav: Bo	IV Cav: Le
7th Uhlans				IV Cav: M, Bv	
8th Uhlans				I Cav: Bo	IV: Le
9th Uhlans				I: Bo	D

UNIT	1806–07	SPAIN	1809	1812	1813–14
10th Hussars				II Cav: Bo	
11th Uhlans				IV Cav: M, Bo	
12th Uhlans				V: S, Bo, W	
13th Hussars				V: Bo, W	
14th Cuirassiers				IV Cav: Bo	VIII: Le
15th Uhlans				IV Cav: M	
16th Uhlans				IV Cav: M, Bo	D
17th Uhlans					
18th Uhlans					
19th Uhlans					
20th Uhlans					
21st Chasseur à Cheval					
22nd Uhlans					
Krakus					VIII: Le

Where there are no engagements shown for the newly raised units of Lithuanian troops for 1812, it was because most fell apart during the retreat out of Russia.

Gaps in the list of units for 1813–14 indicate either that the unit was not reformed during this period, or that the remnants of the existing unit were besieged or blockaded in one of the many fortresses in Central or Eastern Europe.

9. TACTICS

One cannot but be amazed at the size of the army fielded by the Duchy of Warsaw, bearing in mind that it was originally based on largely volunteer formations.

Fighting from a sense of idealism, Poles fought from Russia down to the Iberian Peninsula, gaining a reputation for professionalism and aggression that a more established army would envy. At Fuengirola, for instance, whilst one company of the 4th Regiment held off attacks against their fortifications, other companies launched individual attacks against British and Spanish battalions that rocked them back on their heels and eventually forced them to retreat to their boats.

By 1814, their homeland re-occupied by the Russians and Prussians, Polish units were reduced to a shadow of their former strength, but they still stood in the line of battle, almost reduced to mutiny when forced to give up a position due to superior numbers.

It will be noted that the Duchy of Warsaw did not form any significant numbers of dedicated light infantry units. French eyewitnesses noted that the Polish infantry were proficient in the 1791 Règlement, so it may be supposed that, where necessary, either the voltigeur companies or whole line battalions would carry out any required light infantry duties.

CHAPTER 14

The Army of the Kingdom of Westphalia, 1807–13

1. INTRODUCTION

LIKE THE GRAND DUCHY of Berg in an earlier chapter, the Kingdom of Westphalia was an artificial state constructed by Napoleon for the explicit purpose of cementing Imperial power in Northern Germany.

Historically, the Westphalian Kreis of the Holy Roman Empire ran along the border with the Dutch Republic, and encompassed not only the Prussian holding of Westphalia, but parts of Berg, Münster and East Frisia. The new Kingdom would include only part of this area, but subsume Hesse-Kassel, Brunswick and parts of Hanover; effectively, Westphalia was displaced to the east.

This large state was seen as a valuable contributor of troops to the various Imperial armies. Fighting under its flag, Germans would die in huge numbers in the breaches of Gerona, the Great Redoubt at Borodino and along the corpse-strewn roads of Russia.

2. BACKGROUND

The genesis of the Kingdom, as was so much of change brought about in Germany, were the defeats suffered by Austria at Austerlitz in 1805, and by Prussia at Jena and Auerstadt the following year. The first led to the Treaty of Pressburg which replaced the Holy Roman Empire with the Confederation of the Rhine, whilst the second led to the Treaty of Tilsit under which Prussian lands were given up for disposal as Napoleon saw fit.

The Prussian defeat was comprehensive, involving other German rulers beyond Friedrich Wilhelm III. Both the Duke of Brunswick and the Elector of Hesse-Kassel had either actively supported Prussia or, perhaps more importantly, had failed to support the French Army. This made their continued existence suspect.

In addition, the Electorate of Hanover, the German homeland of the King of England, had fallen under French control in 1803. Subsequently passed over to Prussia, Napoleon's offer to give it back was one ostensible cause of the war that broke between France and Prussia in 1806. Napoleon's victory meant that it became once more spoil for disposal.

The merging of these three principal areas into the Kingdom of Westphalia would serve two purposes: as a French client state it would act as a model of good planning for the rest of Germany, and it would act as a permanent threat to any Prussian resurgence should this be contemplated. To cement this idea, Napoleon appointed the youngest Bonaparte brother, Jérôme, as the new King. Jérôme, newly married to Catherine of Würtemburg, entered his new capital of Kassel on December 7 1807. He was to reign for only six years.

3. COMMAND STRUCTURE

It was a major task to produce one regime for what were once three independent, if interrelated, states. The appointment of Jérôme as King, someone with no previous relationship with any of the ruling houses, was expected to provide a new focus for patronage, etc. In addition, the introduction of the Code Napoléon as an enlightened system of law would unify the state, whilst the departmentalization of the kingdom as a new form of local government was expected to break down the old loyalties.

In order to help this process, experienced French administrators were appointed to oversee the initial process, but it was expected that native bureaucrats would be trained to take over; indeed, the promotion of non-nobles to this was seen as a way of building up support for the new state. Napoleon encouraged Jérôme to work with the local nobility, either by confirming their positions as advisors or local leaders, but also to provide officers for the new army that would need to be formed.

There was a representative assembly that was expected to provide a degree of legitimacy for the executive's decisions, but this only met once. Effective government was therefore in the hands of the King and his ministers. Jérôme could, if he chose to, be an effective ruler, capable of giving good leadership and not afraid to make hard choices. Too often, however, he chose an easier option, and was renowned (and accordingly castigated by Napoleon) for a dissolute lifestyle that he could little afford.

4. OFFICER CORPS

As might be expected, by inheriting the armies of three different states, the Westphalian Army could call on the service of a large number of officers. Unfortunately (for Jérôme), most of the ex-Hanoverian officers had elected to keep their oath to their Elector and were currently in Britain helping to form the King's German Legion, destined to blaze a trail of brilliant service through Portugal and Spain.

The bulk of the officers came from the Hessian service, but there was a significant French presence, notably at the senior command levels where Westphalian units could expect to co-operate with Imperial forces.

The expansion of the army after 1807 required more officers than could be provided from the nobility, and non-nobles were therefore encouraged to join, another way of gaining loyalty for the regime. Perhaps the best indicator that, all in all, the officer corps was settled was that when the opportunity came to join the three rebellions and one invasion during the crises of 1809, few took the opportunity to do so.

5. OTHER RANKS

The nucleus of the Westphalian Army came from the disbanded Hesse-Kassel forces, which had been formed into an auxiliary corps; these were used to form the 1st and 2nd Line Regiments. Non-native Prussians, captured by the French in 1806, were used to form the 1st Light Battalion, but most of the expansion used conscripts with a leavening of volunteers.

Like other states within the Confederation of the Rhine, the need to find more and more men for the voracious Imperial armies meant that the possible population to support this had to be expanded. One way was either to abolish or ameliorate serfdom and feudalism, where the rural population was tied to the soil.

Similarly, guild rules and the role of apprentices removed large numbers of the urban population from the pool, as well as ensuring that trades were closed to new entrants. Abolition of these privileges again brought new cadres forward, as well as ensuring that there were employment opportunities for either time-served or discharged soldiers.

Opening up the standard beyond the poor, the destitute and the unemployable allowed a better type of soldier, likely to respond to training and the opportunities for advancement, to come forward. These were the men who would respond well to the enlightened soldiering that followed French practice, especially where it led to the promotion of suitable candidates.

In 1809, the first campaign fought by the new army, was destined to reveal several weaknesses, however, not least that the officer cadres did not have the experience to lead their unsteady conscripts. That they were capable of fighting hard would be seen in Spain and Russia.

6. THE MILITARY ESTABLISHMENT

Organization

1809 GUARD		
Garde du Corps	1 company of 206 officers and men	–
Chevau-léger-Garde	3 field squadrons, plus 1 depot company; total 660 officers and men	Each squadron approx. 188 officers and men, plus depot company of 104
Garde-Grenadiers	1 field battalion of approx. 700 officers and men, plus depot company	6 field companies of approx. 116 officers and men, plus depot company of 116 officers and men
Garde-Jäger	1 field battalion of approx. 700 officers and men, plus depot company	6 field companies of approx. 119 officers and men, plus depot company of 119 officers and men
Guard Horse Artillery	1 company	4 x 6 pdr guns, plus 2 howitzers

LINE INFANTRY		
6 infantry regiments	Each of 2 field battalions and 1 depot battalion, totalling approx. 2,250 officers and men	Each field battalion of 1 grenadier, 1 voltigeur and 4 fusilier companies, each approx. 140 officers and men, plus depot of 4 fusilier companies each of approx. 140 officers and men
1 light infantry battalion	1 field battalion, plus a depot company, totalling approx. 600 officers and men	The field battalion consisted of 1 carabinier, 1 voltigeur and 4 chasseur companies, each of approx. 80 officers and men, plus a depot of approx. 85 officers and men
Jäger-Karabiniers[1]	1 field battalion of approx. 400 officers and men	4 field companies each of approx. 100 officers and men
LINE CAVALRY		
Kuirassiers	4 field squadrons, each of 2 companies, plus 1 depot company; totalling 735 officers and men	Each field squadron was approx. 158 officers and men, plus the depot company of approx. 79 officers and men
Chevau-légers	4 field squadrons, each of 2 companies, plus 1 depot company; totalling 734 officers and men	Each field squadron was approx. 158 officers and men, plus the depot company of approx. 79 officers and men
LINE ARTILLERY		
Foot Artillery	1 battalion of 3 companies	Each company 4 x 6 pdr guns and 2 howitzers
1812 **GUARD**		
Garde du Corps	1 company of 206 officers and men	–

[1] Although not formally part of it, the Jäger-Karabiniers operated as part of the Guard infantry brigade. It was considered to be an elite formation, composed of the sons of foresters. Service in the unit led to preferment in the state forestry service.

1812 **GUARD (Cont.)**		
Chevau-léger-Garde	4 field squadrons, plus 1 depot company; total 874 officers and men	Each squadron approx. 188 officers and men, plus depot company of 104
Garde-Grenadiers	1 field battalion of approx. 837 officers and men, plus depot company	6 field companies of approx. 139 officers and men, plus depot company of 139 officers and men
Garde-Jäger	1 field battalion of approx. 836 officers and men, plus depot company	6 field companies of approx. 139 officers and men, plus depot company of 139 officers and men
Régiment-Konigin	2 field battalions totalling approx. 1,700 officers and men	Each field battalion of 1 grenadier, 1 voltigeur and 4 fusilier companies, each approx. 140 officers and men
Guard Horse Artillery	1 company	4 x 6 pdr guns, plus 2 howitzers
LINE INFANTRY		
6 infantry regiments (1st, 3rd, 4th, 5th, 6th & 8th)	Each of 2 field battalions and 1 depot battalion, totalling approx. 2,250 officers and men	Each field battalion of 1 grenadier, 1 voltigeur and 4 fusilier companies, each approx. 140 officers and men, plus depot of 4 fusilier companies each of approx. 140 officers and men
2 infantry regiments (2nd & 7th)	Each of 3 field battalions and 1 depot battalion, totalling approx. 3,125 officers and men	Each field battalion of 1 grenadier, 1 voltigeur and 4 fusilier companies, each approx. 140 officers and men, plus depot of 4 fusilier companies each of approx. 140 officers and men
1 infantry regiment (9th)	2 field battalions and 1 depot battalion, totalling approx. 1,700 officers and men	Each field battalion of 1 grenadier, 1 voltigeur and 4 fusilier companies, each approx. 140 officers and men

LINE INFANTRY (Cont.)		
3 light infantry battalions (1st–3rd)	1 field battalion, plus a depot company, totalling approx. 970 officers and men	The field battalion consisted of 1 carabinier, 1 voltigeur and 4 chasseur companies, each of approx. 139 officers and men, plus a depot of approx. 139 officers and men
1 light infantry battalion (4th)	1 field battalion, totalling approx. 836 officers and men	The field battalion consisted of 1 carabinier, 1 voltigeur and 4 chasseur companies, each of approx. 139 officers and men
Jäger-Karabiniers	1 field battalion of approx. 600 officers and men	4 field companies each of approx. 150 officers and men
LINE CAVALRY		
2 kuirassier regiments	4 field squadrons, each of 2 companies, plus 1 depot company; totalling 735 officers and men	Each field squadron was approx. 158 officers and men, plus the depot company of approx. 79 officers and men
2 chevau-légers regiments	4 field squadrons, each of 2 companies, plus 1 depot company; totalling 734 officers and men	Each field squadron was approx. 158 officers and men, plus the depot company of approx. 79 officers and men
2 hussar regiments	As above	As above
LINE ARTILLERY		
Horse artillery	1 company	Consisted of 4 x 6lb guns and 2 howitzers
Foot artillery	1 battalion of 5 companies	Each company had 4 x 6lb guns and 2 howitzers
1813 **GUARD**		
Garde du Corps	2 squadrons, totalling 280 officers and men	Each squadron consisted of 2 companies of 70 officers and men

GUARD (Cont.)		
Chevau-léger-Garde	4 field squadrons, plus 1 depot company; total 874 officers and men	Each squadron approx. 188 officers and men, plus depot company of 104
Jérôme Hussar Regiment	4 field squadrons, each of 2 companies totalling 600 officers and men	Each field squadron was approx. 150 officers and men
Garde-Grenadiers	1 field battalion of approx. 837 officers and men, plus depot company	6 field companies of approx. 139 officers and men, plus depot company of 139 officers and men
Garde-Jäger	1 field battalion of approx. 836 officers and men, plus depot company	6 field companies of approx. 139 officers and men, plus depot company of 139 officers and men
Garde-Fusilier Regiment	2 field battalions totalling approx. 1,100 officers and men	Each field battalion consisted 4 fusilier companies, each approx. 140 officers and men
Guard Foot Artillery	1 company	Consisted of 4 x 6lb guns and 2 howitzers
LINE INFANTRY		
8 infantry regiments (1st – 5th, 7th – 9th)	Each of 2 field battalions and 1 depot battalion, totalling approx. 2,250 officers and men	Each field battalion of 1 grenadier, 1 voltigeur and 4 fusilier companies, each approx. 140 officers and men, plus depot of 4 fusilier companies each of approx. 140 officers and men
4 light infantry battalions	1 field battalion, plus a depot company, totalling approx. 970 officers and men	The field battalion consisted of 1 carabinier, 1 voltigeur and 4 chasseur companies, each of approx. 139 officers and men, plus a depot of approx. 139 officers and men
Jäger-Karabiniers	1 field battalion of approx. 600 officers and men	4 field companies each of approx. 150 officers and men

LINE CAVALRY		
2 Kuirassier regiments	4 field squadrons, each of 2 companies, plus 1 depot company; totalling 735 officers and men	Each field squadron was approx. 158 officers and men, plus the depot company of approx. 79 officers and men
1 Chevau-léger regiment	1 field squadron, of 2 companies totalling approx. 150 officers and men	The squadron consisted of 2 companies of approx. 79 officers and men
2 hussar regiments	4 field squadrons, each of 2 companies, plus 1 depot company; totalling 734 officers and men	Each field squadron was approx. 158 officers and men, plus the depot company of approx. 79 officers and men
LINE ARTILLERY		
Horse artillery	1 company	Consisted of 4 x 6lb guns and 2 howitzers
Foot artillery	1 battalion of 3 companies	Each company had 4 x 6lb guns and 2 howitzers

In addition to these units, whilst the cadres of the 2nd Division returned to Westphalia to reform, the remnants of the original 7,500 officers and men were reduced to 1,500 by the end of the siege of Gerona and were reformed as a single battalion shortly after! The 300 survivors returned to Westphalia in March 1813 to be used to reform the 3rd Light Battalion.

A unit that is sometimes confused with this composite regiment was the Régiment de Westphalie, although it never formed part of the Westphalian Army. Originally to consist of four battalions, it was raised in 1806 to soak up men released from the Prussian Army. It never reached the authorized strength and recruiting ceased at two battalions; the 1st Battalion served as the field battalion and the 2nd acted as a depot.

In 1808 the 1st Battalion was sent to Spain as part of the initial invasion force and served at the abortive storm of Valencia in June–July 1808. It spent two remaining years in dispiriting garrison duties, losing its 2nd Battalion which was used to cadre units in Jerome's army before, in September 1810, going into the Légion Hanovrienne.

7. UNIFORMS

THE GUARD

The Guard du Corps wore a steel, French-style cuirassier helmet with a black comb and white plume. The service uniform was blue, with a red collar, cuffs and piping. The kuirass was iron, with a sunburst design on the front. Breeches were white, and the unit wore knee boots. The shabraque was dark blue, with a yellow border.

The Chevau-léger-Garde was issued with a black leather helmet with a black crest and red plume. The jacket was green, with red collar, cuffs and piping, with yellow litzen on the collar and across the chest. The green breeches had yellow trim. The shabraque was green with a yellow border. The first squadron carried a lance, probably with a red over white pennon as the regiment was based on a contingent of Polish light horse that accompanied Jérôme to Cassel.

The Guard Hussar regiment was uniformed in the French style. The shako was red with a white plume, and the top band and cords were yellow. The dolman was red, and the pelisse and breeches were dark blue.

The senior foot regiment of the Guard was the Garde-Grenadiers. They wore a bearskin cap with red plume and cords, and the rear patch was red with a yellow grenade.

The white jacket had red collar, cuffs, lapels and turnbacks, with red epaulettes. The breeches were white, with black gaiters for service wear.

The Jäger-Garde wore a shako, with the Karabinier company issued with a peaked bearskin. Plumes were yellow over green (some sources say white) with yellow (white) cords. The green jackets had yellow collar, cuffs, turnbacks and lapel piping. Epaulettes were green with yellow hoops. Breeches were green.

The Régiment-Konigin were uniformed as the line units. The shako had a red plume and cords for the grenadiers and the voltigeurs a yellow over green plume with green cords. The jacket was white with dark blue collar, cuffs and lapels; the grenadiers had red epaulettes and the voltigeurs yellow with green hoops. The fusiliers had white straps edged dark blue. Breeches or trousers were white.

THE LINE INFANTRY

Originally, the line regiments wore their previous Hesse-Cassel uniforms, but these were quickly replaced by a national uniform.

The grenadiers of the 1st Line wore bearskin caps, with red plumes and cords, with a red back patch with a white grenade. All other companies of the 1st and all companies of the remaining eight regiments wore shakos. The grenadier shako had red plumes and cords, the voltigeurs had a yellow over green plume and green cords, and the fusiliers had company distinctives as in the French Army.

The tunic was white. Initially the regiments were distinguished by coloured collars, cuffs, lapels and turnbacks: 1st and 2nd dark blue, 3rd and 4th light blue, 5th and 6th yellow and 7th and 8th black, but in 1810 this sequence was dropped and all regiments adopted dark blue distinctives. The breeches or trousers were white.

The light infantry also wore the shako, with the carabinier companies having a red plume and cords, the voltigeurs green over yellow with yellow cords, and the chasseurs company pom-pons and white cords.

Originally, the tunic was cornflower blue with initially green (later orange) collar, cuffs, lapels and turnbacks. This was changed to a more traditional dark green faced light blue, with green breeches and black gaiters or half boots.

The Jäger-Karabiniers had a shako with a red over green plume and red cords for all companies. The coat was dark green with red piping on the collar, cuffs, coat front and turnbacks. The breeches were green with a red stripe and black gaiters or half boots. As it was raised from foresters, the unit was completely equipped with rifles.

THE LINE CAVALRY

The two kuirassier regiments had a steel, French-style cuirassier helmet with a brass comb and a black crest (instead of a mane); the plume was white. On formation the 1st Regiment wore a white tunic faced crimson at the collar, cuffs, lapels and turnbacks. The breeches were white and the regiment had knee boots. The steel kuirass was not issued until 1810. The 2nd Regiment wore the same uniform.

In 1812, the regiments adopted a blue tunic, with the 1st retaining crimson and the 2nd adopting orange distinctives. Breeches remained white. In 1812 shabraques were dark blue with edging in the regimental distinctives.

The chevau-léger regiments both wore a black leather helmet with white metal fittings. The crest was black, and the plume red. The coat was green with orange collar, cuffs, piping and turnbacks. The breeches were green with orange thigh knots, and the unit wore hussar boots.

When formed, the 2nd Regiment adopted buff as its distinctive colour. The shabraque was dark green with edging in the regimental colour.

The hussar regiments wore French-style uniforms. The shakos of the 1st Regiment had a green plume and white cords, whilst the 2nd had a white plume and cords.

The 1st Regiment wore a green dolman with red collar and cuffs, green pelisse (black fur edging) and green breeches. The 2nd replaced the dark green with light blue, and the pelisse had grey fur edging. The sabretaches for both regiments were black.

Shabraques were in the dolman colour edged white.

ARTILLERY

The Guard Artillery wore a uniform based on that of the French line horse artillery. The black shako had a red plume and cords, the jacket was dark blue with red collar, cuffs and turnbacks with red lacing across the front. The breeches were dark blue with red thigh knots. Belting was buff.

The line companies also mimicked the French line regiments with a red collar, cuffs and turnbacks, with red piping to the lapels. Breeches were dark blue. The line horse battery had red thigh knots and white belting.

8. BATTLE HISTORY

(Roman numerals indicate original Corps affiliation; these often changed during the campaign.)

1809

Do	Dodendorf, 4 May 1809
H	Halberstadt, 29 July 1809
O	Oelper, 1 August 1809

Spain

G	Siege of Gerona, 6 June–10 December 1809
T	Talavera, 27–28 July 1809
U	Ucles, 13 January 1809
V	Villafranca, 13 September 1813

1812

Be	Beresina, 26–28 November 1812

Bo Borodino, 7 September 1812
R Blockade of Riga, 24 July–18 December 1812
V Valutina-Gora, 19 August 1812
Ve Vereja, 10 October 1812

1813
D Siege of Danzig, 16 January–29 November 1813
De Dennewitz, 6 September 1813
Dr Blockade of Dresden, 13 October 1813–11 March 1814
G-B Grossbeeren, 23 August 1813
K Katzbach, 26 August 1813
Le Leipzig, 16–19 October 1813

UNIT	1809	SPAIN	1812	1813
Garde du Corps	X		VIII: (returned to Westphalia with Jérôme after his replacement)	
Chevau-léger-Garde	X		VIII: V, Bo, Be	IV: G-B, De, Le
Guard Hussars				
Garde-Grenadier	X		VIII: V, Bo, Be	
Jäger-Garde	X		VIII: V, Bo, Be	
Garde-Fusilier				Imp Gd: Le
1st Line	X: Do (4 cos), O		X: R	D
2nd Line		VII: G	VIII: V, Bo (2 bns only), Be	Dr
3rd Line		VII: G	VIII: Bo, Be	Dr
4th Line		VII: G	XI:	XI: K
5th Line	X: H (captured)		VIII: Be	

UNIT	1809	SPAIN	1812	1813
6th Line	X: O		VIII: V, Bo, Ve (I Bn only), Be	
7th Line			VIII: Bo, Be	
8th Line			X: Be	XI: K, Le
1st Light		VII: G	VIII: V, Bo, Be	
2nd Light			VIII: V, Bo, Be	XI: K, Dr
3rd Light			VIII: V, Bo, Be	
4th Light				XI: Le
Jäger-Karabiniers	X		VIII: V, Bo, Be	
1st Kuirassiers	X: O		IV Cav: Bo, Be	
2nd Kuirassiers			IV Cav: Bo, Be	
1st Chevau-léger		I: U, T, V (disbanded)		
2nd Chevau-léger				
1st Hussars			VIII: V, Bo, Be	II: Deserted to Austrians 22 August
2nd Hussars			VIII: V, Bo, Be	As above

9. TACTICS

The formation and continued strengthening of the Westphalian Army was a remarkable achievement. Just as the state itself was expected to be a standard for other German principalities to emulate, so the army was expected to provide a large auxiliary formation for the Imperial armies – witness the provision of an entire corps in 1812.

Napoleon complained that Jérôme had formed two expensive kuirassier regiments instead of the perhaps more useful light units, but the attack of the largely foreign IV Cavalry Corps at Borodino was a feat that few native regiments could emulate. This integration of the

Westphalian Army with French forces was deliberate, and both drill and grand tactics were adopted wholesale.

With the defeat of Napoleon's Army in Autumn 1813, and the subsequent retreat to the Rhine, opening Westphalia to invasion to the triumphant eastern allies, the remnants of the army faded back into civilian life, probably with little regret. The Elector of Hesse-Cassel returned and summoned those soldiers still owing him allegiance back to the colours to reform his army, but too late to take any significant part in the war. During the Hundred Days, the army mobilized in time to take part in some of the sieges and blockades of the French fortresses.

CHAPTER 15

The Army of the Kingdom of Würtemburg, 1805–15

1. INTRODUCTION

WÜRTEMBURG WAS ONE of the larger states of the Holy Roman Empire, and was part of the Swabian Kreis. The capital was Stuttgart and it was bordered by the Baden duchies to the west, and a host of small principalities and ecclesiastical states to the east and south.

Like most states of the Empire, Würtemburg left her security to the collective will of the Reich, supporting Austria when necessary. As such, the standing army could be kept small as there was no perceived outside threat. With the rise of Prussia in the middle of the eighteenth century, Würtemburg chose to align with Austria, and much of her available army was deployed at Leuthen on 5 December 1757, where they received plaudits for trading volleys with the otherwise victorious Prussians.

During the Revolutionary Wars, Würtemburg deployed her forces to defend along the Rhine frontier, slowly increasing the number of men available through raising militia. The 'cabinet wars' of the earlier part of the century had left her ill-prepared for the intensity of 'wars of nationalism' and by 1795 she had started negotiations with the French to declare neutrality. Although these came to nothing, an armistice was signed in July 1796, only to see the French Army defeated and sent back across the Rhine.

This proved to be only an interlude, as France once more took the offensive and by 1800 (after victories at Marengo and Hohenlinden) was almost in a position to dictate the peace terms at Luneville. Under additional treaties with individual states, including Würtemburg, the previously independent imperial knights and the states of the church were taken over by their more powerful neighbours. Previously, the German states had grown through dynastic marriages; now it was through aggrandizement. Through this accretion of power, Würtemburg became an electorate in April 1803.

2. BACKGROUND

The Elector Friedrich II proved to be a ruthless ruler. With the resumption of war in 1805, he signed a treaty of alliance with newly Imperial France in recognition that Napoleon was now dominant in central Europe. Würtemburg troops provided rear area security during the autumn 1805 envelopment of the main Austrian Army at Ulm, which used the Black Forest as cover.

The reward for this was the Treaty of Brno (12 December 1805), which confirmed that the end of the Holy Roman Empire was approaching. Through the Treaty of Pressburg, signed with Austria on 26 December, Würtemburg was raised to the level of a kingdom (and Duke/Elector Friedrich II became King Friedrich I), and gained substantial new lands in Swabia. In 1806, Würtemburg was one of the first members of the Confederation of the Rhine.

The articles of confederation required that Würtemburg provide 12,000 men to serve as part of the imperial armies. Whilst this would require some expansion, Friedrich was happy to do so as he saw the army as something that would unify the state and act as a catalyst for modernizing some of its structure.

In the event, the army was to fight with distinction along the Danube in 1809, in Russia in 1812, and in Germany the following year. Indeed, the resources devoted to the army allowed it to be re-formed not once (after the huge losses in Russia) but twice (after the losses suffered in Germany). By 1814, Würtemburg was able to deploy a fresh division in France with the Allies, and again in 1815.

The ability of Friedrich to react to circumstances served his kingdom well. Würtemburg was probably the only German state that was able to keep all of its gains made in the previous ten years!

3. COMMAND STRUCTURE

Friedrich was an enlightened despot, and was impressed by what had happened elsewhere in Europe. To introduce these reforms into his own kingdom he needed to dispense with some of the more obstructionist areas, such as the Estates. Indeed, to drive some reforms through, he avoided using any legislative machinery altogether!

The centralization of power meant that individual towns and cities lost their right to govern themselves, often having had the rights to raise local taxes. The King's commissioners were instructed that 'Whoever among you attracts the most complaints is the most gratfying to me', surely something that should be engraved over every Inland Revenue inspector's desk!

The bureaucracy also ensured that conscription lists were maintained.

4. OFFICER CORPS

Like the French Army, Friedrich wanted to make sure that his army was officered by the most effective means possible. Whilst there was a place for the aristocrat, competence was a much more important factor, and men from the lower levels of society would be promoted if their ability warranted it. An attraction was that officers of the rank of captain and above were given noble rank.

Whilst the King encouraged native-born officers, those from elsewhere in Germany also served in the army; this cross fertilisation of knowledge no doubt engendered positive emulation. As well as on-the-job training with a unit, Friedrich also set up a military academy; the late Colonel John Elting reminds us that Erwin Rommel came from this tradition – a testimonial to its effectiveness.

5. OTHER RANKS

The King paid similar attention to the troops that these officers were to command. By striking at the role of the guilds, potential recruits could not hide behind sometimes spurious apprenticeships. This opened up the pool beyond the normal shiftless and unemployable characters representative of the armies of the *ancien régime*. As originally published, the conscription laws exempted married men from the draft, an oversight that was soon rectified and which required prospective grooms to seek authorization.

Travel outside the borders was severely curtailed, whilst Würtemburgers living abroad or serving in foreign armies were expected to return or face fierce penalties. Similarly, foreign armies were forbidden to recruit inside the borders. Once a soldier's service had expired, he was guaranteed employment, either by the state or through reducing the power of the guilds to dictate work practices. In addition wounded soldiers were given pensions or places in an old soldiers' home.

Rewards for bravery or good service came in a variety of ways, including medals, whilst those who showed marked ability could receive promotion to officer rank with all the opportunities that that opened up.

All told, the Würtemburg Army was to justify, both to itself, its allies and, perhaps most importantly, its enemies, the effort that its king and his people lavished on it.

6. THE MILITARY ESTABLISHMENT

Organization

See tables on pp. 323–7.

7. UNIFORMS

GUARD

The Garde zu Pferd wore a different parade uniform for each squadron, but their service uniform was as follows:

The Leibjäger squadron wore a bearskin bonnet with a white plume, cords and flounders. The jacket was green, faced yellow at the collar, cuffs and turnbacks, and the fringed epaulettes were white. The cuirass was steel. Breeches were white and the unit had knee-high boots.

The other three squadrons wore the same uniform but the jacket was blue.

Horse furniture was a yellow shabraque edged silver.

The Leib-Regiment zu Pferd wore a helmet similar to that worn by

Organization

1805 GUARD			
Garde du Corps	1 squadron		2 companies, with approx. 100 officers and men in total
Leibjäger zu Pferd	1 company		35 officers and men
Garde zu Füss	1 battalion of 967 officers and men	4 companies	Each company had approx. 220 officers and men
LINE			
Chevau-léger Regiments	2 regiments, each with approx. 427 officers and men	Each of 4 squadrons	Each squadron had two companies of approx. 104 officers and men
Leichtes Jäger Regiment zu Pferd	1 regiment, of approx. 315 officers and men	3 squadrons	As above
Musketeer Regiments	6, each of 1 battalion, of approx. 686 officers and men	Each of 1 grenadier and 3 musketeer companies	Each company consisted of approx. 167 officers and men
Fussjägers	2 battalions, totalling 611 officers and men	Each of 3 companies	Each company had 200 officers and men
Leichtes Infanterie	2 battalions, strength as above	As above	As above
Artillery	1 horse battery and 2 foot batteries		The horse battery had 6 x 6lb guns and 2 howitzers and the foot batteries had 6 x 6lb guns and 4 howitzers; all of Austrian construction

1809 **GUARD**			
Garde-Regiment zu Pferd	1 regiment of 4 squadrons, consisting of approx. 530 officers and men	1 squadron of Leibjäger; 1 squadron of Garde-du-Corps; 2 squadrons Grenadiere	Each squadron consisted of approx. 130 officers and men
Garde zu Füss	1 battalion of approx. 800 officers and men	The battalion had 4 companies	Each company consisted of approx. 191 officers and men
Guard artillery	1 horse artillery company		4 x 6lb guns and 2 howitzers
LINE			
Chevau-léger Regiments	2 regiments, each with approx. field strength 520 officers and men	Each of 4 field squadrons and a depot squadron	Each field squadron had four companies totalling approx. 123 officers and men
Leichtes Jäger Regiment zu Pferd	2 regiments, as above	As above	As above
Musketeer Regiments	7 regiments, each of 2 field battalions and one depot company. Total field strength was approx. 1,434 officers and men	Each field battalion consisted of 1 grenadier and 3 musketeer companies	Each company consisted of approx. 166 officers and men
Fussjägers	2 battalions, each with 4 field companies and 1 depot company. Field strength was approx. 664 officers and men	Each field battalion consisted of 4 companies	As above

LINE (Cont.)			
Leichtes Infanterie	As above	As above	As above
Artillery	Two horse batteries and four foot batteries		The horse batteries had 4 x 6lb guns and 2 howitzers; three foot batteries had 6 x 6lb guns and the fourth had 3 x 12lb guns and 2 howitzers[1]
1812 **GUARD**			
Garde-Regiment zu Pferd	1 regiment of 4 squadrons, consisting of approx. 530 officers and men	1 Squadron of Leibjäger; 1 Squadron of Garde-du-Corps 2 Squadrons Grenadiere	Each squadron consisted of approx. 130 officers and men
Garde zu Füss	1 battalion of approx. 950 officers and men	The battalion had 4 companies of grenadiers and 1 Garde Jäger Compagnie	Each company consisted of approx. 191 officers and men
Guard artillery	1 horse artillery company		4 x 6lb guns and 2 howitzers
LINE			
Chevau-léger Regiments	2 regiments, each with approx. field strength 520 officers and men	Each of 4 field squadrons and a depot squadron	Each field squadron had four companies totalling approx. 123 officers and men
Leichtes Jäger Regiment zu Pferd	2 regiments, as above	As above	As above

[1] There is no indication that the 4th (Heavy) company took the field.

LINE (Cont.)			
Dragoner Regiment zu Pferd	1 regiment, approx. strength 520 officers and men	Consisting of 4 squadrons	Each squadron consisted of approx. 123 officers and men
Musketeer Regiments	8 regiments, each of 2 field battalions and one depot company. Total field strength was approx. 1,434 officers and men	Each field battalion consisted of 1 grenadier and 3 musketeer companies	Each company consisted of approx. 166 officers and men
Fussjägers	2 battalions, each with 4 field companies and 1 depot company. Field strength was approx. 664 officers and men	Each field battalion consisted of 4 companies	As above
Leichtes Infanterie	As above	As above	As above
Artillery	Two horse batteries and four foot batteries		The horse batteries had 4 x 6lb guns and 2 howitzers; three foot batteries had 6 x 6lb guns and the fourth had 6 x 12lb guns
1814 GUARD			
Garde-Regiment zu Pferd	1 regiment of 4 squadrons, consisting of approx. 530 officers and men	1 squadron of Leibjäger; 1 squadron of Garde-du-Corps 2 squadrons Grenadiere	Each squadron consisted of approx. 130 officers and men
Leib-Regiment zu Pferd	1 regiment approx. field strength 520 officers and men	4 field squadrons	Each field squadron had four companies totalling approx. 123 officers and men

1814 **GUARD** (Cont.)			
Garde zu Füss	1 regiment of 2 battalions, approx. strength 1,500 officers and men	The 1st battalion consisted of 4 companies of grenadiers, the 2nd 4 companies of jäger	Each company consisted of approx. 191 officers and men
Guard artillery	1 horse artillery company[2]		4 x 6lb guns and 2 howitzers
LINE			
Leichtes Jäger Regiment zu Pferd	3 regiments, each with approx. field strength 520 officers and men	Each of 4 field squadrons and a depot squadron	Each field squadron had four companies totalling approx. 123 officers and men
Kavellerie Regiment	1 regiment, as above	As above	As above
Infanterie Regiments (1–8, 11)	9 regiments, each of 2 field battalions and one depot company. Total field strength was approx. 1,434 officers and men	Each field battalion consisted of 1 grenadier and 3 musketeer companies	Each company consisted of approx. 166 officers and men
Fussjägers (Fussjäger Regiment No. 9)	1 regiment, consisting of 2 battalions and 1 depot company. Field strength was approx. 1,434 officers and men	Each field battalion consisted of 4 companies	As above
Leichte Infanterie (Infanterie Regiment No. 10)	As above	As above	As above
Artillery	Three horse batteries and three foot batteries		The horse batteries had 4 x 6lb guns and 2 howitzers; two foot batteries had 6 x 6lb guns and the third had 4 x 12lb guns and 2 howitzers

[2] A Guard foot company was formed after Napoleon's first abdication.

the Austrian Chevau-légers. The crest was black and the plume was red.

The coat was blue, with yellow collars and cuffs, and yellow piping on the lapels and turnbacks. The overall trousers were grey. The shabraque was blue, edged yellow.

The Garde zu Füss wore different headgear for each of the two battalions. The original grenadiers wore a bearskin cap with a silver front plate, white plume, cords and flounders. The back patch was white, with a black grenade. The jägers wore a shako, also with a white plume and with white cords and flounders.

The jacket was blue, with black facings at the collar (with Guard lace), cuffs, lapels; the turnbacks were white. The grenadiers had white fringed epaulettes and the jägers had green. Belting was white. Breeches were white, and were worn with black gaiters.

The Guard Horse Battery wore a black kasket (a combed helmet) with a black caterpiller crest. A white plume was added for parade wear. In 1813, the battery adopted a shako with a white metal front plate.

The coat was a dark sky-blue with black collar and cuffs (with Guard lace); the turnbacks were yellow piped black; brass shoulder scales. Breeches were also dark sky-blue, but grey overall trousers were worn.

THE LINE

The Chevau-léger Regiments originally wore a black helmet with a flowing horse-hair mane and a plume rising from the front of the comb. The 1st Regiment adopted an Austrian Chevau-léger helmet with a black caterpillar crest topped with yellow in 1811.

The coat was blue, with facings of red for both the 1st and 2nd Regiments. These facings were worn at the collar, cuffs and turnbacks, and the piping to the lapels. The 1st had changed their facing colour to yellow by 1809. Breeches were white, with hussar boots, although grey overall trousers were worn for campaign.

The shabraques were blue edged yellow.

The 1st Chevau-légers became the Leib-Regiment in 1813, whilst the 2nd adopted a Jäger zu Pferd uniform.

The Jäger zu Pferd also wore an Austrian style helmet, but the caterpillar crest was black with a facing colour top. Between 1813 and 1814 the regiments adopted a shako.

The coat was dark green with regimental facings at the collar and lapels, although these were only piped with the facing colour from 1809. The facing colours were yellow for the 3rd Jäger zu Pferd (white in 1814) and pink for the 4th. When the 2nd Chavau-légers adopted a jäger-style uniform, they kept scarlet as their facing colour.

The breeches were white, although grey overall trousers were worn for campaign.

Shabraques were green edged yellow.

The Dragoner Regiment zu Pferd adopted the shako on its formation in 1809. It had white cords. The green jacket had a white collar, and the piping on the lapels and turnbacks was scarlet.

The breeches were white, with black knee boots.

The shabraque was green edged white.

The Line Infantry originally wore a black helmet with a black horse-hair mane, but in 1806 it was gradually replaced by a helmet with a black caterpillar crest. The front plate was brass. From 1812, this was itself replaced by a bell-topped shako.

The coat was dark blue. Facing colours were worn at the collar, cuffs, lapels and turnbacks, but from 1812, the lapels also became dark blue, and the facings were used as piping:

1st Yellow, with white buttons
2nd Orange, with white buttons
3rd White, with white buttons
4th Pink, with white buttons and piping
5th Light blue, with white buttons and piping
6th White, with yellow buttons and red piping
7th Red, with yellow buttons
8th Straw, with yellow buttons

The breeches were white, with black gaiters.

The Fussjäger wore a black shako with a green turban and plume. The coat was green which had black facings for the collar, cuffs, lapels and turnbacks. After 1811 the lapels stopped being in regimental colours and became the same colour as the coat collar, piped white. The two battalions were distinguished by their button colour, yellow for the 1st Battalion and white for the 2nd.

The breeches were green, worn with half-boots. The front rank of each battalion carried rifles and the second rank rifled carbines.

When the two battalions were formed into one regiment – the 9th – the new unit adopted the bell-topped shako and yellow buttons.

The Leichtes Infanterie wore the horse-maned helmet on formation, but adopted the shako in 1807. The plume was red.

The coat was green and had light blue collar, cuffs, lapels and turnbacks but, like the Fussjäger, the lapels changed to coat colour, piped white, in 1811. There were no battalion distinctions.

The two separate battalions were formed into the 10th Infantry in 1813.

The 11th Regiment was formed in 1813 from a Landsregiment rifle unit – the scharfschutzen. There is little information available, but a suggestion is that it was similar to that of the fussjäger, but with white buttons.

The Foot Artillery wore a black kasket with a black caterpillar crest and brass front plate. In 1813, it was changed to a shako.

The coat was dark sky-blue with black collar, cuffs, lapels and turnbacks (piped yellow), but by 1812 the lapels were in coat colour, piped black. The shoulder straps were black, piped yellow. Breeches were originally white, but changed to match the coat in 1811. The calf-length gaiters were black, and belting was white.

The horse artillery wore almost the same headgear and uniform, but the turnbacks were yellow piped black, and brass shoulder scales were worn. The breeches were coat colour, but with hussar boots.

8. BATTLE HISTORY

(Roman numerals indicate original Corps affiliation; these often changed during the campaign.)

1807

Br Siege and capture of Breslau, 6 December 1806 – 6 January 1807

S Siege and capture of Schweidnitz, 10 January–16 February 1807
H Heilsberg, 10 June 1807
N Siege and capture of Neisse, 23 February–16 June 1807
G Storm of Glatz, 20–24 June 1807

1809
A Abensberg, 20 April 1809
L Landshut, 21 April 1809
E Eggmuhl, 22 April 1809
U-L Uhfahr-Linz, 17 May 1809
A-E Aspern-Essling, 21–22 May 1809
V Voralberg, May–July 1809 (D represents the depot company of the units involved); deployment of militia units not shown

1812
Be Beresina, 26–28 November 1812
Bo Borodino, 7 September 1812
S Smolensk, 17–18 August 1812
Da Danzig

1813–14
Ba Bautzen, 20–21 May 1813
De Dennewitz, 6 September 1813
W Wartenburg, 3 October 1813
Le Leipzig, 16–19 October 1813
L-R La Rothière, 1 February 1814 (with Allied forces)
M Montereau, 18 February 1814 (with Allied forces)
A-A Arcis sur Aube, 20–21 March 1814 (with Allied forces)
F-C Fère-Champenoise, 25 March 1814 (with Allied forces)
P Paris, 30 March 1814 (with Allied forces)

Note: In order to provide a benchmark, we have used the unit numbers as given in 1811; prior to this, units were known by their name of their inhaber.

UNIT	1807	1809	1812	1813–14
GUARD				
Garde-Regiment zu Pferd		V (2 Sqns)		
Garde zu Füss		V		
LINE				
Chevau-léger Regiment No. 1 –1805, Chevau-léger Regiment (vacant) –1807, Chevau-léger Regiment Herzog Heinrich –1811, Chevau-léger Regiment No. 1 (vacant) –1812, Chevau-léger Regiment No. 1 Prinz Adam –1813, Leib-Kavellerie Regiment No. 1	Br, S N, G	VIII: A, E, A-E	III: S, Bo, Be	IV: Ba, De, Le
Leib-Chevau-léger Regiment No. 2 –1805, Chevau-léger Regiment Kurfürst –1806, Leib-Chevau-léger Regiment –1811, Leib-Chevau-léger Regiment No. 2 –1813, Kavallerie Regiment No. 4 Jäger Prinz Adam	Br, S, H, N	VIII: A	III: S, Bo, Be	VI: Le (defected) IV: L-R, M, A-A, F-C[1]
Jäger Regiment zu Pferd No. 3 –1805, Jägerregiment zu Pferd Prinz Paul –1806, Jägerregiment zu Pferd (vacant) –1807, Jägerregiment zu Pferd, Herzog Louis –1811, Jägerregiment zu Pferd No. 3 –1813, Jägerregiment zu Pferd, No. 2 Herzog Louis –1814, Kavellerie Regiment No. 2 Jäger Herzog Louis	Br, S, N, G	VIII: A, L, E, U-L	II Cav: Bo, Be	IV: Ba, De, Le IV: L-R, M, A-A, F-C[1]

Footnotes on p. 335.

UNIT	1807	1809	1812	1813–14
LINE (Cont.)				
Jägerregiment zu Pferd No. 4 König –1806, Jägerregiment zu Pferd König –1811, Jägerregiment zu Pferd No. 4 König –1813, Jägerregiment zu Pferd No. 4 –1814, Jägerregiment zu Pferd No. 5 –1814, Kavellerie Regiment No. 5 Jäger König		VIII: L, E, U-L	III: Bo, Be	VI: Le (defected)
Dragonerregiment No. 5 (Krönprinz) –1809, Dragonneregiment zu Pferd –1809, Dragonneregiment Krönprinz –1811, Dragonneregiment No. 5 (Krönprinz) –1813, Kavallerie Regiment No. 3 Dragoner Krönprinz				IV: L-R, M, A-A, F-C[1]
Infanterie Regiment No. 1 –1805, Prinz Paul von Würtemburg Infanterie Bataillon –1806, Von Schroder Infanterie Bataillon –1807, Von Phull Infanterie Regiment –1809, Prinz Paul von Würtemburg Infanterie Regiment –1811, Infanterie-Regiment No. 1 –1813, Leib-Infanterie Regiment No. 1	Br, S, N, G	VIII: U-L V (D)	III: S, Bo, Be	IV: Ba, De, W, Le
Infanterie Regiment No. 2, Herzog Wilhelm –1805, Herzog Wilhem von Würtemburg Infanterie Regiment –1811, Infanterie Regiment No. 2, Herzog Wilhelm	Br, S, N, G	VIII: U-L; V (D)	III: S, Bo, Be	IV: Ba, De, W, Le IV: L-R, M, F-C, P[1]

UNIT	1807	1809	1812	1813–14
LINE (Cont.)				
Infanterie Regiment No. 3 –1805, Seckendorf Infanterie Regiment –1807, Von Camrer Infanterie Regiment –1809, Von Phull Infanterie Regiment –1811, Infanterie Regiment No. 3	Br, S, N, G	VIII: U-L; V (D)		IV: L-R, M, F-C, P[1]
Infanterie Regiment No. 4 –1805, Von Romig Infanterie Bataillon –1807, Franquemont Infanterie Regiment –1811, Infanterie Regiment No. 4		V	III: S, Bo, Be	IV: L-R, M, F-C, P[1]
Infanterie Regiment No. 5, Prinz Friedrich –1805, Von Lilienburg Infanterie Regiment –1808, Prinz Friederich von Würtemburg Infanterie Regiment –1811, Infanterie Regiment No. 5, Prinz Friedrich	Br, S, N, G	V		
Infanterie Regiment No. 6, Krönprinz –1805, Infanterie Regiment Kurprinz von Würtemburg –1806, Infanterie Regiment Krönprinz von Würtemburg –1811, Infanterie Regiment No. 6, Krönprinz	Br, S, N, G	VIII: U-L; V (D)	III: S, Bo, Be	IV: L-R, M, F-C, P[1]
Infanterie Regiment No. 7 –1805, Neubronn Fusilier Bataillon –1808, Neubronn Fusilier Regiment –1811, Infanterie Regiment No. 7 –1813, Infanterie Regiment No. 8		VIII: U-L; V (D)	III: D, Be	IV: Ba, De (destroyed)

UNIT	1807	1809	1812	1813–14
LINE (Cont.)				
Infanterie Regiment No. 8 –1809, Infanterie Regiment von Scharffenstein –1811, Infanterie Regiment No. 8 –1813, Infanterie Regiment No. 7				IV: L-R, M, F-C, P[1]
Fussjäger Bataillon König –1805, Fussjäger Bataillon von Romann –1806, Fussjäger Bataillon von Hugel, No. 1 –1807, Fussjäger Bataillon König –1813, I/Fussjäger Regiment No. 9, König	Br, S, N, G	VIII: A, E, U-L; V (D)	III: S, Bo, Be	IV: Ba, De, W IV: L-R, M, F-C, P[1]
Fussjäger von Neusser, No. 2 –1805, Fussjäger Bataillon Scharfenstein –1806, Fussjäger Bataillon Scharfenstein, No. 2 –1808, Fussjäger von Neuffer, No. 2 –1813, II/Fussjäger Regiment No. 9, König	Br, S, N	VIII: A, L, E, U-L; V (D)	III: S, Bo, Be	IV: Ba, De, W IV: L-R, M, F-C, P[1]
Leichtes Infanterie Bataillon No. 1, Von Wolff –1805, Scheler Leichtes Infanterie Bataillon –1807, Leichtes Infanterie Bataillon No. 1, von Neubronn –1808, Leichtes Infanterie Bataillon No. 1, von Wolff –1813, I/Bataillon, Infanterie Regiment No. 10, Leichte Infanterie	Br S, N	VIII: A, E, U-L; V (D)	III: S, Bo, Be	IV: Ba, De, W IV: L-R, M, F-C, P[1]
Leichtes Infanterie Bataillon No. 2, Von Stockmayer –1806, Leichtes Infanterie Bataillon No. 2, von Bruselle –1810, Leichtes Infanterie Bataillon No. 2, von Stockmayer –1813, II/Bataillon, Infanterie Regiment No. 10, Leichte Infanterie	Br, S, N, G	VIII: A, L, E, U-L	III: Bo, Be	IV: Ba, De, W
Infanterie Regiment No. 11 –1809, Landscharfschutzen zu Fuss –1814, Infanterie Regiment No. 11, Scharfschutzen				

[1] As part of the allied army.

9. TACTICS

Almost alone amongst the French allies, the Würtemburg Army continued to use the two-rank deep line for firing, although it was fully trained in the usage of columns and skirmish screens within its repertoire of tactics.

The light units, formed into a Light Brigade, proved to be an example to the rest of the army in this role; in the 1809 campaign it spearheaded corps attacks and acted with the light cavalry in advance guard work.

The cavalry proved to be versatile, and acted as Napoleon's escort in the early stages of the 1809 campaign, gaining the Emperor's plaudits. At Aspern-Essling, Chevau-léger Regiment Herzog Heinrich had carried out several charges and was exhausted, but pleaded to be allowed to attack once more.

In 1812, the Würtemburg Division was worn down to little more than an understrength regiment but, under the direct command of Marechal Michel Ney, repeatedly turned round and saw off the pursuing Russians. Worn down yet again in 1813, they continued in the French ranks until the Emperor's forces fell back across the Rhine, then advanced to the gates of Paris having changed sides.

One would be hard put to find a record of service like this in any army, at any time.

Bibliography

We have listed here those books which, in our opinion, give a good overview of Napoleonic Armies in general as well as those which treat them individually. There have been occasions where we have had to reconcile differing information, but if we have felt it necessary, explanations have been given in the text.

GENERAL WORKS

Bowden, Scott, *Napoleon's Grande Armée of 1813*, Emperor's Press, 1990

Bowden, Scott and Tarbox, Charlie, *Armies on the Danube*, Empire Games Press, 1980

Broers, Michael, *Europe Under Napoleon, 1799–1815*, Arnold, 1996

Chandler, Dr David, *Dictionary of the Napoleonic Wars*, Arms and Armour, 1979

Chandler, Dr David, *The Campaigns of Napoleon*, Weidenfeld & Nicholson, 1966

Elting, Colonel John R., *Swords Around a Throne – Napoleon's Grande Armée*, The Free Press, 1988

Elting, Colonel John R. & Knotel, Herbert, *Napoleonic Uniforms (4 volumes)*, Vols 1 & 2 published by Macmillan, 1993 and Vols 3 & 4 Emperor's Press, 2000

Emsley, Clive, *The Longman Companion to Napoleonic Europe*, Longman, 1993

Esdaille, Charles J., *The Wars of Napoleon*, (Modern Wars in Perspective Series), Longman, 1995

Funcken, Liliane & Fred, *L'Uniforme et les Armes des Soldats du Premier Empire* (2 vols), Casterman, 1968–69

Gates, David, *The Napoleonic Wars, 1803–1815* (Modern Wars Series), Arnold, 1997

Gill, John H., *'Vermin, Scorpions and Mosquitos – the Rheinbund in the Peninsula*, in *The Peninsular War – Aspects of the Struggle for the Iberian Peninsula* (ed. Ian Fletcher), Spellmount, 1998

Gill, John H., *With Eagles To Glory – Napoleon and his German Allies in the 1809 Campaign*, Greenhill Books, 1992

Gould, Robert W., MBE, *Mercenaries of the Napoleonic Wars*, Tom Donovan Publishing, 1995

Haythornthwaite, Philip, *Uniforms of Napoleon's Russian Campaign*, Blandford Press, 1976

Haythornthwaite, Philip, *Uniforms of the Peninsular War 1807–1814*, Blandford Press, 1978

Haythornthwaite, Philip, *The Napoleonic Source Book*, Arms and Armour Press, 1991

Haythornthwaite, Philip, *Who Was Who in the Napoleonic Wars*, Arms and Armour Press, 1998

Hourtoulle, F-G (trans Mckay, Alan), *Jena, Auerstadt – the triumph of the eagle*, Histoire & Collections, 1998

Hourtoulle, F-G (trans Mckay, Alan), *Borodino – The Moskova, the battle for the redoubts*, Histoire & Collections, 2000

Johnson, Ray, *Napoleonic Armies, a Wargamer's Campaign Directory 1805–1815*, Arms and Armour Press, 1984

Knotel, Richard; Knotel, Herbert and Sieg, Herbert, *Uniforms of the World (Handbuch de Uniformkunde)*, Orig. Frankh Verlagshandlung Kosmos-Verlag; W.Sperman Verlag, Stuttgart; republished New Orchard Editions Ltd, 1988

Lochet, Jean (ed.), *Empires, Eagles and Lions* (various issues), RAFM

Nafziger, George, *Lutzen & Bautzen*, Emperor's Press, 1992

Nafziger, George, *Napoleon at Dresden*, The Emperor's Press, 1994

Nafziger, George, *Napoleon at Leipzig*, The Emperor's Press, 1996

Nafziger, George, *Napoleon's Invasion of Russia*, Presidio Press, 1988

Nafziger, George, *A Guide To Napoleonic Warfare – Maneuvers Of The Battery, Battalion And Brigade During The 1st Empire As Found In Contemporary Regulations*, privately published 1996(?). This was subsequently republished as *Imperial Bayonets* by Greenhill Books in 1997

Oman, Prof, Charles, *The History of the Peninsula War* (7 vols), orig published 1902–1930, recently re-published by Greenhill Books, 1995–1997

Partridge, Richard (ed.), *Age of Napoleon* (various issues), Partizan Press

Sapherson, CA, *1809 – A Year At War* (5 volumes), Raider Games, 1986

Smith, Digby, *The Greenhill Napoleonic Wars Data Book*, Greenhill Books, 1998

Von Pivka, Otto (Digby Smith), *Armies of 1812 – vol 1: The French Army*, Patrick Stephens Ltd, 1977
Von Pivka, Otto (Digby Smith), *Armies of the Napoleonic Era*, David and Charles, 1979
Von Pivka, Otto (Digby Smith), *Navies of the Napoleonic Era*, David and Charles, 1980
Wilson, Peter H., *German Armies – War and German politics 1648–1806* (Warfare and History series), UCL, nd

FRANCE

Blond, G., *La Grande Armée*, Arms and Armour Press, 1995
Bucquoy, E-L., *Les Uniformes du Premier Empire*, (10 volumes) Grancher, 1977–1980
Bukhari, Emir, *French Napoleonic Line Infantry*, Almark Publications, 1974
Bukhari, Emir & Angus McBride, *Napoleon's Cavalry*, Osprey, 1979
Dempsey, Guy, *Napoleon's Soldiers*, Arms and Armour Press, 1994
Haythornthwaite, Philip, *Napoleon's Line Infantry*, Osprey, 1983
Haythornthwaite, Philip, *Napoleon's Light Infantry*, Osprey, 1983
Haythornthwaite, Philip, *Napoleon's Guard Infantry*, (2 vols) Osprey, 1984, 1985
Johnson, David, *The French Cavalry 1792–1815*, Belmont Publications, 1989
Lachouque, Henri and Brown, Anne S.K., *The Anatomy of Glory*, Arms and Armour Press, 1994
Nafziger, George, *The French Army – Royal, Republican, Imperial 1792–1815* (5 vols), self-published, 1997
Petre, F. Loraine, *Napoleon's Last Campaign in Germany – 1813*, originally published, re-printed Arms and Armour Press, 1974
Rogers, Col. H.C.B., *Napoleon's Army*, Purnell Book Services, 1974
Smith, Digby, *Napoleon's Regiments*, Greenhill Books, 2000

BADEN

Rawkins, W.J., *The Armies of Baden and Wurtemburg*, HMR Group, 1977

BAVARIA

Nafziger, George and Gilbert, Martin, *The Bavarian and Westphalian Armies, 1799–1815*, RAFM, 1981
Rawkins, W.R., *The Bavarian Army, 1805–14*, W.J. Rawkins, 1982
Von Pivka, Otto (Digby Smith), *Napoleon's German Allies: Bavaria*, Osprey, 1980

BERG

Rawkins, W.J., *The Armies of Naples & Kleve-Berg 1806–1814*, HMR Group, 1978

Von Pivka, Otto (Digby Smith), *Napoleon's German Allies: Westfalia & Kleve-Berg*, Osprey, 1975, 1992

DENMARK

Cassin-Scott, Jack, *Scandinavian Armies in the Napoleonic Wars*, Osprey, 1976

Snorrason, Torstein, *Danish Uniforms and Equipment 1800–1815*, Bent Carlsens Forlag Aps, nd

HESSE-DARMSTADT

Rawkins, W.J., *The Confederation of the Rhine – Hesse-Darmstadt, Mecklenburg & Nassau*, W.J. Rawkins, 1980

Von Pivka, Otto (Digby Smith), *Napoleon's German Allies: Hessen-Darmstadt & Hessen-Kassel*, Osprey, 1982

HOLLAND

Von Pivka, Otto (Digby Smith), *Dutch-Belgian Troops of the Napoleonic Wars*, Osprey, 1980

ITALY

Currie, J., *The Kingdom of Italy Infantry*, Napoleonic Association, nd

Rawkins, W., *The Italian Army, 1805–1814*, Anschluss, 1982

Von Pivka, Otto (Digby Smith), *Napoleon's Italian and Neapolitan Troops*, Osprey Publications, 1979

NAPLES

Rawkins, W.J., *The Armies of Naples & Kleve-Berg 1806–1814*, HMR Group, 1978

Von Pivka, Otto (Digby Smith), *Napoleon's Italian and Neapolitan Troops*, Osprey Publications, 1979

SAXONY

Nafziger, George; Weslowski, Mariusz & Devoe, Tom, *Poles and Saxons of the Napoleonic Wars*, Emperor's Press, 1991

Rawkins, W.J., *The Army of Saxony 1805–14*, HMR Group, 1979
Von Pivka, Otto, *Napoleon's German Allies: Saxony 1806–1815*, Osprey, 1979

SMALLER GERMAN STATES

Rawkins, W.J., *The Confederation of the Rhine – Hesse-Darmstadt, Mecklenburg & Nassau*, W.J. Rawkins, 1980
Von Pivka, Otto (Digby Smith), *Napoleon's German Allies: Nassau and Oldenburg*, Osprey, 1976

UNITED STATES

Bowler, R. Arthur (ed.), *War Along the Niagara – Essays on the War of 1812 and its legacy*, Old Fort Niagara Assoc., Inc., 1991
Chartrand, Réné, *Uniforms and Equipment of the United States Forces in the War of 1812*, Old Fort Niagara Assoc., Inc., 1992
Kochan, James, *The United States Army 1783–1811*, Osprey, 2001
Kochan, James, *The United States Army 1812–1815*, Osprey, 2000
Urwin, Gregory, J.W., *The United States Infantry – an illustrated history 1775–1918*, Blandford Press, 1988
Weigley, Russell F., *History of the United States Army*, Batsford, 1967

WARSAW

Nafziger, George; Weslowski, Mariusz & Devoe, Tom, *Poles and Saxons of the Napoleonic Wars*, Emperor's Press, 1991
Von Pivka, Otto (Digby Smith), *Napoleon's Polish Troops*, Osprey, 1974

WESTPHALIA

Nafziger, George and Gilbert, Martin, *The Bavarian and Westphalian Armies, 1799–1815*, RAFM, 1981
Von Pivka, Otto (Digby Smith), *Napoleon's German Allies: Westfalia & Kleve-Berg*, Osprey, 1975, 1992

WÜRTEMBURG

Nafziger, George, *The Wurtemburg Army, 1793–1815*, Raider Games, 1987
Rawkins, W.J., *The Armies of Baden and Wurtemburg*, HMR Group, 1977

Index

Note: The index covers the main text. Subject matter within the tables is shown in **bold** typeface.